ENVIRONMENTALLY SUSTAINABLE ECONOMIC DEVELOPMENT

ASAYEHGN DESTA

PRAEGER

Westport, Connecticut
London

Library of Congress Cataloging-in-Publication Data

Desta, Asayehgn, 1944–
    Environmentally sustainable economic development / Asayehgn Desta
  ; foreword by Françoise O. Lepage.
        p. cm.
    Includes bibliographical references and index.
    ISBN 0–275–95741–1 (alk. paper).—ISBN 0–275–96628–3 (pbk.)
    1. Economic development—Environmental aspects.   2. Sustainable
development.   I. Title.
    HD75.6.D4748   1999
    363.7—dc21   98–31368

British Library Cataloguing in Publication Data is available.

Library of Congress Catalog Card Number: 98–31368
ISBN: 0–275–95741–1
        0–275–96628–3 (pbk.)

First published in 1999

Praeger Publishers, 88 Post Road West, Westport, CT 06881
An imprint of Greenwood Publishing Group, Inc.
www.praeger.com

Printed in the United States of America

The paper used in this book complies with the
Permanent Paper Standard issued by the National
Information Standards Organization (Z39.48–1984).
P

In order to keep this title in print and available to the academic community, this edition
was produced using digital reprint technology in a relatively short print run. This would
not have been attainable using traditional methods. Although the cover has been changed
from its original appearance, the text remains the same and all materials and methods
used still conform to the highest book-making standards.

To my mother, my daughters,
Hararta and Hierete, and to the
memory of my father.

Contents

Illustrations

FIGURE

Foreword

While the concepts associated with sustainable development can be topics of heated debate, there is broad consensus on the importance of exploring these concepts. Critical in these discussions are the linkages between economic development and environmental concerns. Inasmuch as these linkages are considered focal points in many intellectual exchanges, we often find ourselves lacking the essential knowledge to further the conversation. What is clear to many of us is the critical nature of the discussion for ourselves and for our students irrespective of our domain of knowledge. Thus we are dependent on a slowly emerging body of literature written for nonspecialists, for those of us without a formal academic background in either economics or environmental sciences.

Asayehgn Desta's new book, *Environmentally Sustainable Economic Development,* fills a vacuum for the nonspecialist. His work not only integrates theoretical approaches with policy implications, it also links these two considerations with examples from a broad range of countries. From the first chapter, "The Stages of Economic Development Paradigms," which addresses the prevailing theories of economic development, to the more issue-oriented chapters such as "Women and the Environment," the reader is guided through the interplay of economic theory and environmental implications.

One of the great strengths of Professor Desta's work is the book's organization. Nothing is left to chance. He sets the stage for an engaging conversation by leading the reader through a series of theoretical discussions followed by a historical perspective of the selected issues and offers country-specific case studies. His case studies are both sound and thought provoking. For instance, his chapter on "Health Services and the Environment," with its case study on AIDS in Thailand, represents that special blend of data presentation, analysis, and conclusions that lead one to reflect on the global implications of the AIDS crisis.

What makes this work especially appealing for students and teachers are Professor Desta's Summary and Review Questions following each chapter's presentation. I found beginning with the review questions an efficient way to focus my attention on the key issues. I was never disappointed by the chapters. Each referred directly and explicitly to the review questions at the end. Similarly, the summaries were in fact summaries of what I had read.

The specialist in economics will appreciate the integration of this field with environmental issues. The environmental scientist will be exposed to the contending theories in economics and economic development. Finally, the novice in both fields will have the opportunity to follow clear and cogent arguments for engagement in pursuit of sustainable development.

Personally, as a concerned global citizen committed to relevant and ethical curricula in higher education, I am thankful to Professor Desta for writing a book that explains the complex relationship between economic development, quality of life and the environment. As a nonspecialist in both economics and environmental science, I found that this book furnished the concepts and arguments that allow me to engage meaningfully in a conversation about the future.

Françoise O. Lepage

Preface

Environmentally sustainable economic development, meeting the needs of the present generation without depleting the future supply of resources from future generations, is one of the new, dynamic areas of the rapidly growing environmental and economic development curricula. Today it is no longer possible to design plans for developing countries without mapping out the effects of the environment on economic development. Yet, crucial as it is, the objective of sustainable development is very difficult to realize. At the least, sustainable development cannot be effectively pursued if there is no change in attitudes toward the environment as reflected in national policies.

Environmentally Sustainable Economic Development attempts to integrate the basic theoretical framework underpinning economic development (which implies the process of quantitative rise in per capita income growth over a long period of time accompanied by output distribution, the well-being of the people, and their participation in the political process) to the sound management of the environment. To accomplish this task, the book makes use of theoretical approaches, draws policy implications, and uses real-country examples to further document the discussions in every chapter.

Each chapter is written in a reader-friendly manner, and the book's orientation is practical, not merely academic. This book has been written specifically to be useful to general readers and policymakers as well as to senior-level undergraduates and master's degree students with some background in principles of economics and environmental sciences. It is hoped that, after thoroughly reading this book, each reader will be able to understand and evaluate economic development information found in major economic and environmental science publications.

Environmentally Sustainable Economic Development attempts to link economic development and environmental issues in a coherent way. I am sure the readers of this book will be challenged in their assumptions about existing economic development paradigms as they discover new ways to think about the role of environmentally sustainable economic development in the Third World countries in the twenty-first century.

ORGANIZATION OF THE BOOK

The concept of environmentally sustainable development is inherently complex. This book attempts to clarify the issues surrounding the subject by answering the following fundamental questions: Given the present global environmental crisis, (1) can the needs of the least advantaged and most vulnerable members of society be met, and (2) can the current form of economic development be sustained?

The position taken in this book is that protection of the environment is an essential part of development; and the best chance for achieving long-term sustainable development is to systematically incorporate environmental issues into key aspects of economic development paradigms.

Thus *Environmentally Sustainable Economic Development* focuses on fourteen highly interrelated areas of environmental viability and economic development. A brief synopsis of each chapter follows.

Chapter 1. Evolution of the idea of sustainable development

Chapter 2. How depreciation of natural "capital" should—and can—be factored into national cost-accounting equations

Chapter 3. How capital formation impacts the environment

Chapter 4. How market forces and the environment interact. How environmental and resource costs can be internalized

Chapter 5. How poverty and environmental degradation are linked in Third World countries

Chapter 6. The relationship between population and the environment

Chapter 7. The relationship between the role of women and the environment

Chapter 8. How rural development impacts the environment

Chapters 9 and 10. How environmental considerations can be incorporated into human capital and health care services in Third World countries

Chapters 11 and 12. How multinational enterprises and technology impact the environment of Third World countries

Chapter 13. The environmental impact of international trade

Chapter 14. The feasibility of environmental solutions to Third World nations' external debts

ACKNOWLEDGMENTS

This book has benefited greatly from the generous support and assistance of many institutions, the suggestions of colleagues, and the reactions of the students who class-tested the manuscript. Each of these forms of assistance proved crucial to the completion of this book.

Specifically, I would like to express my gratitude to the Friedman Fund for Innovation Competition and the Compton Foundation for their financial support, so I could undertake research in Southeast Asia and attend various seminars.

I am grateful to Dominican College of San Rafael for granting me a sabbatical leave to complete my research project. My sincere thanks go to Dr. Denise Lucy, Vice President for Academic Affairs; Dr. Françoise O. Lepage, former Dean of the School of Business and International Studies; and all my students and colleagues who gave me detailed reviews and helpful suggestions. Special acknowledgments go to both undergraduate and graduate students of Dominican College for showing interest in the relationship between economic development and the environment and for researching and writing up the case studies presented here.

I am grateful to Diana Walsh for invaluable assistance with the earlier manuscript. My special thanks go to Larry Boggs, who cheerfully took on the editing, proofreading, and indexing of this book, as well as handling the permissions process; and to Barbara Powell Pelosi of Bay View Publishing Services, whose typesetting and excellent design ideas made this book visually attractive. I greatly value the assistance of Dr. Zahi Haddad, Dawit Atsbeha, Elsa Berhe, Sara Wolde Aragai, Berhane Atsbeha, and Lete Atsbeha. I am indebted to the entire staff at Greenwood Publishing Group, especially Cynthia Harris for her support in guiding this manuscript to its completion, and Maureen Melino for her invaluable guidance with securing permissions. Thanks are also due to Meg Fergusson for a detailed manuscript review and style standardization, and for ongoing assistance in the prepublication stages. Finally, I am indebted to my family for understanding, supporting, and putting up with me in my long absences while doing research for this book.

chapter 1

The Stages of Economic Development Paradigms

S ince the eighteenth century, economists have been attempting to discern the factors that contribute to sustained economic growth. This chapter discusses the evolution of development economics, from income growth-based to sustainable development. The first section presents the classical view and neoclassical paradigm, followed by the opposing view as expressed by a leading critic, Karl Marx. The second section presents other development theories formulated for Third World countries since World War II. Finally, neoclassical counterrevolutionary and current paradigms of sustainable development are discussed.

THE CLASSICAL PERSPECTIVE

Orthodox development economics, emerging out of Western modes of thought, measured economic growth in terms of per capita income or product. David Hume, an earlier proponent of the orthodox paradigm, conceptualized a nation's output as a function of labor, land, and manufactures. According to Hume, the productivity of labor and land is determined by the scale of manufactures, which in turn is determined by the scale of domestic and foreign trade. Hume argued that poor nations have the capacity to catch up with rich nations because during their period of transition they enjoy the advantage of lower money wages and a backlog of unapplied technology.[1]

Adam Smith's analysis of the British economy developed a general theory of economic factors responsible for economic progress and the policy measures that need to be undertaken in order to create an environment favorable to rapid growth.[2] According to Smith's argument, everyone pursues his own interest and acts to increase personal wealth (not just money but all the necessities and conveniences of life); the effect of this principle is to increase the wealth of a nation. Once set in motion by the exploitation of capital, division of labor, and a regional or international absolute trade advantage, economic progress will result in economic development.[3]

In 1817 David Ricardo refined Smith's analysis by including land, capital, and international trade (based on comparative advantage) along with the division of labor as the driving force for economic growth. In addition, Ricardo speculated on the limits to growth caused by finite land sources due to population increase. According to Ricardo's "iron law of wages," workers would receive very low wages because population growth would force them to work for less.[4] It can be argued that the Ricardian model of growth is especially relevant to Great Britain, as an island with limited arable land. As Pari Kasliwal points out, "the most productive land is brought into cultivation first, then the lesser productive, and so on. . . . [M]arginal productivity of labor declines as more land is brought into production."[5]

John Stuart Mill's version of economic growth was based upon the productivity of the three factors of production: labor, capital, and land. Mill investigated the economic contents of the steady state of the three factors of production.[6] Based on the law of diminishing returns, the classical theorist Thomas Malthus projected that rapid population growth relative to a fixed amount of land could threaten economic growth. Malthus developed his theories in reaction to existing economic philosophies which he felt were overly optimistic. His doctrine assumed that the unchecked breeding of man would cause human population to grow at a geometric rate (i.e., 2, 4, 8, 16), whereas food supplies could grow only at an arithmetic rate (i.e., 1, 2, 3, 4). Malthus failed to foresee a rapid increase in industrial and agricultural productivity due to improved technology after the industrial revolution. He also failed to predict the drop in birthrate as family income increased.

THE MARXIST VIEW

Based on materialism and the Hegelian dialectic of inherent change, Karl Marx developed the theory of dialectical materialism. According to Marx, every society is built on a class system and on an economic base comprising the mode and means of production. Above this is the superstructure that encompasses laws, ethics, government, religion, and education.[7] Using this argument Marx theorized that economic growth could be achieved only when capitalism was transformed into socialism by a revolution, engineered and led by the suppressed working class, the proletariat. In a communist society, the proletariat would seize political power and would own the means of production, distributing the resultant output according to need.[8] As noted by T. N. Srinivasan, Marx proclaimed that

> the forces of production, represented by available technology at any point in historical time, and the existing relations of production, represented by the institutions governing ownership and access to the means of production, determine an "equilibrium." In this linear view of history, capitalistic production relations supplanted feudal relations in the historical context because changes in technology made the feudal relation obsolete. In turn, the recurrent crises that Marx so confidently predicted for mature capitalism were expected to lead to socialism and, eventually, to communism.[9]

Especially during the 1970s, some Marxists developed the neocolonial dependency model, hoping to explain underdevelopment in Third World countries. According to the dependency theorists' argument, the Third World countries are underdeveloped because the international division of labor favors the mother countries (the "core"). Less-developed countries (LDCs—the "periphery") rely on exporting primary goods (agriculture, fuel, raw materials, etc.) and must import manufactured products from the industrialized countries. This leads to an unfavorable trade pattern for LDCs since manufactured goods are generally more expensive than primary products.[10]

In addition, the industrialized nations form alliances with a precapitalist, local elite to obtain access to vital resources and scarce capital, and accumulated surplus is then expropriated by the local elite. In this way the developing countries are effectively condemned to remain underdeveloped, peripheral players in the international capitalist system. Their reliance on the demand from the developed countries (or the "center") for their volatile export commodities renders them vulnerable to fluctuations in international markets.[11] Dependency theorists believe the only solution for these countries is to sever relations with the international capitalist system in order to develop internally.[12]

Although the dependency model was accurate in revealing the causes of world poverty and adequately described the situation of Latin American countries in the 1970s, it failed to describe how wealth is created and to account for the situation of many other less developing countries in the 1980s and 1990s. For example, in contradiction to the dependency theory, South Korea's economy, which is extremely dependent on the developed nations for export markets, produced a per capita growth rate of more than 7 percent annually between 1965 and 1990.[13]

THE NEOCLASSICAL APPROACH

During the 1870s, a group of economists known as neoclassicists surfaced. Completely abandoning the concept that fixed proportions of capital, labor, or land are required in productions within a given state of technology to spur economic growth, the neoclassicists recognized the possibility of the substitution of capital for labor and argued that as capital stock grows in relation to a given population, national income increases.[14] In addition, neoclassical economics argued that "utility, rather than tangibility, was the true standard of production and wealth. Lawyers' fees, commissions, all the paper shuffling of an abstracted commercial economy, were essentially no different from sacks of potatoes or carloads of iron."[15]

The role of the market is stressed in neoclassical economic theory. The implication is that nonrenewable resources, such as fossil fuels and ores, are easily dealt with, but clean air and water, as well as functions of ecosystems, are labeled as free goods. The main result of this theory is that such goods require governmental intervention that corrects the functioning of the market process.

Otherwise, a disoptimal level of such goods will result. Generally, one can say that the market can only deal with the optimal allocation of private goods.[16]

In addition, the neoclassicists argued that

> in early stages of development, externalities are pervasive and scale economics are significant, particularly in sectors such as transport and communications which provide the infrastructure for the functioning of an economy. Capital markets are likely to be segmented and imperfect: and the financial system primitive and not performing intermediation to any significant extent. The entrepreneurial class is likely to be minuscule, if not altogether absent or alien and unassimilated. Under such circumstances, . . . the state would then have to perform the role of the . . . entrepreneur as well as intervene in existing markets, through appropriate taxes and subsidies, to ensure that externalities were appropriately reflected in private calculations.[17]

Ernst Lutz notes that Alfred Marshall, the father of neoclassical economics and among the first to note the contribution of nature to the production of goods and services, would no doubt have considered the degradation of nature in the process of the production of goods and services.[18]

Although the orthodox economists and neoclassicists contributed to laying the conceptual perspectives necessary to conceptualize economic growth, their theories were ahistorical and did not lend themselves to empirical testing, much less to policy implications. They particularly focused on the optimal use of factors of endowments, such as natural and human resources and changes in population, and capital stock as the key ingredients to economic progress. Moreover, they stressed that the factors of production need to be privately owned, and therefore markets are required in which goods and services are freely bought and sold. Nonetheless, the conditions under which these factors might contribute to economic growth, why many nations remain poor, and how poverty can be reduced were not empirically demonstrated. Also, the neoclassicists did not include the notion that growth could also undermine the ecological foundations on which economic growth can be sustained.

THE KEYNESIAN APPROACH

In response to chronic unemployment and low levels of national output during the Great Depression of the 1930s, economic theorists shifted development economics in a new direction. The leading economist of the period, John Maynard Keynes, revolutionized economic theory. Keynes's model rested on the assumption that the demand for capital, which he regarded as the engine of growth, is a function of the growth of population, the rate of growth of the standard of living, and the rate of increase and character of technology. In contradiction to the classical paradigm, Keynes argued that a positive rate of population increase enlarges the demand for investment. Concerning the poor countries, Keynes proposed that by maximizing the rate of growth of the gross national product (GNP), Third World countries could maximize their rate of labor absorption.[19]

Keynes's work inspired future theorists to sharpen their economic development paradigms. One of these theorists was Joseph Schumpeter, who highlighted the importance of private initiative, citing such areas as innovation in production, entrepreneurship, introduction of new goods, the opening of new markets, the conquest of new sources or supplies of raw materials or partially manufactured goods, and the breaking up of monopolies.[20]

THIRD WORLD DEVELOPMENT VIEWS

The economics of developing countries evolved during the eighteenth century and was generally regarded as an extension of conventional orthodox economics. Development economics emerged as a discipline in its own right in the 1950s with the establishment of the Bretton Woods institutions (the World Bank and the International Monetary Fund) and the United Nations.

Sir Arthur Lewis, regarded as the grandfather of economic development, took the classical approach to economic growth, arguing that surplus labor available at subsistence wages in the backward sector of the economy could enhance capitalistic development.[21] For economic growth to be achieved, Lewis proposed a structural transformation of a subsistence-based agricultural economy into a modern industrial economy. As stated by Christopher Pass and colleagues, Lewis also stressed the need for "economic infrastructure in developing countries" and "such social overhead capital as transport networks, communications systems, and educational facilities as prerequisites for growth."[22]

Lewis's model of economic development asserted that as the relative size of the capitalistic sector grows due to imported capital or state capitalism, the national income will grow, even in economically dependent countries. Though instructive, Lewis's two-sector model neglected the importance of agriculture. In addition, Lewis placed "more emphasis on the problem of capitalist infusion than on the means to its achievement."[23] Nonetheless, it can be argued that Lewis's model of development was freed from the classical economists' argument of diminishing marginal productivity of inputs. Instead, capital was found to be the most significant input for increasing output.

Sir Roy Harrod and Evsey Domar concurrently but independently developed a variant theory of economic growth. In their model they argue that for nations to grow, a certain proportion of their GNP must be saved and invested; that the rate of growth of GNP is determined jointly by the national savings ratio and the national capital-output ratio; and that the faster a nation can save and invest in capital, the faster its economy can grow.[24]

The Harrod-Domar model is limited by the assumption that output must grow at the same rate as capital formation. On the other hand, it assumed that labor is not essential for growth. Thus, for many agriculturally based developing nations with low levels of new capital formation, the Harrod-Domar model "became a rationale and an opportunistic tool for justifying massive transfers of capital and technical assistance from the developed to the less developed nations of the Third World."[25]

The growth theories of the 1950s evolved in the soil of imperial planning initiatives.

> The origins of development theory are part of the process by which the "colonial world" was reconfigured into a "developing world" in the aftermath of World War II. Africa, for example, only became an object of planned development after the Great Depression of the 1930s. The British Colonial Development and Welfare Act (1940) and the French Investment Fund for Economic and Social Development (1946) both represented response to the crises and challenges which imperial powers confronted in Africa, providing a means by which they could negotiate the perils of independence movements on the one hand and a perpetuation of the colonial mission on the other.[26]

Structuralist institutionalists of the 1960s developed the import-substitution model. They theorized that production by domestic industries could replace the need for expensive imports, thereby expanding output and achieving full employment in Third World countries. Many countries adopted this policy, only to discover unintended negative externalities.

> Selective trade barriers built industrial sectors highly dependent on imported capital goods and petroleum. Industrial concentration in urban centers contributed to multiple environmental ills. In agriculture, the "green-revolution" technology increased yields of food grains, but at the price of intensive use of agrochemicals and losses of genetic diversity.[27]

In response to the Lewis and Harrod-Domar models, Walt Whitman Rostow, an eminent economic historian, conceptualized economic growth into five linear stages: the traditional society, the preconditions for takeoff, the takeoff, the drive to maturity, and the age of high mass consumption. Rostow suggests that economic growth is a process of transformation in which a society proceeds from a traditional level (output is limited by the lack of modern science and technology) to a transitional one in which the foundations for growth are developed. Accelerated growth occurs during the takeoff period (that is, the rapid expansion of new industries in turn stimulates the creation of support service industries); finally the society moves to mature and high mass consumption of durable goods and services while at the same time allocating more of its resources to social welfare and security. Based on Rostow's theories, mobilization of domestic and foreign saving is necessary to generate sufficient investment to accelerate economic growth.[28]

Barbara Ingham comments that Rostow's "view of history is patently misleading. Economies may miss stages, become locked in one particular stage, or even regress. Moreover, there may be alternative paths. . . . European history itself has been traumatic and aberrant, not smooth and sequential."[29] According to E. Wayne Nafziger, Rostow's approach is ethnocentric and "implies a change from an underdeveloped economy to one similar to those in North America and Western Europe . . . "[30] Finally, Rostow's definitions of the stages of growth are too broad and general. For instance, his definition of traditional society would include all the dynasties of China and the civilizations of Africa, the Middle East, and the Mediterranean on a single stage.

By the 1960s earlier approaches to economic development were met with strong criticism. Theorists advocated the importance of modernization and the complete transformation of economic, cultural, social, and political life.

> Modernization is a broad social science concept and many of its critics adopt a social science perspective. In economic terms, modernization implies industrialization and urbanization and the technological transformation of agriculture. Socially, it involves the weakening of traditional ties, and the rise of achievement as the basis for personal advancement. Its political dimension is in the rationalization of authority and the growth of the bureaucracy. Culturally, modernization is represented by increased secularization of society arising from the spread of scientific knowledge. Taken together, modernization means change toward those types of economic and political systems that developed in western Europe and North America in the 18th and 19th centuries.[31]

GROWTH-WITH-EQUITY PARADIGMS

By the beginning of the 1970s there was a call for the dethronement of GNP as the major objective of economic activity. In its place concerns for the problems of poverty and equality became the major theme.[32] "Development professionals had become so operationally preoccupied with growth that they lost sight of poverty."[33] Therefore, in contradistinction to the trickle-down theory of economic growth, economists focused on the satisfaction of basic needs and growth-with-equity approaches to development. Historically accepted as a measure of purchasing power, gross domestic product (GDP) per capita as a benchmark for economic progress began to be replaced by the Physical Quality of Life Index (PQLI). Created in 1977 by the Overseas Development Council, PQLI was considered as an alterative measure of social welfare. It is an aggregate of three measures: literacy rate, life expectancy at age one, and infant mortality rate. Each country is rated on a scale of 1 to 100 on each of the three variables. However, the rationale for giving equal weight to the three indicators in the construction of the PQLI composite scale is not clearly justified. In addition, Nafziger argues that "PQLI indicators are of limited use in distinguishing levels of development beyond middle-income countries. All three PQLI variables—life expectancy, literacy and infant mortality—are highly related to per capita income until nutrition, health, and education reach certain high levels, then the value of the variables levels off."[34]

It should be noted here that the "basic needs" concept is country-specific and is a function of culture. Also, as argued by Ingham, income distribution as a variable does not take into account gender distribution of income. As males are usually the primary income generators, widows and single mothers often do not

8   Environmentally Sustainable Economic Development

share in the indicated income gains, and they have always been among the most impoverished groups.[35]

Though there were obvious methodological flaws in the growth-with-equity paradigm, the "grow now, trickle down later" approach was riddled with perhaps even more basic flaws.

- The "trickle-down" approach assumed a country could grow now and redistribute income later. But those benefiting from the present growth will never permit the mechanisms of redistribution to take place down the road.
- The poor moved into cities in far greater numbers than growth theory assumed.
- The growth theory focused on industrialization and gave little or no attention to agriculture, which was the mainstay of the Third World economies.[36]

Although they shared a common understanding of the issues surrounding the disenfranchised in Third World countries, the proponents of growth-with-equity espoused a wide variety of strategies for addressing these problems. "Employment generation, the redirecting of investment, the meeting of basic needs, human resource development, agriculture-first development, integrated rural development, and the New International Economic Order"[37] were put forth as major policy components.

More recently, there has been an attempt to define development as people oriented. The United Nations Development Programme generated the Human Development Index (HDI) in 1990, which encompasses the social indicators of life expectancy, literacy, and purchasing power. According to the United Nations Development Programme, the HDI is "best seen as a measure of people's ability to live a long and healthy life, to communicate and to participate in the life of the community, and to have sufficient resources to obtain a decent living."[38] Within this composite scale countries are ranked into three groups: low human development (0.0 to 0.50), medium human development (0.51 to 0.79), and high human development (0.80 to 1.0). As a single index of human or social development, HDI is constructed in three steps:

1. *Define a measure of deprivation* that a country suffers in each of the three basic variables—life expectancy, literacy, and (the log of) real GDP per capita. A maximum and a minimum value are determined for each of the three variables given the actual values. The deprivation measure then places a country in the range of zero to one as defined by the difference between the maximum and the minimum.
2. *Define an average deprivation indicator* by taking a simple average of the three indicators.
3. *Measure the HDI as one minus the average deprivation index.*

To illustrate, the application of the formula to Indonesia is as follows.

Maximum life expectancy	= 78.40
Minimum life expectancy	= 41.80
Maximum adult literacy rate	= 100.00
Minimum adult literacy rate	= 12.30

Maximum real GDP per capita (log)   =   3.68
Minimum real GDP per capita (log)   =   2.34
Indonesia life expectancy   =   57.00
Indonesia adult literacy   =   73.80
Indonesia real GDP per capita (log)   =   3.22
Indonesia's life expectancy deprivation $(78.4 - 57)/(78.4 - 241.8)$ =   0.585
Indonesia's literacy deprivation $(100 - 73.8)/(100 - 12.3)$ =   0.299
Indonesia's GDP deprivation $(3.68 - 3.22)/(3.68 - 2.34)$ =   0.343
Indonesia's average deprivation $(0.585 + 0.299 + 0.343)/3$ =   0.409
Indonesia's HDI $= 1.00 - 0.409$ =   0.591[39]

Although HDI provides a broader perspective on relative human development and can be used to analyze the comparative status of socioeconomic development of countries, Michael P. Todaro points out the following limitations of HDI:

> (1) [I]ts creation was in part motivated by a political strategy designed to refocus attention on health and education aspects of development; (2) the three indicators used are good but not ideal (e.g., the U.N. team wanted to use nutrition status of children under age 5 as their ideal health indicator, but the data were not available); (3) the national HDI may have the unfortunate effect of shifting the focus away from the substantial inequality within countries; (4) the alternative approach of looking at GNP per capita rankings and then supplementing this with other social indicators is still a respectable one; and, finally, (5) one must always remember that the index is one of *relative* rather than *absolute* development, so that if all countries improve at the same weighted rate, the poorest countries would not get credit for their progress.[40]

To summarize, while the orthodox economic growth approach focused on growth as the ultimate goal to which all nations aspire, the growth-with-equity paradigm concentrated on fulfilling basic needs of the poor and on income redistribution. Another group, the political economists, focused on development as a means of attaining "the progressive emancipation of peoples and nations from control of nature and from the control of other peoples and nations."[41]

As mentioned before, neo-Marxist theorists squarely attribute the continuing underdevelopment in the "periphery" to the penetration of modern capitalism from the "center."[42] They strongly suggest that the peripheral economies (mostly LDCs) can only develop by delinking themselves from the world capitalist system. The main argument of the neo-Marxist states that "the economic development of the rich countries contributes to the underdevelopment of the poor. Development in an LDC is not self-generating or autonomous but ancillary. The LDCs are economic satellites of the highly developed regions of Northern America and Western Europe in the international capitalist system."[43]

THE NEOCLASSICAL COUNTERREVOLUTION APPROACH

The astonishing economic growth during the 1980s in the newly industrializing countries (NICs) of Asia and Latin America, in conjunction with the political ascendancy of conservative governments in the United States, Canada, Britain, and West Germany, gave birth to a neoclassical counterrevolution in economic theory and policy.[44] The central argument of the neoclassical theorist attributes the lack of economic growth in the Third World countries to poor resource allocation (due to unrealistic domestic pricing policies), overvalued exchange rates, and excessive state intervention.

Neoclassical strategies for economic development included the adoption of competitive free markets, the privatization of state-owned enterprises, promotion of free trade, export promotion of nontraditional agricultural products, and creation of conducive environments for foreign direct investment.[45] But the export-promotion model fails to account for the social costs of natural resource depletion. Moreover, South Korea's development experience under Park Chung Hee, an authoritarian but benevolent "social guardian," presents a stark contrast to laissez-faire policies promoted by advocates of unregulated markets. For example, Anne O. Kruegar, one of the prominent neoclassical economists, argues that the rise of democracy does not necessarily lead to economic reform.[46] Similarly, Lee Kuan Yew, former Prime Minister of Singapore, believes that discipline more than democracy contributes to a country's development. As he stated it, "the exuberance of democracy leads to undiscipline and disorderly conduct which are inimical to development."[47]

During the 1970s, development strategies viewed grassroots participation not only as a means of reducing poverty but also as a means of self-actualization. Failures of past development projects were seen to result from "the fact that the populations concerned were kept out of all the processes related to their design, formulation and implementation. In their great majority, they started to advocate the end of 'top-down' strategies of action and the inclusion of participation and participatory methods of interaction as an essential dimension of development."[48]

Participation was viewed as a means of promoting democracy by enfranchising the economically weak. A special claim was made that participation would harness the talents of women, and has often been seen as having a special relevance to the gender dimension of development.[49] Citing this argument, the World Bank began to carry out participatory poverty assessments (PPAs) in all borrower countries as an optional component of poverty assessments. As discussed by Lawrence Salmen, the idea of PPA was

> to bridge the gap between policymakers and the poor, by systematically bringing the human, social dimension into this analysis. PPAs address a wide range of critical questions, [such as] how do the poor perceive the relative importance of the various manifestations of poverty, such as low income, lack of food security, and propensity to ill health?...The answers to these questions are vital because they bring out the role of the poor as actors, not merely passive recipients of government largesse or nongovernment organizations' (NGOs) attention. Put in terms of neoclassical economics, the development community knows best what it can supply to meet the needs of the poor, but the poor know best what they need [demand] and what resources and services are available.[50]

Although it is very difficult to discern the linkage between democracy and development, the World Bank, using African countries with multiparty systems (for example, Botswana and Mauritius), argues that democracy is not only valuable in its advocacy of human rights but that democracy also helps sustain growth.[51]

NEW GROWTH THEORY AND HUMAN DEVELOPMENT

As mentioned earlier, the classical, dualistic-development, and neoclassical counterrevolution models of development mainly emphasized that economic growth is largely the accumulation of physical capital and the expansion of the labor force. On the other hand, the new growth theory, developed by Paul Romer and Robert Lucas in the late 1980s and early 1990s, stressed that the real motive force of long-term economic growth is largely related not to exogenous factors (such as technology) but to endogenous factors that can affect the behavior of people responsible for the accumulation of productive factors and knowledge.[52]

But while some of the new economic theorists argue that human capital is the crucial factor in economic growth, others argue that the key source of productivity growth is research and development (R&D). For example, the human capital theorists argue that educated people use capital more efficiently, so it becomes more productive. Educated people are also more likely to innovate—to devise new and better forms of production. Moreover, educated people spread the benefits to their coworkers, who learn from them and also become more productive. Thus the rising levels of education cause a rise in the efficiency of all factors of production.

On the other hand, the new growth theories emphasize the role of investment in research and development in terms of long-term growth. Research and development models argue that "R & D can clearly increase the productivity of the firms making the investments. But here too there can be positive externalities. Many innovations are difficult to keep secret, so other firms learn of these advances, and total factor productivity rises."[53]

The new growth (endogenous) model of economic development discards the conventional model of diminishing marginal returns to capital investments, but it is only limited to a set of easily quantifiable factors.

> Other factors—such as people's habit, their social groups and networks, and the nature of institution and government policies—are more difficult to measure but nonetheless vitally important in explaining differences in growth rates across countries. The family and the formal education system, for example, help impart many skills beyond literacy and numeracy.[54]

SUSTAINABLE DEVELOPMENT PARADIGM

In the past, development economists believed that environmental concerns retarded economic growth. Also, developing countries were of the opinion that environmental agendas could detract from the achievement of developmental goals. The debate between economists and environmentalists was reduced to "trees versus jobs." For instance, prior to the late 1960s, environmental issues focused on the control of unwanted emissions through improvement in technology. The rapid pace of industrialization and societal issues were not yet perceived as problems to be addressed.[55]

In the 1970s and early 1980s it became clear that economic growth may have been consuming its foundations through pollution and depletion of natural resources. Clearer notions of the environment and a sense of the need to protect it grew following the European Nature Conservation Year in 1970, the United Nations Environmental Conference at Stockholm in 1972, and the report issued by the Club of Rome *(The Limits to Growth)* in 1972. Moreover, new and more complex environmental threats (such as deforestation, ecosystem damage, acid precipitation, ozone depletion, contaminated sites, air pollution, hazardous wastes, and global warming) were perceived.[56]

During the past decade, development economists began to tackle other vital questions, such as the impact of the staggering world population on the earth's natural systems and the sustainability of economic development strategies over the long term. The idea of environment as constraint has given way to an acceptance that environmental concerns and development issues are closely related. Recent development strategies focus on simultaneously eradicating poverty and creating sustainable development. In the same vein, it is imperative that policymakers recognize that failing to take the costs of environmental damage into account will prove inefficient and often ineffectual in raising incomes and well-being. Analysts and policymakers acknowledge that if development is to be sustainable the environment needs to be protected. Similarly, it is axiomatic that without development there is no chance of environmental protection. Empirical research (see Table 1.1) undertaken in some of the OECD countries shows that expenditures on environmental programs would contribute to an increase in GNP the first year, but effects in the final year may be positive in some cases and negative in others.

In 1980 the World Conservation Union, United Nations Environmental Programme (UNEP), and Worldwide Fund for Nature coined the term *sustainable development,* and the United Nations General Assembly appointed its World Commission on Environment and Development. The conference is better known as the Brundtland Commission after its chairperson, Mrs. Gro Harlem Brundtland, then prime minister of Norway. This commission signaled that the world community had come to accept the premise that economic development can coexist alongside sound environmental policies. In its April 1987 report, the Brundtland Commission stressed that "growth, poverty alleviation, sound environmental management and the conservation of natural resources are all important objectives of society and must be considered complementary when drafting economic development plans and policies."[57]

At the June 1992 "Earth Summit" (United Nations Conference on Environment and Development, or UNCED) in Rio de Janeiro, more than 178 nations established that the damage being inflicted by human activities on the natural environment can prevent the achievement of a sustainable future. "It has become

Table 1.1
Impact of Environmental Expenditures
on GNP in Select OECD Countries, Various Years
(percentage gain or loss of absolute GNP)

Country, Year, and Nature of Program	First Year	After Several Years	Final Year	After the Program Ends
Austria, 1979–85				
Base program	—	—	–0.2	—
Increased program	—	—	–0.6/+0.5	—
Finland, 1976–82				
Water pollution	+0.3	+0.5	+0.6	—
France, 1966–74				
Actual program	—	—	+0.1	—
Increased program	—	—	+0.4	—
Netherlands, 1979–85	+0.1	—	–0.3/–0.6	–0.4/–0.7
Norway, 1974–83	—	—	+1.5	—
United States, 1970–87	+0.2	—	–0.6/–1.1	—

Source: David W. Pearce and Jeremy J. Warford, *World without End: Economics, Environment, and Sustainable Development* (New York: Oxford University Press, 1993): 45.

Note: Dashes indicate data are unavailable.

clear that the activities cannot be projected to continue into the future, either because they will have destroyed the environmental condition necessary for that continuation, or because their environmental effects will cause massive, unacceptable damage to human health and disruption of human ways of life."[58]

Thus they accepted Principle 4, which stated that environmental protection needs to be incorporated into the development process. A program of action for sustainable development worldwide for the twenty-first century was created. Appropriately named Agenda 21, this program "stands as a comprehensive blueprint for action to be taken globally from now into the Twenty-First Century by governments, United Nations organizations, development agencies, nongovernmental organizations and independent-sector groups in every area in which human activity impacts on the environment."[59]

The first section of Agenda 21 outlines a structure for attaining sustainable development together with estimates of the costs and scale of the implementation recommendations. The second section includes conservation and resource management proposals. The third section is devoted to recognizing and strengthening the role of women, youth, and indigenous peoples. The last section outlines the steps necessary for implementation and costs out the capital requirement for each job to be performed.[60]

During Earth Summit talks, many representatives from the developing countries were concerned that principles and policies contained in Agenda 21 and the Rio Declaration

> could be made use of by the industrial North to impose new forms of control over the economic and social policies and structures of the South. This could be done, for instance, by using the environment as a new form of conditionality attached to grants or loans which the North would in future provide the South, either through bilateral or multilateral channels.[61]

However, as discussed by Mohamed El-Ashry,

> Representatives from more than 80 developed and developing countries meeting in Geneva on March 14–16 [1994] agreed to transform the Global Environment Facility (GEF) from an experimental program into a permanent financial mechanism that will provide grants and concessional funds to developing countries for programs aimed at protecting the global environment.[62]

So the question that needs to be addressed is, What is sustainable development? A review of the literature indicates there is strong agreement at the conceptual level on the need to simultaneously address environment and developmental imperatives. However, the perspectives of sustainable development are quite multidimensional. The Brundtland Commission defines sustainable development as "development that meets the needs of the present without compromising the ability of the future generations to meet their own needs."[63] To make more concrete the concepts of development, needs, and future generations that are within the Brundtland Commission definition of sustainable development, these concepts need to be expanded further. For example, development needs to include not only economic growth but also improvement in sociocultural and political dimensions. Needs should include fair redistribution of resources among the various groups in the society. Finally, the concept of protecting future generations should include the principle of intragenerational, intergenerational, and international equity.[64]

The World Bank approaches environmentally sustainable development in terms of any technical proposal that they fund. Thus, environmentally sustainable development is defined as any proposal that

> has to be *economically and financially sustainable* in terms of growth, capital maintenance, efficient use of resources and investments. But it has to be *ecologically sustainable,* and here we mean ecosystem integrity [and] carrying capacity, including biodiversity. Ecological sustainability is the domain of the biologist and the physical scientist. The units of measurement are different, the constructs are different, and the context and time scale are different. However, equally important is the *social side,* and here we mean equity, social mobility, social cohesion, participation, empowerment, cultural identity, and institutional development. The social dimension is the domain of the sociologist, the anthropologist, and the political scientist.[65]

UNEP explains sustainable development as "development that does not destroy or undermine the ecological, economic or social basis on which continued development depends."[66] The ecological perspective of sustainable development, on the other hand, deals with the structure and function of the natural environment and focuses more on the preservation of biological diversity and the protection of ecological process and life-support systems. Using a systemwide approach, ecologists suggest the following threefold strategy to achieve sustainable development.

1. Encourage the integration of ecological considerations into economic and sectoral development policies.

2. Devise anticipatory and preventive strategies for development projects.

3. Demonstrate that sound ecological policies also benefit development.[67]

The sociocultural and political aspect of sustainability, also referred to as "cultural capital," addresses the centrality of the social actors and their institutions in the governance and ownership of resources, and the stability of social and cultural systems. It considers questions regarding the alleviation of poverty and the reduction of intragenerational, intergenerational, and international inequalities.[68]

Environmental economics treats the environment as an asset or a form of natural capital and stresses the efficient use of natural resources, as well as manmade capital and human resources, to enhance ecosystem productivity and integrity.[69] According to Barbier's analysis, "an overriding feature of recent economic analysis in environment and development has been 'how much to draw down stocks of natural capital to reinvest in other economic assets (i.e., reproducible, man-made capital, foreign assets, and human resources), in order to meet both current and future economic demands.'"[70]

Ingham, however, argues that there will be little demand for sustainable productive systems in those developing countries where most of the population is marginally subsistent. In these countries, demand for basic commodities and services will take precedence over demand for environmental protection.[71]

Given the complexity of the concept of sustainable development, it is no surprise that researchers have taken multidimensional approaches to systematically incorporate environmental concerns into conventional paradigms of economic development. Nonetheless, quoting David W. Pearce and Jeremy J.Warford, it is imperative that the following functions be fulfilled in all development models:

- Direct contributions to the quality of life. Environments act as amenities. They are appreciated and enjoyed as a beautiful landscape [and] as an essential ingredient of recreational activity . . .

- Indirect contributions to the quality of life. . . . Air and water pollution directly affect health, which, in turn, affects both the enjoyment of life and the ability of labor to support economic processes.

- Direct contributions to real income (GNP) through [the] environmental sector. The environmental sector—expenditures to protect the environment and provide [amenities]—creates income and employment. . . .

- Direct contributions to economic activity as environmental inputs. Natural environments supply raw materials and energy in the form of oil, coal, gas, fuelwood, and minerals. . . .
- Contributions to sustaining life-support systems generally.[72]

As Pearce and Warford succinctly summarize, "natural environments serve three major economic functions: they supply direct utility to individuals, they supply inputs to the economic process, and they supply services that support life. These three functions have direct relevance to how sustainable development is interpreted."[73]

Environmentally sustainable economic development may be defined as a long-term objective that ensures continuous economic development in which the quality of the environment is not negatively affected by the use mankind makes of it for economic growth. Thus a sustainable future depends on taking precautionary action now.[74]

SUMMARY

Orthodox theories of economic development, which originated in Western countries, assessed economic growth in terms of per capita income. Economic growth was based upon the productivity of labor, capital, and land. Neoclassical economists, on the other hand, completely abandoned the classical economist point of view that fixed proportions of capital, labor, or land are required in production within a given state of technology to spur economic growth. They argued that as capital stock grows in relation to a given population, national income might increase. Although orthodox and neoclassical economics contributed to laying the foundation of economic growth, the theories could not be empirically tested and were not directly related to the conditions of the developing countries.

Development economics emerged as a discipline in the 1950s with the establishment of the Bretton Woods institutions (i.e., the World Bank and International Monetary Fund) and the United Nations. Arthur Lewis in his "dual economic model" argued that surplus labor available at subsistence wages in the backward sector of the economy could enhance capitalistic development. To help achieve economic growth in Third World countries, Lewis proposed a structural transformation of the agricultural sector into a modern industrial economy.

In the 1960s Walt Whitman Rostow attempted to conceptualize economic growth in five linear stages: the traditional society, the precondition for takeoff, the takeoff, the drive to maturity, and the age of high mass consumption. However, the ethnocentric bias of this overly linear model has been noted.

In contradistinction to the then-existing "trickle-down" theory of economic growth, in the 1970s economists focused on the satisfaction of basic needs and on growth-with-equity approaches to development. GDP per capita as a benchmark for economic growth was replaced by the PQLI and HDI as measures of people-oriented development.

The astonishing economic growth during the 1980s in the NICS of Asia and Latin America gave birth to a neoclassical counterrevolution in economic theory and policy. Neoclassical strategies for economic development include establishment of competitive free markets, privatization of state-owned enterprises, promotion of free markets, export promotion of nontraditional agricultural products, and creation of a conducive environment for foreign direct investment.

Following the debate between economists and environmentalists in the 1970s and early 1980s on environmental issues, the idea of environment as constraint gave way to an acceptance that environmental concerns and development issues are closely related. Both analysts and policy makers acknowledge that if development is to be sustainable, environmental needs must be systematically incorporated into conventional paradigms of economic development. At the Earth Summit in 1992, there was strong agreement that environmental protection needs to be incorporated in the development process, and the Global Environmental Facility was established to provide grants and concessional funds to developing countries for programs aimed at protecting their environments.

REVIEW QUESTIONS

1. Define economic growth.

2. How does economic growth differ from economic development?

3. Briefly discuss the evolution of development paradigms.

4. What is sustainable development? Briefly review the evolution of sustainable development.

CASE STUDY: SOUTH KOREA

Prior to its economic crisis in the late 1990s, the Korean economy had experienced strong growth for some forty years. Mimicking the pace-setting example of Japan, South Korea was long hailed as a "miracle" economy—one of the "four tigers" making up the newly industrialized nations in Asia. Despite the devastation of the Korean War and the burden of large and persistent defense costs, South Korea's annual GNP growth rate was 10 percent each year from the mid-1960s to 1973 and more than 7 percent each year during the 1973-to-1982 period. Development transformed Korea's industrial structure, the lifestyles of its people, and its standard of living. Growth was concentrated in the manufacturing sector. Increasing access to governmental and other new employment opportunities shifted Korea from a rural, agrarian economy into an urban, industrial economy. The rapidity of the change had contradictory effects: crowding, pollution, and inefficiency in the economy, contrasted with an expansionary psychology, business confidence, and receptivity to change.

Paul W. Kuznets attributes Korea's long period of rapid and successful developmental accomplishments to two significant factors: the government's planning and credit allocation policies and its heavy emphasis on export expansion. His analysis begins with 1948, when a government capable of independent political and economic control came into being with the establishment of the Republic of Korea under president Syngman Rhee. U.S. emergency relief and reconstruction aid (which lasted until 1958), assistance, and influence following the Korean War led to a "liberalization program that would free the economy of restrictions."[75] But the economy performed only at an average of 3.7 percent GDP annual growth rate between 1953 and 1962. Political instability and the lack of an overall economic strategy characterized the period. Import substitution

> created the usual web of controls that perverted entrepreneurial incentives by making avoidance of controls rather than increased productivity the main source of profit. Furthermore, substitution was becoming increasingly difficult as the opportunities were exhausted for the sort of easy substitution that suited domestic factor proportions (abundant labor, scarce capital) and employed simple technology.[76]

The presidency of Park Chung-hee initiated a new economic strategy which included a series of liberalization measures that unleashed entrepreneurial forces and expanded output for export. Rapid industrialization progressed, marked by a doubling of capacity in the industrial sector by 1980. Export opportunities were abundant and Korea possessed the elements to exploit them. Foreign borrowing following the oil shock of 1973 was used to expand industrial capacity. Heavy industry expansion (including rapid growth of chemical industries) to the point of overcapacity strained the economy and led to bouts of inflation that destabilized economic growth into the early 1980s.

Development goals of the regime included (1) the improvement of living standards for the population, (2) the preservation of political power, and (3) the maintenance of national security-fostered policies to achieve self-sufficiency in food production and heavy industry.

The Korean government relied most heavily on credit allocation to control the economy. Kuznets wrote in 1986: "In recent years allocation has favored export activity, heavy and chemical industry projects, and the chaebol, or large conglomerate enterprises."[77]

During its early expansion efforts, Korea favored labor-intensive products and manufactures that were in line with its factor endowments, centering on textiles, apparel, and so on. Facing tariffs, quotas, and other protectionist devices by advanced industrial economies, Korea was forced to move up the technological learning curve as lower-wage competitors began making inroads on Korea's market shares for these products. Korea's inherent factor endowments encouraged the government to emphasize and expand the heavy and chemical industries that were capable of producing more skill-intensive products. Research institutes and consortiums, utilizing Korea's human-capital endowment (Korea has the world's highest per capita Ph.D. ratio and one of the highest-scoring student bodies in math and science) sprouted as government policy makers began to favor semi-conductor, bioengineering, and other technologies.

Again, government policy and capital allocation continued to favor the chaebol and further exacerbated the development of a two-tiered economic system, effectively denying smaller firms access to new technologies and equipment by maintaining high capital costs. This lack of access also confined them to local markets and further production limitations of scale when they could not compete in world markets.

There are many important factors that bear upon the developmental processes. Our investigation into Korea's economic development path is limited to the industrial sector because this is where the major environmental issues are generated. For thirty years, Korea pursued high growth policies for rapid industrialization, often with deleterious effects upon the environment. Exacerbating Korea's historical neglect of the environment is a lack of commitment. In the late 1980s there was still no "ambassador-at-large" for the environment, and no office within the Ministry of Foreign Affairs dedicated to environmental issues; and any presidential proclamations on the environment were notably lacking.[78] It is no surprise that a government pushing for rapid industrialization at any price, and a production sector doing all that it could and more to accomplish that goal, have forced environmental concerns to take a back seat to economic expansion.

For years environmental degradation was considered an acceptable fact of life in Korea. Urban air pollution, caused mainly by automobile and residential heating emissions, is quite severe, yet only in the 1990s was unleaded gasoline finally made available. Until recently, home heating utilized bunker-c and diesel oil instead of propane or other low-pollution fuels.[79] The development-first philosophy has prevailed so completely among both policy makers and businessmen that those who raised environmental questions were treated as antinational or antigovernmental.

Only recently has the Korean government made attempts to reduce carbon dioxide emission levels and to increase investment in environmentally friendly technologies; previously it claimed to have lacked the resources and the technology to implement more environmentally sound manufacturing procedures. Korean industries have opposed any changes that resulted in increased costs and made Korean products less competitive in world markets.

Suspecting that the other industrialized nations would begin to use environmental progress as a condition for trade, President Roh Tae Woo in a June 1992 speech warned that "the environment issue is likely to emerge as another barrier in international trade and our firms should positively cope with the situation."[80] The government projected a domestic market for environment-related industries of around $6.41 billion by 2001. The incentive for companies is purely profit oriented.

The Korean government has made regional and international commitments by signing the biodiversity and global warming treaties and the Montreal Protocol for the reduction of chlorofluorocarbons (CFCs). Several major ministries, especially the Ministry of Trade and Industry and the rather weak Ministry of the Environment, have formulated an "environmental industrial policy."[81] This policy aims at (1) minimizing the adverse effects international environmental regulations will have on domestic industries; (2) fostering an environment that preserves industry while restructuring existing industries; and (3) establishing detailed sectoral plans for the effective disposal of industrial pollution and wastes.

In March 1991 eight managers of the Doosan Electro-Materials Company in Taegu were arrested after it was discovered that many tons of untreated phenol waste had been dumped from their plant in the Kumi Industrial Complex into the Naktong River northwest of Pusan, Korea's second-largest city. The river feeds a wild bird sanctuary below the spill site and supplies drinking water to some 10 million people. Phenol is used in the production of printed circuit boards, and Doosan's market share is 80 percent of the nation's total. Phenol is known to cause cancer and damage to the nervous system. People throughout Southern Korea were forced to drink imported bottled water.

The leader of the nation's largest opposition party, Kim Dae-Jung, called the pollution spill a "result of the government's failure to have an environmental policy."[82] To underscore the lack of an effective environmental policy, within days of this incident, three food companies in Taejon were closed due to pollution violations. Environmental investigators and prosecutors let it be known that many other factories in the Kumi and other industrial complexes had contributed to the water contamination in the region. It was reported that surveillance officials sometimes accepted bribes from companies, and other industrial complexes throughout Korea had also contributed to environmental contamination.

Other areas of pollution in Korea that we have not touched upon include the buildup of garbage and industrial wastes and the CFC crisis in manufacturing. The main elements of the problem are quite clear: government industrialization goals have neglected adequate environmental safeguards; the business sector resists responsibility for cleaning up the pollution that it generates; and the population is unwilling to push environmental issues on a broad front.

DISCUSSION QUESTIONS

1. Briefly assess whether or not South Korea has achieved sustainable development.

2. What is the Korean ideological viewpoint on the environment? If it is changing, how much change is there and in what direction is the change?

3. Discuss the strengths and weaknesses of the Korean case study.

4. What lessons did you learn from the Korean case study?

NOTES

The introductory chapter was prepared with the assistance of Laura Van Galen and Russ Scherf, both of Dominican College, San Rafael, California.

1. See, for example, W. W. Rostow, *Theories of Economic Growth from David Hume to the Present* (New York: Oxford University Press, 1990).

2. Irma Adelman, *Theories of Economic Growth and Development* (Palo Alto, California: Stanford University Press, 1961): 25.

3. Henry William Spiegel, *The Growth of Economic Thought* (Englewood, New Jersey: Prentice-Hall, 1971): 244.

4. Ibid.

5. Pari Kasliwal, *Development Economics* (Cincinnati, Ohio: South-Western College Publishing, 1995): 95.

6. See, for example, Rostow, *Theories of Economic Growth from David Hume to the Present.*

7. David Mclellan, *Karl Marx: Selected Writings* (New York: Oxford University Press, 1990): 345–50.

8. Ibid.

9. T. N. Srinivasan, introduction, in Hollis Chenery and T. N. Srinivasan (ed.), *Handbook of Development Economics,* vol. 1 (Amsterdam: Elsevier, 1988): 5.

10. Michael P. Todaro, *Economic Development,* 5th ed. (New York: Longman, 1994): 52–53.

11. Gerald M. Meir, *Leading Issues in Economic Development* (New York: Oxford University Press, 1989): 105.

12. Todaro, *Economic Development,* 81–82.

13. Ibid., 124.

14. Gerald M. Meier and Robert E. Baldwin, *Economic Development: Theory, History, Policy* (New York: John Wiley & Sons, 1962): 67.

15. Clifford Cobb et al., "If the GDP is up, why is America down?" *The Atlantic Monthly* (October 1995): 62.

16. Jeroen C. J. M. van den Bergh and Jan van der Straaten, "The significance of sustainable development for ideas, tools, and policy," in van den Bergh and van der Straaten (eds.), *Toward Sustainable Development: Concepts, Methods, and Policy* (Washington, D.C.: Island Press, 1994): 3.

17. T. N. Srinivasan, introduction, in Hollis Chenery and T. N. Srinivasan (ed.), *Handbook of Development Economics,* vol. 1, 4.

18. Ernst Lutz, overview in Ernst Lutz (ed.), *Toward Improved Accounting for the Environment* (Washington, D.C.: The World Bank, 1993): 3.

19. Michael P. Todaro, *Economic Development in the Third World,* 4th ed. (New York: Longman, 1989): 23.

20. Rostow, *Theories of Economic Growth from David Hume to the Present,* 235.

21. Ibid., 392.

22. Christopher Pass et al., *The HarperCollins Dictionary: Economics* (New York: HarperCollins, 1991): 130.

23. Ranjani Kanth, *Paradigms in Economic Development* (New York: M. E. Sharpe, 1994): 6.

24. Todaro, *Economic Development in the Third World,* 66.

25. Ibid., 67.

26. Richard Peet and Michael Watts, "Introduction: Development theory and environment in an age of market triumphalism," *Economic Geography,* 69(3) (July 1993): 227–53.

27. Olman Segura and James K. Boyce, "Investing in natural and human capital in developing countries," in AnnMari Jasson et al. (eds.), *Investing in Natural Capital* (Washington, D.C.: Island Press, 1994): 480.

28. Ibid., 64.

29. Barbara Ingham, "The meaning of development: Interactions between 'new' and 'old' ideas," *World Development* 21(11), 1803–21.

30. E. Wayne Nafziger, *The Economics of Developing Countries* (Belmont, California: Wadsworth, 1984): 154.

31. Ingham, "The meaning of development: Interactions between 'new' and 'old' ideas."

32. Pass et al., *The HarperCollins Dictionary: Economics,* 130.

33. John P. Lewis and Valeriana Kallab, *Development Strategies Reconsidered* (New Brunswick, New Jersey: Transaction Books, 1986): 7.

34. Nafziger, *The Economics of Developing Countries,* 27.

35. Ingham, "The meaning of development: Interactions between 'new' and 'old' ideas."

36. Charles K. Wilber and Kenneth P. Jameson, "Paradigms of economic development and beyond," in Charles K. Wilber (ed.), *The Political Economy of Development and Underdevelopment* (New York: Random House, 1984): 11.

37. Ibid., 12.

38. United Nations Development Programme, *Human Development Report: 1993* (New York: Oxford University Press, 1993): 104.

39. "Guidelines for social analysis of development projects," *Asian Development Index* (June 1991): 34.

40. Todaro, *Economic Development,* 65.

41. Ibid., 13.

42. Ian M. D. Little, *Economic Development: Theory, Policy, and International Relations* (New York: Basic Books, 1982): 218.

43. Nafziger, *The Economics of Developing Countries,* 164.

44. Todaro, *Economic Development,* 85.

45. Ibid.

46. Anne O. Kruegar, *Political Economy of Policy Reform in Developing Countries* (Cambridge, Massachusetts: MIT Press, 1993).

47. "Democracy and growth," *The Economist* (August 27, 1994): 15.

48. Majid Rahnema, "Participation," in Wolfgang Sachs (ed.), *The Development Dictionary* (London: Zed Books Ltd., 1992): 117.

49. Ingham, "The meaning of development: Interactions between 'new' and 'old' ideas."

50. Lawrence Salmen, "Listening to the poor," *Finance and Development* (December 1994): 45–48.

51. Ibid.

52. United Nations Development Programme, *Human Development Report 1996* (New York: Oxford University Press, 1996): 50.

53. Ibid.

54. Ibid., 51.

55. Organization for Economic Cooperation and Development (OECD), "Science responds to environmental threats" (1992): 16.

56. Ibid.

57. S. V. S. Juneja, foreword to *Economic Policies for Sustainable Development* (Manila: Asian Development Bank, 1990): iii.

58. Paul Ekins, "The environmental sustainability of economic processes: a framework for analysis," in Jeroen C. J. M. van den Bergh and Jan van der Straaten (eds.), *Toward Sustainable Development* (Washington, D.C.: Island Press, 1994): 26.

59. Noel J. Brown and Pierre Quiblier, *Ethics and Agenda 21* (New York: United Nations Environment Programme, 1994): 6.

60. "UN conference on environment and development: Earth Summit puts future of rich and poor alike in our hands," *UN Chronicle* (March 1992): 81.

61. Martin Khor, "Earth Summit ends with both disappointment and hope," *Third World Economics* (June 16–July 15, 1992): 2–5.

62. Mohamed El-Ashry, "The new global environment facility," *Finance and Development* (June 1994): 48.

63. World Commission on Environment and Development, *Our Common Future* (Oxford: Oxford University Press, 1987): 8.

64. Andrew Blowers, *Planning for a Sustainable Environment* (London: Earthscan, 1993): 5.

65. Ismail Serageldin, "Sustainability and the wealth of nations: First steps in an ongoing journey," *Environmentally Sustainable Development Studies and Monographs Series No. 5* (Washington, D.C.: The World Bank, 1966): 3. *(Emphases added.)*

66. Noel J. Brown and Pierre Quiblier, *Ethics and Agenda 21*, 5.

67. Colin Rees, "The ecologist's approach to sustainable development," *Finance and Development* (December 1993): 14–15.

68. See, for example, Michael M. Cernea, "The sociologist's approach to sustainable development," *Finance and Development* (December 1993): 11–13.

69. Mohan Munasinghie, "Environment issues and economic decisions in developing countries," *World Development* 21(11) (1993): 1729–48.

70. Edward B. Barbier, "Natural capital and the economics of environment and development," in Ann Mari Jansson et al. (eds.), *Investing in Natural Capital* (Washington, D.C.: Island Press, 1994): 292.

71. Ingham, "The meaning of development: interactions between 'new' and 'old' ideas."

72. David W. Pearce and Jeremy J. Warford, *World without End: Economics, Environment and Sustainable Development* (New York: Oxford University Press, 1993): 43.

73. Ibid., 44.

74. See, for example, Andrew Blowers, *Planning for a Sustainable Environment* (London: Earthscan, 1993).

75. Paul W. Kuznets, "Economic development in South Korea," in Iipoyong J. Kim (ed.), *Development and Cultural Changes: Cross-cultural Perspectives* (New York: Paragon House, 1986): 37–64.

76. Ibid., 42.

77. Ibid., 51.

78. "Environmental trends in Korea," *East Asian Executive Reports* (August 15, 1992): 8, 13–16.

79. Clayton Jones, "Water shocks rouse South Korea," *The Christian Science Monitor* (May 29, 1991): 12.

80. Ibid.

81. Ibid.

82. "Alarms sound over the environment," *Business Korea* (April 1991): 21.

chapter 2

An Environmentally Adjusted System of National Accounts

By itself the GDP tells very little. Simply a measure of total output (the dollar value of finished goods and services), it assumes that everything produced is by definition "goods." It does not distinguish between costs and benefits, between productive and destructive activities, or between sustainable and unsustainable ones.

—Clifford Cobb et al.[1]

The economy should not be considered only in terms of its being a part of the environment nor should the natural environment be viewed only in terms of its economic usefulness. The natural environment and the economy could be interpreted as constituting two sides of the same coin. An accounting framework should therefore assist in identifying strategies of sustainable development that balance the satisfaction of human needs with the long-term maintenance of environmental functions.

—UN report, 1993[2]

The universally applied measure of the economic activity of a nation is the aggregate GDP (gross domestic product).

—UN report, 1993[3]

In spite of its clear limitations, GDP remains the primary indicator by which we measure a nation's economic success. Whereas GNP is the sum of domestic and foreign value of all production claimed by a nation's residents in a given year, GDP assesses the sum of the money values of all goods and services produced in the domestic economy by both residents and nonresidents within a given year. For example, a Toyota assembly plant in the United States is not included in the calculation of the U.S. GNP, but it is included in the U.S. GDP.

For the last fifty years, GDP per capita, which takes population into account, has also been used to rank the relative wealth of countries and has been the primary measure for assessing a country's relative degree of development. In recent years, development economics has taken into account the importance of sustainability and has identified a serious shortcoming in the current national accounting system.

The aim of this chapter is to discuss the limitations of the GDP as a measure of the national accounts and to demonstrate (using a case study) how environmentally adjusted GDP can be assessed in the LDCs.

SOME LIMITATIONS OF THE GROSS DOMESTIC PRODUCT

The first estimates of national accounts in the Western world were made by the English economist Thomas Petty in 1665. Whereas Petty was interested in ascertaining the taxable capacity of the nation,[4] it was not until the nineteenth century that national accounts were expanded to include income distribution, welfare, and unemployment. And only in 1968 was the system of national accounts (SNA) for measuring national wealth put to use.[5]

GDP data are a far from perfect measure of economic activity and there are limitations to its use as a tool for comparison between countries. There are five major problems with GDP.

1. GDP includes basically one thing: the monetary value of goods and services traded in the marketplace. This is an inaccurate measurement for the following reasons. First, most of the goods and services in developing countries are produced within the home by family members for their own use, rather than for sale in the marketplace.[6] Second, because GDP deals in monetary values rather than in physical units, it does not adjust for inflation. Finally, a large portion of the transactions in the underground economy escape inclusion in the GDP estimation.

2. GDP does not correctly take into account improvements in the quality of goods. For example, in a technologically advanced society, goods are usually improved over time, and new goods are constantly being introduced. The reverse situation—reduced quality of goods—may also occur.[7]

3. GDP places no value on leisure, although as a country's disposable income increases it is likely that its citizens will have more leisure time.[8]

4. Per capita income as a monetary measure of well-being fails to reflect that the measurements of purchasing power and increased GDP are being distributed across the population, and thus give disproportionate weight to the wealthiest segments of society. "Since in a typical DMC (Developing Member Country) around 75% of GNP is accounted for by the wealthiest 40 per cent of the population, it is essential to have a measurement of the relative changes in income of the poorest section of population."[9] Similarly, a rich country may have a disproportionate number of poor people.[10]

5. Standard measures of national accounts do not factor in the environmental cost of growth. Although items like machinery and tools are depreciated, natural resources are not depreciated as they are used up. If rain forest timber is clear-cut and sold in Indonesia, this is counted as "income." However, no debit is shown for a resource that has been consumed and cannot be replaced. Thus a country can show growth in GNP and yet be headed for ecological (and economic) disaster.[11] Lester Brown cites many countries in Africa and South America which experienced considerable economic growth that has now been reversed. For example, Nigeria was once one of the world's largest tropical timber exporters, but by 1988 it had a net trade deficit of $94 million in forest products.[12]

RATIONALE FOR ENVIRONMENTALLY ADJUSTED GROSS DOMESTIC PRODUCT

According to Ernst Lutz, the increasing consensus that environmental factors need to be considered in estimating national income is based on the following factors.

- Environmental damage not only affects psychic or non-economic welfare, but also translates into lost production. These costs can be large—up to 5% or more of GNP.

- Past development policy has been influenced by the theory of optimal growth without reference to sustainable growth; there is a critical need to determine under what conditions so-called optimal growth is also sustainable growth.

- Although raising real per capita income must remain a major objective of development policy, sustainable growth can be achieved only by systematically considering and addressing the environmental effects of growth strategies.[13]

Though it might be difficult to assess the direct environmental effects of the complex ways that national income is produced, it is possible that cost data can be used as a rough means of indirect measurement. To cite one example, in the case of disposal of wastes and other residuals, an opportunity-cost approach could be used by calculating the expenditures that would have to be made to prevent the emission of residuals. Similarly, the actual cost of health damages that could be caused by environmental deterioration could be subtracted from the national income to avoid the negative health effects of a deteriorated natural environment. In short,

> actual damage costs caused by environmental deterioration could also be assessed on the basis of so-called defensive expenditures or costs. Defensive environmental costs comprise the actual environmental protection costs involved in preventing or neutralizing a decrease in environmental quality, as well as the actual expenditures that are necessary to compensate for or repair the negative impacts of an actually deteriorated environment. The advantage of this approach is that estimates can be based on observable costs in monetary terms.[14]

But it needs to be emphasized that valuation of environmental deterioration in monetary terms may require the inclusion of physical data.

> This is especially true for the description of the flow of materials and nutrients within the natural environment, and from the natural environment to the economy and back to the environment as residuals. The concepts of material/ energy balances can be used as a suitable instrument for analyzing the material flows between the environment and the economy.[15]

AN ENVIRONMENTALLY ADJUSTED SYSTEM OF NATIONAL ACCOUNTS

Improved accounting procedures for the environment originated with Sir John Hicks in 1946. According to Hicks's definition, income is the maximum value a person can consume in a period of time and still expect to be as well off at the end of the period as at the beginning. When a person saves, he or she plans to be better off in the future; when a person lives beyond his or her income, he or she plans to be worse off.[16] Similarly, Salah El Serafy attempted to apply Keynes's "user cost" notion to environmental accounting in his effort to elaborate a method of accounting for flows of mineral extraction.[17]

As mentioned above, the environmental costs of economic production are not fully included in measures of economic production and national income because of outdated accounting procedures. Lutz points out three major deficiencies in the SNA, the national accounting framework developed in 1968.

> First, although national accounts usually record the depreciation of certain forms of capital, such as plant and machinery, they neglect other forms of capital, as represented by a nation's stock of water, soil, air, nonrenewable resources, wildlands, and the like, which provide not only the raw materials a society needs, but also essential waste-absorbing and life-support capabilities. Second, natural and environmental resources are generally not included in balance sheets or assessed by environmental quality indicators. And, third, cleanup costs (for example, to restore environmental assets) often fail to take into account previous environmental damages. For private firms, increased defensive environmental expenditures mean less value added. In contrast, when such cleanup costs are incurred by the public sector or by households, national output increases.[18]

The SNA framework failed to consider that GDP, conventionally measured, was increased at the expense of the environment, and by consuming limited resources faster at the expense of future generations. Even now, although there is a general consensus that standard national income be adjusted for environmental concerns, two diametrically opposed methods exist for doing so.

The first method advocates a holistic (or "totally integrated") system,

> starting with a complete inventory of environmental assets and setting money values on these in order to construct a balance sheet of all assets, whether nature- or man-made. Changes in such a balance sheet from year to year—as a result of degradation, renovation, locating new deposits, as well as economic exploitation—would be reflected in the end-period balance sheet.[19]

The second method argues that

> the gross domestic product (GDP) as conventionally calculated needs no adjustment at all. All that is needed is to reflect environmental degradation only in net income, by deducting from gross values calculated a magnitude for "depreciation." This course would leave the GDP . . . as previously calculated, without change, and adjust only the net domestic product (NDP) and the net national product (NNP).[20]

More recently, several alternative approaches redress some of the shortcomings in accounting procedures. To accurately record the costs of environmental damage and protection, the most basic approach is to estimate costs for pollution abatement programs such as those used in the United States and Germany. Another approach is to account specifically for natural resource capital depletion. For example, Indonesia's net domestic product (NDP) was estimated by subtracting petroleum, timber, and soil depletion from GDP (See Table 2.1). The study finds that "the conventionally measured GDP substantially overstated net income and its growth by ignoring the consumption of natural resource capital. It suggested that while GDP increased at an average annual rate of 7.1 per cent, they estimated net domestic product (GDP) rose by only 4.1 per cent per year."[21]

Table 2.1
Indonesia's Gross Domestic Product (GDP) and Net Domestic Product (NDP) at Constant 1973 Billion Rupiah from 1971 to 1984
Net Change in Natural Resource Sector

Year	GDP	Petroleum	Forestry	Soil	Net Change	NDP
1971	5,545	1,527	−312	−89	1,126[a]	6,671
1972	6,067	337	−354	−83	−100	5,967
1973	6,753	407	−591	−95	−279	6,474
1974	7,296	3,228	−533	−90	2,605[a]	9,901
1975	7,631	−787	−249	−85	−1,121	6,510
1976	8,156	−187	−423	−74	−684	7,472
1977	8,882	−1,225	−405	−81	−1,711	7,171
1978	9,567	−1,117	−401	−89	−1,607	7,960
1979	10,165	−1,200	−946	−73	−2,219	7,946
1980	11,169	−1,633	−965	−65	−2,663	8,506
1981	12,055	−1,552	−595	−68	−2,215	9,840
1982	12,325	−1,158	−551	−55	−1,764	1,056
1983	12,842	−1,825	−974	−71	−2,870	9,972
1984	13,520	−1,765	−493	−76	−2,334	11,186

Source: Robert Repetto and William B. Magrath, *Wasting Assets: Natural Resources in the National Income Accounts* (New York: World Resources Institute, 1989).

[a] The adjustment is positive in 1971 and 1974 because of new additions to petroleum reserve.

As shown in Table 2.2, based on a full physical accounting of natural resources, some countries (including Norway, the United States, and France) are attempting to fully compile inventories of their natural resources to better and more realistically plan for the future.[22]

At the international level in November 1988, the Joint UNEP-World Bank Export meeting on environmental accounting and the SNA met in Paris and agreed on the following.

• Natural resources and the environment are increasingly critical factors that should be properly accounted for in economic measurements.

- Replacing GDP with a more sustainable measure of income is not yet feasible. For the time being, therefore, satellite accounts that include environmental concerns in the computation of income linked to SNA should be created in which adjustments and alternative computations can be made.

- As a gauge of environmental health, net measures such as net domestic product (NDP) may be more meaningful than gross measurements such as GDP.

- Two NDPs should be computed: NDP as GDP minus consumption/depreciation of man-made capital, and NDP as GDP minus consumption/depreciation of natural capital.[23]

A consensus emerged to the effect that enough progress had been achieved to develop the links between environmental accounting and the SNA and to elaborate certain aspects of environmental accounting revision of the SNA.[24]

Table 2.2
National Approaches to Environmental Accounting by Three Countries: Norway, United States, and France

Norway

- Longest running interest in environmental and resource accounting, actually began in 1974.
- Focus is not on adjustment of GDP.
- Intent is to assist the government in making decisions on managing resources that are economically and politically most important.

United States

- Accounting is limited to collection of data on pollution abatement expenditure.
- Strong lobbying by environmental groups promoted the calculation of a measure called "gross sustainable productivity." This measure would seek revisions in the current accounting systems to take into account the depletion or degradation of natural resources.
- Sizable resources will be required for data gathering.

France

- For many years French experts have been trying to set up a system known as "patrimony accounting." This will analyze and describe the natural environment in its three basic functions: economic, ecological, and social.
- Limited resources have led to slow progress.
- Concentration has been on establishment of resource accounts similar to those in Norway.

Source: Ernst Lutz and M. Munasinghe, "Some national approaches to environmental accounting," *Finance and Development* (March 1991): 20.

In the same vein, Herman E. Daly approaches environmentally adjusted income or sustainable social net national product (SSNNP) "as net national product (NNP) minus both defensive expenditures (DE) and depreciation of natural capital (DNC); thus, SSNNP = NNP − DE − DNC."[25]

In February 1993 the Statistical Commission of the United Nations formally adopted a management-oriented approach to natural resource accounts known as the Satellite System of Integrated Environmental and Economic Accounting (SEEA). This system, which included many principles outlined in the System of National Accounts (SNA), attempts also to account for changes in the quality of the environment and depletion of natural resources. According to the SEEA, the concept of capital included "natural" in addition to "man-made" capital and also incorporated nonmonetary data on the stocks and flows of natural resources into the accounting system.

Although countries would not be required to fully integrate environmental concerns into the core accounts, it is suggested that they prepare "satellite" accounts, comprising both physical and monetary units, consistent with the core accounts. For this purpose, in December 1993 the United Nations Statistical Office issued detailed guidance in a handbook on integrated environmental and economic accounting.[26]

This approach was further backed up in Agenda 21 issued by UNCED (the Earth Summit) held in Rio de Janeiro, Brazil, on June 3–14, 1992. Agenda 21 stated that the Statistical Division of the United Nations Secretariat should, *inter alia*:

> a) Make available to all member States the methodologies contained in Integrated Environmental and Economic Accounting;
> b) In collaboration with other relevant United Nations organizations, further develop, test, refine and then standardize the provisional concepts and methods such as those proposed by the present handbook;
> c) In close collaboration with relevant United Nations organizations, strengthen existing mechanisms for technical cooperations among countries, including exchange of experience in the establishment of integrated environmental and economic accounting; and
> d) Provide the necessary technical support to member States to ensure the application of integrated environmental and economic accounts.[27]

Using the recently updated version of the SNA, in 1993 the United Nations Statistical Division (UNSTAT) in collaboration with the World Bank undertook two studies in Mexico and Papua New Guinea, to relate the 1968 SNA to the environment.[28] To measure sustainable income in the Mexican study the following four environmental adjustments were made.

1. GDP = consumption expenditure + gross investment expenditure + government expenditure (in a closed economy)
2. NDP = GDP − depreciation on manufactured capital
3. Environmentally adjusted net domestic product (EDP1) = NDP − Resource Depletion estimates (e.g., oil, mineral, timber extraction)
4. EDP2 = EDP1 − environmental degradation estimates (e.g., soil erosion, solid wastes, groundwater use, water pollution, air pollution)[29]

Although the natural damages costs would not be included in calculating the EDP, they would be considered in the calculation of an environmentally adjusted net income (ENI) by subtracting the following five items from the EDP.

1. Government and household environmental protection expenditure
2. The costs of environmental effects on health and other facets of human capital
3. Environmental costs of household and government consumption activities
4. The costs of environmental damage caused by discarding capital goods
5. The costs of negative environmental effects in the country that are caused by another country[30]

Though instructive, SEEA is mainly based on natural capital such as land and subsoil assets insofar as they provide economic benefits and can have approximate market prices. But from an ecological point of view,

> such coverage may be incomplete: Tropical forests, for instance, might have a market value because of their yield of tropical wood commanding high market prices, while other functions of such forests that could have non-market value from an ecological point of view are not registered. Among the other functions may be mentioned the role of those forests in the global climate balance, as well as their cultural and spiritual use for indigenous people. From an ecological point of view, tropical forests are one of the most important habitats for a great variety of animals and plants. Furthermore, market valuation for assets is not the only type of valuation possible.[31]

Also, the SEEA is

> a more ambitious undertaking because it requires physical information on stocks and flows of natural resources, disaggregated by economic sector, including the consumption and non-market activities of households. It can then be used in the input-output modelling framework currently used for national accounts, to integrate economic and environmental sectors, to determine trade-offs among development strategies, and to determine the implications of alternative economic valuation methods. A uniform classification scheme can also integrate data gathered in different government agencies and political jurisdictions into a common analytical framework that can be used to identify inconsistencies and interrelationships.[32]

SUMMARY

Since 1968 the United Nations has been using GDP (the sum of the market value of all goods and services produced in the domestic economy by both residents and nonresidents within a given year) as the primary means of assessing the system of national accounts or the economic health of a country. But it can be argued that GDP was largely increased by consuming natural resources at a progressively faster rate at the expense of future generations.

With the emergence of sustainable development paradigms in the 1972 Stockholm Conference on the Human Environment, the assessment of the SNA is attempting to show the interrelationships between the natural environment and the economy using the SEEA.

Though instructive, the SEEA is largely based on the market values of natural capital with little or no attention given to nonmarket values. To be complete in its enumeration, the SEEA would require complete information on stocks and flows of natural capital in each country (a situation that is not possible in practice).

REVIEW QUESTIONS

1. Are economic growth and sustainable development complementary or competing goals for a developing country? Give specific examples from Southeast Asian countries.
2. In what ways might the revised version of the SNA be inadequate in assessing EDP or EDI?

CASE STUDY: A SATELLITE SYSTEM OF NATIONAL ACCOUNTS FOR MEXICO

In 1990 and 1991 the UNSTAT, the World Bank, and Mexico's National Institute of Statistics, Geography and Informatics attempted to create environmentally adjusted national income aggregates for Mexico based on the SEEA. Mexico was chosen not only because Mexican officials were concerned about the environmental problems that their country was facing, but also because they wished to halt the depletion of Mexico's oil reserves, upon which it relies very heavily.[33] Given the host of conceptual and methodological hurdles that existed, the focus of the study was not so much to achieve quantitative accuracy as to see how the discipline, concepts, and data could be integrated and where the difficulties would arise. The study focused on the following three main elements:

1. oil extraction and depletion
2. deforestation and land use
3. degradation

Depletion, deforestation, and land use are quantitative measures based on the amount of resources used (e.g., barrels of oil extracted, hectares of forest removed). These amounts are given a monetary value based on their current market value. In the case of oil and timber, the net rent value (market value minus profit and extraction cost) was used. The level of degradation was given an economic value based on the amount of money required to reverse the damage to the environment (e.g., the costs of cleaning contaminated water, replacing lost soil and groundwater). Once all the values were determined, they were combined with traditional economic indicators in an SNA, which is called *capital accumulation*. Capital accumulation attempts to incorporate environmental resources into the traditional accounting framework by looking at the total accumulation of "produced" and "nonproduced" economic capital. For example, factories and machinery are considered *produced economic capital,* whereas environmental resources, like oil reserves and forest lands, are considered *nonproduced economic capital.* By these means, environmental resources are now included in the total economic picture and their consumption and depreciation can be accounted for.[34]

Four stages were used in the compilation of the satellite SNA (as described by Ernst Lutz).

> First, the standard SNA analysis that derives the GDP was expanded to include produced asset balances. The depreciation of those assets was estimated and the resulting figures were deducted from the GDP to arrive at the (standard) NDP. Second, attention turned to oil depletion and forest and groundwater assets. Oil depletion represents an economic cost (so-called user cost) that needs to be subtracted from gross product along with other corrections to arrive at the adjusted net product. Additional finds of oil reserves contribute to capital accumulation (but without being reflected in the flow accounts). Third, an effort was made to assess degradation, not only that caused by air and water pollution, but also by soil erosion, groundwater use, and the deposit of solid wastes. Degradation affects the quality of non-produced assets (such as water and air), which have complex ties to the economy. In general, degradation affects the quality of life more immediately than economic production. Fourth, land-use concerns and deforestation were added to the accounting framework. Forests are essentially a renewable resource, but if they are depleted over and above their maximum sustainable yield, a depletion cost must also be calculated.
>
> ... One is to calculate the value of stocks of assets as the sum of discounted values of future income streams; the value of changes in the stock of natural assets is derived from changes in future income streams as a consequence of additions to the reserves of natural assets, or depletions. Another is to calculate the user-cost of depletion. ... The third type of valuation, which is only used for assessing quality changes in the natural assets, is concerned with the cost of avoiding such changes (avoidance-cost approach).[35]

As shown in Table 2.3, while Mexico's EPD1 for 1985 was estimated to be 94 percent of NDP, the EPD2 was estimated at 87 percent of NDP. Although the figures are not fully reliable, the application of satellite accounts to Mexico and other developing countries is an important step toward the eventual incorporation of environmental factors to national income estimation. However, as David W. Pearce and Jeremy J. Warford point out, the valuation of natural capital assumes a full knowledge of each of the following.

- the cost of extraction or harvesting
- any environmental costs involved in extraction, harvesting, and use
- the benefits forgone in the future from using a unit of the resource today[36]

Ascribing the correct economic value to natural capital, especially in developing countries, is not that easy. Markets do not function efficiently. Data on resource depletion and their nonmonetary impacts (such as on living systems or biological mechanisms, economic productivity or ecological systems) are very difficult to

Table 2.3
Mexico's Environmentally Adjusted National Account (1985)

	In Million Pesos	Index
NDP	42,060	100.0
Minus resource depletion		
Oil	1,470	3.5
Timber	164	0.4
Land use change	764	1.8
Equals EDP1	39,662	94.3
Minus environmental degradation		
Soil erosion	449	1.1
Solid wastes	197	0.5
Ground water use	191	0.5
Waste pollution	662	1.6
Air pollution	1,656	3.9
Equals EDP2	36,507	86.7

Source: Andrew Steer and Ernst Lutz, "Measuring environmentally sustainable development," Finance and Development (December 1993): 22.

obtain. Inferences and indirect estimates may lead to faulty conclusions. Contingent valuation (estimating the willingness-to-pay response from an individual) requires a certain level of literacy and sophisticated interview techniques.[37]

Although this case study is an attempt in the right direction, it does not include elements such as biodiversity, ecosystem services, or the marine environment. In addition, since data were compiled from several government and private institutions, the data collected to assess the system of national accounts were neither accurate nor comprehensive. For example, solid wastes were calculated for the household sectors but not for the industrial sectors.[38] Also, the value of forestlands was not broken down into types of trees. Neither soil erosion caused by the industrial sector nor pollution caused by oil extraction were accurately calculated.

Moreover, as shown in Table 2.4, calculations using the above-noted adjustment did not necessarily make changes in the values of all industries. For example, the tourism industry, which accounts for 31 percent of the NDP, increased to 36 percent when depletion and degradation were applied, though it could be argued that since tourism contributes to pollution and energy degradation, it should have been reduced substantially. On the other hand, though oil contributed 3.5 percent to Mexico's NDP, after adjustments were made it contributed only negative 0.20 percent to the EDP1. If Mexico can see that oil depletion is detrimental to its development, it can focus its efforts on creating more efficient uses of oil resources. This case study appears to show that although environmental accounting is in its infancy, it is nonetheless a very important step toward achieving sustainable development for the benefit of future generations.

Table 2.4
Changes in Mexico's Net Domestic Product
when Environmentally Adjusted

Industry	% NDP	% EDP1[a]	Difference	% EDP2[b]	Difference
Agriculture	5.61	5.61	0.00	5.57	−0.04
Animal farming & breeding	2.64	1.49	−1.15	0.93	−1.71
Forestry	0.54	0.15	−0.39	−0.08	−0.62
Fishing, hunting, etc.	0.32	0.34	0.02	0.37	0.05
Oil	3.50	0.00	−3.50	−0.20	−3.70
Other mining	0.97	1.03	0.06	1.12	0.15
Manufacturing	20.88	22.15	1.27	22.76	1.88
Electric, gas, water	0.78	0.83	0.05	0.05	−0.73
Construction	4.09	4.20	0.11	4.57	0.48
Trade, hotels, restaurants	31.09	32.96	1.87	35.87	4.78
Transport, storage, communication	5.72	6.06	0.34	4.55	−1.17
Other services					
(excluding government)	20.66	21.91	1.25	23.82	3.16
Government services	3.21	3.26		3.49	
Total Production Activities	100.00	100.00		100.00	

[a] EDP1 = NDP minus resource depletion

[b] EDP2 = NDP minus EDP1 minus environmental degradation

Source: Adapted from Jan Van Tongeren, Stefan Schweinfest, Ernst Lutz, Maria Gomez Luna, and Guillen Martin, "Integrated environmental and economic accounting: A case study for Mexico," in Ernst Lutz, ed., *Toward Improved Accounting for the Environment: An UNSTAT-World Bank Symposium* (Washington, D.C.: The World Bank, 1993): 105, Table 6-12.

DISCUSSION QUESTIONS

1. What are the strengths and weaknesses of the above case study?
2. Choose a country and estimate its EDP for two years.

NOTES

This chapter was prepared with the assistance of John Stayton, David Robertshaw, and Juliet Meehan, students at Dominican College, San Rafael, California.

1. Clifford Cobb et al., "If the GDP is up, why is America down?" *The Atlantic Monthly* (October 1995): 65.

2. United Nations, Department for Economic and Social Information and Policy Analysis Statistical Division, *Integrated Environmental and Economic Accounting* (New York: United Nations, 1993): 3.

3. Udo E. Simmonis, "Industrial restructuring: Does it have to be 'jobs vs. trees'?" *Work in Progress of the United Nations University* 14(2) (1993): 6.

4. Cobb et al., "If the GDP is up, why is America down?": 62.

5. W. W. Rostow, *Theories of Economic Growth from David Hume to the Present* (New York: Oxford University Press, 1990): 221–22.

6. E. Wayne Nafziger, *The Economics of Developing Countries* (Belmont, California: Wadsworth Publishing, 1984): 23.

7. Robert Heilbroner and Lester Thurow, *Economics Explained* (New York: Touchstone/Simon & Schuster, 1994): 83.

8. Ibid.

9. Asian Development Bank, "Guidelines for social analysis of development projects" (1991): 5.

10. Heilbroner and Thurow, *Economics Explained*, 84.

11. Ernst Lutz (ed.), UNSTAT-World Bank Symposium, *Toward Improved Accounting for the Environment* (Washington, D.C.: The World Bank, 1993): 1.

12. Lester R. Brown et al., *Saving the Planet: How to Shape an Environmentally Sustainable Global Economy* (New York: W. W. Norton, 1991): 123.

13. Lutz (ed.), *Toward Improved Accounting for the Environment*, 1–2.

14. United Nations, Department for Economic and Social Information and Policy Analysis, Statistical Division, *Integrated Environmental and Economic Accounting*, 5.

15. Ibid., 6.

16. John Hicks, *Classics and Moderns: Collected Essays on Economic Theory* (Cambridge, Massachusetts: Harvard University Press, 1983).

17. Salah El Serafy, "The environment as capital," in Ernst Lutz (ed.), *Toward Improved Accounting for the Environment*, 17.

18. Lutz (ed.), *Toward Improved Accounting for the Environment*, 1–2.

19. El Serafy, "The environment as capital," in Lutz (ed.), *Toward Improved Accounting for the Environment*, 19.

20. Ibid.

21. United Nations, "Natural resource accounting: a case study in Indonesia," *State of the Environment in Asia and the Pacific* (Bangkok, Thailand: Economic and Social Commission for Asia and the Pacific, 1990): 264.

22. E. Lutz and M. Munasinghe, "Some national approaches to environmental accounting," *Finance and Development* (March 1991): 20.

23. Ernst Lutz and Salah El Serafy, "Recent developments and future work," in Yusuf J. Ahmad et al. (eds.), *Environmental Accounting for Sustainable Development* (Washington, D.C.: The World Bank, 1989): 89.

24. United Nations, Department for Economic and Social Information and Policy Analysis, Statistical Division, *Integrated Environmental and Economic Accounting*, iii.

25. Herman E. Daly, "Toward a measure of sustainable social net national product," in Ahmad et al. (eds.), *Environmentally Accounting for Sustainable Development*: 8.

26. Andrew Steer and Ernst Lutz, "Measuring environmentally sustainable development," *Finance and Development* (December 1993): 20–23.

27. United Nations, Department for Economic and Social Information and Policy Analysis, Statistical Division, *Integrated Environmental and Economic Accounting*, iv.

28. Lutz (ed.), *Toward Improved Accounting for the Environment*, 5–6.

29. Steer and Lutz, "Measuring environmentally sustainable development," 20–23.

30. United Nations Environmental Programme (UNEP), *Poverty and the Environment* (Nairobi, Kenya: UNEP, 1995): 107.

31. United Nations, Department for Economic and Social Information and Policy Analysis, Statistical Division, *Integrated Environmental and Economic Accounting,* 4.

32. UNEP, *Poverty and the Environment,* 107.

33. Jan van Tongeren et al., "Integrated environmental and economic accounting: A case study for Mexico," in Lutz (ed.), *Toward Improved Accounting for the Environment,* 85.

34. Ibid.

35. Lutz (ed.), *Toward Improved Accounting for the Environment,* 6–7.

36. David W. Pearce and Jeremy J. Warford, *World without End: Economics, Environment and Sustainable Development* (Oxford: Oxford University Press, 1993): 60.

37. Ibid.

38. Ibid., 88.

chapter 3

The Environmental Impact of Capital Formation

P revious chapters have concentrated on sustainable development and the new system of estimating national accounts. Of equal importance, however, is the theory of capital formation and its linkage to the environment. Capital formation is regarded as a major component in the economic development of a nation. Also referred to as capital accumulation, it includes all new investments in natural capital, physical equipment and technology, infrastructure, and human resources. When some proportion of the GDP is reinvested as capital (man-made, natural, and human) every year, a nation achieves an increase in output and income. Until recently, development economists have not been able to clearly delineate the environmental spillover effects of capital accumulation on the productivity of a nation.

The discussion of capital accumulation in this chapter is organized as follows. First, the various theories of capital formation are summarized. Second, the linkage between capital formation and other environmental concerns is shown. Finally, trade-offs between economic growth and environmental degradation are illustrated in a case study of China.

THEORIES OF CAPITAL FORMATION

The most widely known simple one-sector model of economic growth was developed by Sir Roy Harrod and Evsey Domar during the 1940s. The Harrod-Domar growth model is an offshoot of the simple Keynesian income determination model in which the identity of output produced is equal to output sold (consumption + investment = consumption + savings). The model, also known as Dynamic Theory, examines the relationship between growth and capital requirements. As described by Rostow, the "Dynamic Theory . . . is likely to retain its present place as a landmark in economic analysis in general, and growth analysis in particular. Its status derives from the fact that it crystallized and rendered explicit a way of looking at growth and fluctuations toward which a number of economists were tending."[1]

While developed to explain the macroeconomic performance of advanced industrial economies, this model become a very important planning tool for developing countries in the 1950s.[2]

The Harrod-Domar model is based on the assumption that a combination of higher savings rates and the resultant physical capital accumulation on the one hand, and the rise in the capital-output ratio (i.e., the physical productivity of new investment) on the other hand, would bring about aggregate growth. To grow an economy must not only save and invest a certain proportion of its national income, but net additions to the capital stock in the form of new investments are necessary. Net addition to the capital stock will lead to increased GDP. The rate of growth resulting from new investments is determined by the combination of two factors: the savings ratio and the capital-output ratio. Thus investment constitutes an important component of aggregate demand for output as well as a change in the capital stock available to the business sector from the supply side.

In the Harrod-Domar model, capital plays a strategic role in economic growth, creating both income and output. "The relationship which equates the rate of growth of income to the savings ratio divided by the capital output ratio has been one of the chief vehicles by which Western economic thought has been carried into the plans and discussions of the plans of underdeveloped countries."[3]

In its simplest form the Harrod-Domar model states that the growth rate of GDP is determined jointly by a nation's savings rate and the incremental capital-output ratio (ICOR) or marginal capital-output coefficient.[4] The relationship between output and capital stock can be specified as

$$Y = K/k \tag{3.1}$$

where Y = output, K = stock of capital, and k = capital-output ratio. When converting Equation 3.1 to growth of output, increases in output and capital are rewritten as ΔY and ΔK. Hence,

$$\Delta Y = \Delta K/k \tag{3.2}$$

where $1/k$ is a change in output (GDP) due to a one-unit change in the capital stock, also referred to as ICOR.

The growth rate of output (g) is obtained by dividing both sides of Equation 3.2 by output (Y). Thus we rewrite Equation 3.2 as

$$g = \Delta Y/Y = \Delta K/Y.1/k \tag{3.3}$$

For the entire economy, ΔK is the same as net investment (I). As shown above, according to the Keynesian equilibrium condition, net investment (I) must equal savings (S). Thus,

$$\Delta K/Y = I/Y = S/Y = s \tag{3.4}$$

where s is average savings rate of GDP.

Therefore Equation 3.3 can be converted to the basic Harrod-Domar growth model

$$g = s/k \tag{3.5}$$

According to the Harrod-Domar model, the more a nation saves and invests, the faster it can achieve economic growth. The rate of growth of GDP is determined by both the national saving ratio (s) and the national capital-output ratio (k). As mentioned above, the ICOR is a measure of the productivity of capital or investment.[5] For example, an economy that saves 15 percent with a capital-output ratio of 5 will have a 3 percent growth rate. If an economy wants to grow at a faster rate, investment must be increased.

The model predicts that economic growth is dependent on saving more and increasing investment in the economy. However, the model fails to show the impact that investment might have on income growth. As stated by Celso Furtado, by leaving investment as an autonomous figure, the Harrod-Domar model does not illustrate that investment by definition leads to a growth in income.[6] While savings and investment in capital stock are necessary for high rates of economic growth, other institutional structures and human capital must exist in order for a nation to grow.

There are also some fundamental problems in applying the Harrod-Domar model to developing nations. In poor countries where sufficient new capital is not being generated, the model assumes that the solution is to increase investment in the economy through foreign government aid or private foreign investment. However, such additional investment does not always work. According to Michael P. Todaro, there are several assumptions about development in Third World countries that are not accurate. Western economic theories assume that all developing economies follow the same path or stages of growth as the more developed countries. There is also the expectation that because an infusion of capital into postwar Europe was successful in reviving those economies, a similar strategy would hold true in the Third World. While it is true that investment is needed, it is not sufficient by itself.[7]

Though widely used in the development planning process of a number of developing countries, ICOR has the following limitations.

- The model assumes that s and k are independent of output.

- Complementary factors such as entrepreneurship, management, labor, technical knowledge, and efficiency in capacity utilization are not included in calculating growth.

- The interdependencies among different projects are ignored. Due to time lags, different types of capital will have quite different gestation periods.

- The simple calculation that a certain amount of investment inevitably leads to an increase in income ignores the variable time values of money in various projects.[8]

- The proportion of saved NDP and the capital-output ratio is assumed to be a constant.

- There is a faulty assumption that resources are fully employed which an underdeveloped country is unlikely to achieve.[9]

In the 1950s the role of capital formation in the development process was taken for granted. In view of this underlying assumption, various United Nations economists considered capital shortage (plant, equipment, inventory, etc.) the greatest limitation to the economic growth of LDCs.[10]

W. W. Rostow attempted to extend the Harrod-Domar model. Rostow argued that investment and savings are integral parts in moving an economy from a pre-condition stage to a takeoff stage, and that an economy must achieve a rise in savings from 5 percent to 15 percent to reach the takeoff stage. If the domestic savings rate has not reached a level of 15 percent to 20 percent of the national economy, then the difference can be made up through foreign capital flows. Rostow endorsed a new era for the economic development of LDCs based on plans similar to those used in the Marshall Plan in Europe, without understanding the complex social and human conditions of developing countries. Investments in human capital occupied an increasing percentage of development budgets in the developed countries, a fact largely ignored by Rostow. In the 1950s and 1960s Alec Moses Abramovitz, Robert Solow, Benton Massell, and others undertook econometric analyses to determine the relative importance of capital accumulation and technical progress in economic growth. As shown in Table 3.1, in the United States it was found that between 5 percent and 33 percent of growth in output was attributable to an increase in capital per worker-hour. The residual was attributed to technical progress. A similar study conducted in the developing countries after the 1960s indicates that the major source of growth is increased capital per worker. However, as cited by Hogendorn, World Bank data covering 125 LDCs from 1973 to 1987 show that "on average . . . a 1 percentage point increase in the ratio of investment to GDP would raise the rate of growth by 0.1 of 1 percentage point."[11] Policies based on Rostow's model failed significantly to contribute to the economic growth of the developing countries.

THE RESIDUAL

As stated above, the residual (technical progress) rather than physical capital was the major contributor to economic growth in the industrial countries. According to Edward Dension's neoclassical sources of growth analysis, the residual developed as the major determinant of real income per worker in the United States from 1909 to 1973 (Table 3.2).

Although it succeeded in isolating the determinants of growth as measured by real per capita income, Dension's study suffers from disaggregation. For example, it is axiomatic that the allocation of capital is highly dependent on a key variable: advances in knowledge (i.e., technological change and improvements in managerial and organizational knowledge). Also, with experience, efficiency in the allocation of capital is likely to improve. However, Dension's analysis sounds a cautionary note: Pinpointing the explanatory variables in the growth process of the LDCs is extremely difficult. The lack of infrastructure to support data collection in the LDCs can lead to faulty policy development. Growth accounting must focus only on identifying the most crucial elements in the growth process.

Table 3.1
The Share of Growth in Output per Worker
from Increased Capital per Worker

Author, Year of Study	Country	Measure of Output per Worker or Person	Period	Percentage of Growth in Output per Worker Attributed to Increases in Capital per Worker
Abramovitz (1956)	United States	Net National Product (NNP) per capita	1869–78 to 1944–53	.05–.20
Solow (1957) with correction by Hogan (1958) and Levine (1960)	United States	Gross private nonagricultural output per man-hour	1909–59	.10–.19
Massell (1960, 1962)	United States	Manufacturing output per man-hour	1919–57	.10–.33
Niitamo (1958)	Finland	Output per man-year	1925–52	< .50
Aukrust and Bjerke (1959)	Norway	NNP per capita	1900–56	.38
Reddaway & Smith (1960)	United Kingdom	Net manufacturing output per worker	1948–54	.33
Gaathon (1961)	Israel	GNP per capita	1950–59	.60
Bruno (1962)	Israel	GNP per capita	1958–60	.50–.60
Bruton (1967)	United States, Northwest Europe, Japan, Israel	Output per man-hour	1940–64	.42
Bruton (1967)	Argentina, Brazil, Chile, Colombia, Mexico	Output per man-hour	1950–65	.74
Maddison (1970)	22 developing countries	Output per man-hour	1950–65	.90
Robinson (1971)	39 developing countries	Output per man-hour	1958–66	.88

Source: E. Wayne Nafziger, *The Economics of Developing Countries,* 2d ed. (Paramus, New Jersey: Prentice-Hall, 1990).

Table 3.2
Contribution to Growth in Real Income per Worker, 1909–1973 (in percent)

Residual	1909–1929	1929–1957	1948–1973
Volume of capital	29	9	15
Reduction in hours worked	−19	−33	−8
Education	29	42	19
Effects of fewer hours on labor quality	19	21	
Change in age and sex composition of labor force			−8
Technical progress (knowledge)	20	36	54
Economies of scale	23	21	15
Improved allocation of resources			15

Source: Edward F. Dension's calculations in Jan S. Hogendorn, *Economic Development,* 2d ed. (New York: HarperCollins, 1992): 90.

Note: Column totals do not add up exactly because of rounding off and omission of several minor items.

GOVERNMENT INTERVENTION IN CAPITAL FORMATION

As mentioned above, Rostow's stages of economic growth deal with capital formation in the developing countries. Countries that save and invest 15 percent to 20 percent of their GNP will reach a takeoff stage in their economic growth. Other than providing a strong argument for justifying technical and capital assistance from the developed to the developing countries, Rostow's economic growth model concentrated only on national savings as an important vehicle for economic growth in the developing countries. On the other hand, as John Page analyzed the development models of East Asian economies, he found that the East Asian NICs achieved dynamic development because they were extremely successful in their efforts to increase real savings and to give primary and secondary schooling to their school age population. He stated:

> Macroeconomic performance was unusually stable, providing the necessary framework for private investment. Policies to increase the integrity of the banking system and make it more accessible to nontraditional savers increased the levels of financial savings. Education policies that focused on primary and secondary education generated rapid increases in labor force skills.[12]

The East Asian economies organized financial systems to provide positive interest rates to borrowers. To attract foreign investors Asian economies employed two methods. First, infrastructure was created to complement investment. Second, tariffs on imported capital goods were reduced to encourage importation of foreign goods. Providing the greatest return for dollars invested, allocations to primary and secondary education became the focus of social investment. In Indonesia, Korea, and Thailand, Page documented that more than 80 percent of the educational budget was targeted towards primary and secondary education.[13] To address the argument that technology cannot advance without postsecondary education, the East Asian countries spent scarce public funding in this educational sector, especially on technology training. A large portion of training in the humanities was left to private universities. By stressing primary and secondary education, the Asian countries increased human capital and developed a workforce with the skills necessary for industrial expansion.

Government intervention in capital formation in the NICs is common. For example, mild suppression of interest rates in Japan, Korea, Malaysia, Taiwan, and Thailand lowered real interest rates to borrowers, increasing incentives for investment. Financial institutions were created, and institutional reform was implemented to encourage domestic savings. Credit policies favored large corporations, leading to an increase in the volume of exports. Tax policies were designed to encourage both foreign and domestic investment. Thus, the main argument of Page's analysis is that in order for a nation's economy to experience high levels of economic growth, basic economic fundamentals should be the focus of government's attention.[14]

CAPITAL FORMATION AND THE ENVIRONMENT

Capital formation can lead to economic growth. However, as discussed before, capital formation almost always comes at the expense of the environment. The limitation of capital accumulation as a prescription for growth has prompted interest in the accumulation and preservation of natural capital. Classical economics outlines three factors of production: land, labor, and capital. Today the terms *man-made capital* (machines, tools, buildings, technologies, infrastructure), *natural capital* (forests, fisheries, oil, minerals, waste assimilation, water, and impact of the biosphere), *human capital* (health, knowledge, skill, and motivation), and *social and organizational capital* (community involvement and grassroots organization) have replaced the original triad.[15]

The six-capital model differs significantly from the conventional triad. The new model assumes that an increase in production due to capital accumulation will contribute to a decrease in intergenerational welfare. Capital is now linked to unacceptable costs of environmental degradation and to negative impacts on human well-being. This new model deals with the costs of environmental cleanup and maintaining environmental assets. Investment in natural capital focuses on the preservation and sustenance of the existing level of biological diversity so that society can receive a return from capital in perpetuity.[16]

Quantification and accurate valuation of biodiversity is very complicated. It requires use of a combination of surrogate market techniques (such as travel costs); discrete choice techniques (opportunity costs for non-marketed goods, attaching unit costs per visit to recreational sites); construction of shadow pricing (valuing damage to life using wage premia); use of contingent valuation methods (e.g., asking consumers how much they are willing to compensate for an impact on environmental quality); and dose-response relationship (the rate at which the surface of a material decays as estimated by the costs of repairs).[17]

SUMMARY

Capital formation, also known as capital accumulation, includes all new investments in natural capital, physical equipment and technology, infrastructure, and human resources. When some proportion of the GDP is reinvested as capital every year, a nation achieves an increase in output and income.

The one-sector model of economic growth was developed to explain the macroeconomic performance of the advanced countries. However, it become an important tool for predicting economic growth in the LDCs. That is, the model assumed that poor developing countries could increase their investments through foreign government or foreign direct investments if they followed the footsteps of postwar European countries.

It is axiomatic that capital formation with well-developed infrastructure and well-focused primary and secondary education could lead to economic growth. But capital formation can also bring environmental disaster and a decrease in intergenerational welfare. The Chinese case study presented below demonstrates how development strategies based on capital formation can contribute to environmental destruction.

REVIEW QUESTIONS

1. What is incremental capital-output ratio (ICOR)? What are the limitations of using ICOR to estimate capital requirements in developing countries?

2. What is capital formation? Does capital formation necessarily contribute to sustainable development?

3. How can environmental protection be included in development strategies based on capital formation?

CASE STUDY: CAPITAL FORMATION IN THE CHINESE EXPERIENCE

Since the formal establishment of the People's Republic of China in 1949, China followed the Soviet Union's central planning system and attempted to modernize its economy by creating heavy industries. However, the Big Push industrialization programs were disappointing until 1978. China's GNP continued to grow around 4 to 5 percent per year in the decades prior to 1976, "but the economy was by some measures becoming much less efficient. A growing share of GNP was going into capital formation and more energy per unit of GNP was required just to maintain this GNP growth rate."[18] In contrast, the piecemeal and experimental approach adopted since 1979 seems to have resulted in remarkable economic success, but at the considerable expense of the environment. Below is a brief review of China's industrialization based on a capital formation strategy.

During the period known as the Great Leap Forward, Mao Zedong's Second Five-Year Plan (1958–61) was launched to catch up with a "race against time."

The period earmarked an extensive increase in production, represented by heavy investments in industry and the creation of socialist agricultural communes, referred to as "people's production communes." In 1958 alone, "investment in capital construction increased by 87.9%, and the rate of accumulation leapt from 24.9% to 33.9%."[19] In 1959, the rate of capital accumulation jumped again to a staggering 43.9 percent.[20]

Between 1952 and 1960, China imported some 256 turnkey projects from the Soviet Union.[21] However, between 1958 and 1960, China incurred a deficit of 20 billion yuan. In 1960 a massive 8.18 yuan was added to the existing budget deficit because of severe losses incurred by the misuse of resources, a withdrawal of Soviet assistance, and a succession of natural disasters. All this culminated in administrative confusion, extensive closing of factories, the collapse of agricultural organization, and, in many parts of China, severe malnutrition.[22]

In 1964 Mao once again announced that China must undergo another Great Leap Forward, and that every effort must be made to use advanced technology to build the nation. The Fourth Five-Year Plan (1971–1975) defined output quotas for items such as steel, wage outlays, and grain consumption. This forced march of capital accumulation contributed to an increase in the money supply. High inflation plagued the market.

In 1978, two years after Mao's death, his "Great Achievements Within Three Years" slogan was revived. Another leap was launched, but this time it involved China's opening to the outside world.[23]

It was announced that China would embark on a modernization of agriculture, industry, national defense, science, and technology, designed to propel China into the front rank of the industrial countries of the world.[24] This drive toward modernization and reform led to the implementation of China's famous open door policy, designed primarily to bring in foreign capital and technology.

In 1978 alone investment in capital construction rose 32 percent over the preceding year. In the wake of this, a balance of payments deficit of 29.8 billion yuan developed between 1979 and 1980. In 1984, as another wave of economic reform swept through China, capital construction rose 34 percent; in 1985 it rose another 22 percent. Capital investment exploded from 84.5 billion yuan in 1982 to 116 billion yuan in 1984. Of this, 73.5 percent was capital construction investment.[25] Actually, the reality behind these impressive figures was "an endless stream of duplicated projects, policy mistakes, unproductive investments, extended production time, and poorly coordinated engineering projects, with little to show for all that was invested."[26] Moreover, "the surge of investment in capital construction provoked a shortage of energy, transportation, and raw materials. Electric circuits were overloaded and faulty electrical generators continued in service."[27]

In 1992 China recorded broad-based strong economic performance. Real agricultural output rose 4 percent, and the grain harvest was the second highest on record. Industrial output rose 20 percent, on top of a 14 percent increase in 1991. Most remarkable was the phenomenal 60 percent output growth in rural and township industries, which in 1992 employed a total of 100 million workers and accounted for about 17 percent of the nation's total labor force. Foreign trade also grew rapidly. Exports rose by 18 percent and imports increased by 27 percent. Attracted by a booming economy and availability of low-cost labor and land, foreign direct investment reached $11 billion, more than double the volume in 1991. The boom in 1992 was an acceleration of recovery from a prolonged recession in 1989 and 1990. The recession was brought on by a severe austerity program launched in September 1988 in order to fight inflation.[28]

In the course of rapid economic development based on capital formation strategies, China neglected some major infrastructure changes to protect the environment. A major area of neglect was the conversion from highly polluting coal energy to other environmentally friendly sources of energy. With intensive industrialization, old eco-insensitive machines and equipment were overmaximized to meet production quotas. As reported in *China Today*, "According to statistics provided by the Beijing Environmental Protection Administration, 23 million tons of coal are burned annually in Beijing and the sulfur dioxide and dust in the atmosphere over the city come mainly from coal smoke released by boilers and civil stoves (coal-burning stoves)."[29]

Another city where the effects of coal-burning are evident is Benxi, "an important industrial city in the northeast, which is heavily draped in a veil of smoke and dust and once even was invisible in pictures of the earth's surface taken by a satellite."[30]

Concentrations of suspended particulate matter have been relatively high throughout China, but "the highest levels are recorded in the northern cities, with Beijing and Shenyang reporting an annual average value of 870 and 690 micrograms per cubic meter of ambient air respectively."[31]

In many Chinese cities, pollution resulting from coal burning has been aggravated by the high sulfur content expelled, leading to acid rains which damage crops, seriously corrode metal structures, and damage concrete works. Southwestern China has been subjected to the worst of such acid rains. In view of the fact that a great majority of the people in China depend on coal for fuel, it is essential that other environmentally friendly alternative energy sources are identified. For example, by substituting honeycomb briquettes, "an average of over one-fifth of the coal can be saved, reducing smog by two-thirds, carbon monoxide by three-fifths to four-fifths and the discharge of carbon dioxide by about two-fifths."[32]

To summarize, although China's growth performance since reforms began in 1979 has been impressive, the nation faces formidable environmental challenges. China's takeoff to sustainable development will depend critically on whether it will take a more proactive approach to maintaining and investing in natural capital. Existing barriers to sustainability need to be identified in order to make the necessary structural changes.

DISCUSSION QUESTIONS

1. What are the strengths and weaknesses of the case study?
2. What lessons did you learn from the Chinese case study?

NOTES

This chapter was prepared with the assistance of Laura van Galen and Mike Misemer, both of Dominican College, San Rafael, California.

1. W. W. Rostow, *Theories of Economic Growth from David Hume to the Present* (New York: Oxford University Press, 1990): 254.

2. A. Hirschman, "The rise and decline of development economics," in Rajani Kanth (ed.), *Paradigms in Economic Development* (New York: M. E. Sharpe, 1994): 199.

3. Gerald M. Meier, *Leading Issues in Economic Development* (New York: Oxford University Press, 1976): 63–64.

4. Michael P. Todaro, *Economic Development,* 5th ed. (New York: Longman, 1994): 70–72.

5. Malcolm Gillis et al., *Economics of Development,* 2d ed. (New York: W. W. Norton, 1987): 45.

6. Celso Furtado, *Development and Underdevelopment* (Berkeley, California: University of California Press, 1964): 60.

7. Todaro, *Economic Development,* 70–73.

8. Jan S. Hogendorn, *Economic Development* (New York: HarperCollins, 1992): 412–14; and E. Wayne Nafziger, *The Economics of Developing Countries* (Belmont, California: Wadsworth, 1984): 336.

9. Michael P. Todaro, *Economic Development in the Third World,* 4th ed. (New York: Longman, 1989): 245.

10. Nafziger, *The Economics of Developing Countries* (Belmont, California: Wadsworth, 1984): 275.

11. Hogendorn, *Economic Development,* 91.

12. John Page, "The East Asian miracle: Building a basis for growth," *Finance and Development* (March 1994): 2–5.

13. Ibid., 3.

14. Ibid.

15. Paul Ekins et al., *The GAIA Atlas of Green Economics* (New York: Doubleday, 1992): 49.

16. Ralph C. d'Arge, *Investing in Natural Capital* (Washington, D.C.: Island Press, 1994): 114.

17. See, for example, David W. Pearce and Jeremy J. Warford, *World without End: Economics, Environment and Sustainable Development* (Oxford: Oxford University Press, 1993): 139–143.

18. Gillis et al., *Economics of Development,* 119.

19. He Bochuan, *China on the Edge: The Crisis of Ecology and Development* (San Francisco: China Books and Periodicals, 1991): 139.

20. Ibid.

21. See, for example, Asayehgn Desta, *International Political Risk Assessment for Foreign Direct Investment and International Lending Decisions* (Needham Heights, Massachusetts: Ginn Press, 1993): 105.

22. Price Waterhouse, *Doing Business in the People's Republic of China* (San Francisco: Price Waterhouse, 1988): 8.

23. Bochuan, *China on the Edge,* 140.

24. Price Waterhouse, *Doing Business in the People's Republic of China,* 5.

25. Bochuan, *China on the Edge,* 141.

26. Ibid., 142.

27. Ibid.

28. Hang-Sheng Cheng, "China on the fast track," *Federal Reserve Bank of San Francisco Weekly Letter,* No. 93–22 (June 4, 1993): 1–3.

29. "Coal and air pollution," *China Today,* 30(4): 19.

30. Ibid., 18.

31. United Nations, *State of the Environment in Asia and the Pacific* (Bangkok, Thailand: Economic and Social Commission for Asia and the Pacific, 1990): 128.

32. Ibid., 129.

The Market-Oriented Approach to Development and the Environment

> There is also increased recognition that natural capital is a scarce and limiting factor rather than a free good, and that new socially and ecologically based methods of economic analysis are needed that account for the depreciation of natural as well as human capital. Until recently, the language of the mainstream in economics has defined the economy mainly in market terms, without giving much attention to non-market elements such as subsidies provided by eco-system services, subsistence activities, household labour or cultural aspects of human social systems.
>
> —UN report, 1995[1]

> Ecological damage is often irreversible. Cleaning up later is not an option when terrestrial and aquatic biodiversity has been lost because of habitat destruction.
>
> —Vindo Thomas and Tamara Belt[2]

Some economists argue that economic development in Third World countries resides in an unfettered market. Other economists, however, argue that market discipline cannot be relied on to function properly, and that even when it does, the results often prove undesirable. Citing market failures as the underlying cause of environmental degradation, they argue that the state has a duty to intervene and correct market failures.[3] This chapter examines various development theories related to the market mechanism as well as the negative environmental consequences of a market-oriented approach. Finally, the effects of the market system of development on the environment are illustrated in a case study of economic development in Malaysia.

THE MARKET SYSTEM

A market system is that part of an economy in which basic decisions about what to produce, how to produce it, and how products (incomes) are to be distributed are determined by the interaction of buyers and sellers in product and factor markets. Based on the determinants of market structures—the number of sellers (buyers), the nature of the product, entry/exit conditions, and pricing strategies—markets are classified as being either perfect competition, oligopoly, monopolistic competition, or monopoly. Given these structural distinctions, market system analysis examines how market structures interact with market conduct to produce particular patterns of market performance.[4]

According to Harry G. Johnson,

> [T]he market rations supplies of consumers; this rationing is governed by the willingness of consumers to pay. . . . Secondly, the market directs the allocation of production between commodities, according to the criterion of maximum profit, which, on the same assumption, corresponds to social usefulness. Thirdly, the market allocates the different factors of production among various uses, according to the criterion of maximizing their incomes. Fourthly, it governs the relative quantities of specific types of labour and capital equipment made available. Fifthly, it distributes income between the factors of production and therefore between individuals.[5]

PROMARKET ARGUMENTS OF ECONOMIC DEVELOPMENT

The market system also provides incentives for economic growth. As argued by Johnson, consumers can maximize their utility by acquiring more goods and services at lower prices. Entrepreneurs and inventors profit from the market. The market serves as a vehicle for accumulating both material and human capital, very essential for economic growth.[6] Similarly, neoclassical economics assumes that each consumer is rational and makes decisions to purchase goods and services according to price. Based on the law of diminishing returns, it further assumes that the value a consumer places on additional consumption of a good declines with increasing consumption. "Economic rationality dictates that consumption of a good continues up to the point at which the value placed on an additional unit is just equal to the price."[7]

In the same vein, adherents of the neoclassical counterrevolution argue persuasively that freely functioning markets ration supplies of consumer products and that the willingness of consumers to pay governs this rationing process. Maximization of profit directs the allocation of production which corresponds to social usefulness. The market regulates the amount of specific types of labor and capital equipment that are available in the economy. Finally, the market distributes income between the various factors of production and therefore between individuals.[8]

Applying the same concept to development economics, the neoclassical counterrevolutionary economists argue that "underdevelopment results from poor resource allocation due to incorrect pricing policies, and too much state intervention by overly active Third World governments."[9] Based on this reasoning, neoclassical counterrevolutionary economic theories suggest that markets be permitted to be free and perfectly competitive. State-owned enterprises must be privatized, free trade promoted, exports expanded, foreign investors welcomed, and government regulations and price distortions in factor, product, and financial markets eliminated.[10] In short, the government should allow "the magic of the marketplace" and the "invisible hand" to guide resource allocation and stimulate economic development.[11]

Pursuing market-oriented policies, the World Bank utilizes structural adjustment programs and the International Monetary Fund employs stabilization packages, encouraging developing countries to undertake market-friendly types of development. "[T]he examples of South Korea, Taiwan, Singapore, and Brazil, all of which sustained rapid growth for close to two decades with market-oriented economies, convinced many that the market was worth another look."[12] From a socialist point of view, "China's economic reforms of the 1980s have made the market a respectable proposition even for socialist-oriented third world countries."[13]

ARGUMENTS AGAINST MARKET-ORIENTED GROWTH

Over the past quarter of a century, economic growth per capita in the southeast part of East Asia—Indonesia, Malaysia, Singapore, and Thailand—averaged 5 percent a year. . . . At the same time, environmental losses in East Asia have surpassed in many respects those of other regions. For example, 9 of the world's 15 cities with the highest levels of particulate air pollution are in this region. About 20 percent of land covered by vegetation suffers from soil degradation owing to water logging, erosion and overgrazing at levels above world averages. Fifty to 75 percent of coastlines and marine protected areas are classified as areas with highly threatened biodiversity, and the region has witnessed some of the highest deforestation rates in the world.[14]

Despite impressive arguments in favor of market-oriented development, there are adamant objections to the market system. Because of imperfect information, competitive markets do not exist in the developing countries. Given the institutional, cultural, and historical contexts of many of these countries, markets may not be desirable from either a long-term economic or a long-term social perspective. For instance, distribution of income produced by the market is uneven and socially undesirable. It encourages the well-off to prosper at the expense of the downtrodden masses.[15] Income distribution produced by the market benefits the highly skilled and the privileged. According to Michael P. Todaro, "Due to the rationing of resources, high-income households have frequently been the predominant beneficiaries of energy, water, and agricultural subsidies."[16]

Stated differently, markets are imperfect because wealthy consumers "vote" with their dollars for goods the economy should produce. In addition, geographic remoteness and illiteracy prevent many rural laborers and farmers from influencing goods and capital markets. The impoverished masses, therefore, have little influence on which goods and services should be supplied in the economy, while the wealthy, based in urban centers, benefit from the rationing quotas of underdeveloped financial institutions.[17]

Markets tend to ignore externalities accruing to third parties as a result of exchanges. "As a simple example, the buyer and seller of a packaged good do not consider that the packaging material must be disposed of in some way. The costs of a garbage collection and disposal scheme, if one exists, are not reflected in the price of the packaged good, and someone else—the local or national taxpayer—pays that cost."[18]

It can be argued that environmental degradation is due in part to the existence of open markets and to the exploitative transfer of resources from underdeveloped to industrialized countries. Since rapid growth through an open market does not necessarily improve the environment, environmental policies must be openly declared. To mitigate the environmental consequences of these forms of exploitation, a number of policy initiatives have been put forward.

INCORPORATING AN ENVIRONMENT-FRIENDLY APPROACH TO THE MARKET MECHANISM

The green approach attributes the environmental crisis to both market and policy failures. "After all," state David W. Pearce and Jeremy J. Warford, "governments can alter market prices to reflect, albeit approximately, the external costs of production and consumption."[19] This school of thought advocates management of markets. Ecodevelopment economics argues that, without state mitigation of negative externalities on the environment caused by market failures, the "invisible hand" will not consciously deliver value for money or meaningful quality of life to a society.[20]

Based on the ecodevelopment approach, Ernesto M. Perina calls for an "economic policy that promotes rapid economic growth while paying serious attention to alleviating poverty and sustaining the environmental resource base."[21] More specifically, Perina's environmental recommendations include four components.

1. Macroeconomic growth policies that allow the market mechanism to work and to foster institutions, infrastructure, and technology conducive to labor-intensive growth. (These policies have few distortionary effects on the economy.)

2. Policies that account for the provision of essential social services

3. Urban management policies that address such problems as transport, water, sanitation, and housing

4. Environmental policy[22]

Market-based environmental proposals can be classified into those that create environmental awareness, those that internalize the full cost of externalities, and those that restructure the governance of environmental policymaking and administration. These market-based environmental proposals are discussed below.

ENVIRONMENTAL AWARENESS PROPOSAL

Under green capitalism (a free-market system), environmental awareness and consciousness of consumers, investors, and firms is expected to influence market forces. As stated by Pearce and Warford, the three sets of decisions made in light of environmental awareness and consciousness include

1. Changed patterns of consumer demand for products that are less, rather than more, damaging to the environment
2. Altered patterns of investment and a shift toward buying shares in companies with green images
3. Altered production processes based on environmental consciousness as well as on concern for shareholders and customers[23]

A case in point is *The China Environmental News,* which was started under the auspices of the Environmental Protection Commission of the State Council and the National Environmental Agency in 1984 and which raises public awareness by publicizing information and knowledge on environmental protection nationally and internationally.[24]

INTERNALIZING EXTERNALITIES

Externalities occur when the actions of one economic agent affect other economic agents, and the market fails to exert sufficient controls over the behavior of its economic actors. As stated by A. P. Thirlwall, "[E]xternalities have two related causes: lack of individual property rights, and jointness in either production or consumption. . . . [A]lso, externalities may have positive and negative impacts."[25]

Thus internalization strategies include environmental taxes, scrutiny of existing subsidy regimes, and transferring the social costs of resource use to consumers. These policies contribute to discouragement of environmentally damaging activities and result in long-term sustainability by altering the behavior of consumers and producers.

The polluter-pays principle says that environmental costs of pollution should be accounted for and *internalized* into the cost of producing goods or services, instead of being discounted and *externalized* as a free right to pollute. A number of European countries levy externality taxes (often called effluent charges). Because removing lead from gasoline improves health, especially in children, and also reduces the cost of maintaining vehicles, gasoline containing lead additives is priced higher than gasoline without lead. For example, "In January 1986, Sweden lowered the tax on unleaded petroleum 14 ore per liter and increased the tax on leaded petroleum 2 ore per liter, producing a price differential of 16 ore per liter."[26] Similar taxes were levied on carbon (to reduce greenhouse gas effects), diesel fuel, sulphur, and domestic transportation. Subsidies on nitrogen and phosphate fertilizers and other pesticides were discontinued to reduce water pollution.

Other variants of pollution taxes include deposit-refund systems for returned or properly recycled products (for example, cans, bottles, plastic bags).[27] In order for taxes to be effective, the demand for the product must be price-responsive. Also, taxes must be higher than abatement costs. Abatement policies (such as taxation of emissions and tradable emissions permits) are very effective when they give incentives to the most efficient producers.

Additional incentives to adopt clean technologies may be provided through tax credits and subsidies specifically tied to the purchase or development of pollution abatement technologies. Ironically, the hardest industries to regulate are those run by governments themselves because the profit motive is often not a consideration and, as a general rule, it is difficult for any group to regulate itself.[28]

Based on the above analysis, a number of techniques such as possible (contingent) valuation, replacement cost estimation, and the use of surrogate markets can be used to develop the nonmarketed values of environmental services. However, in arguing against these strategies Morris Miller states that allocating externality costs, subsidies, and taxes may indeed seem very logical and attractive, but "it is operationally an empty box. Many who endorse the market system approach do so without a conception of the market process as it actually operates."[29]

RESTRUCTURING GOVERNANCE

Developing countries are advised to restructure the levels of governance and policymaking so that environmental concerns are integrated into the policymaking process. As noted by Miller, restructuring environmental governance implies "the incorporation of environmental policy-making functions into a central ministry, say finance or planning, so that fiscal policy, budgetary, and major project and programme investment decisions can be made on a longer-term basis . . . that includes environmental factors."[30] Also, it is suggested that programs to improve environmental conditions are effective when operating in tandem with community networks and matched to local customs.[31]

It needs to be emphasized here that developing countries lack the necessary infrastructure—legal system, training, and pricing mechanisms—to implement the above proposals. Restructuring governance and policymaking in developing countries requires not only profound institutional changes but political will and commitment as well. But a coherent system of environmental authorities needs to be established at the federal, regional, and local levels to develop and implement effective environmental policies. Particularly at the national level, the environmental authorities should try to integrate environmental requirements into economic policies by

- Formulating environmental objectives, policies, plans and programmes, and following them up

- Preparing relevant legislative proposals and setting standards

- Developing environmental policy and management instruments (permit systems, environmental impact assessment procedures and methodology, economic instruments, etc.)

- Promoting the integration of environmental and sectoral policies

- Coordinating and supervising environmental monitoring, standardizing monitoring methods and reporting, maintaining environmental data and information centres
- Promoting environmental research and development and the introduction of environmental technologies
- Coordinating environmental education and public information
- International cooperation[32]

Stated differently, the aim of the environmental authorities should be to prevent environmental degradation and inefficient use of natural resources with little or no direct regulations and administrative interventions in environmental policy. For instance, as mentioned above, the general principles that should guide the use of economic instruments in the long run are the polluter-pays principle and the user-pays principle. However,

> compensation schemes may be introduced to offset the effect of steep cuts in income on the disadvantaged sections of society. Ways and means should be identified to cope not only with the high economic and social costs borne by all economic actors and the public at large, but also with other constraints resulting from the application of economic instruments during the transition process, such as underdeveloped markets and the limited capacities of environmental and fiscal institutions.[33]

To reduce pollution and to improve resource use, resource prices and charges should be high enough to induce changes in behavior and foster clean technologies. Also, proper pricing of energy and appropriate energy taxes can contribute significantly to reducing air pollution. Sewage disposal from enterprises and households should be charged according to marginal treatment costs. Waste disposal fees, hazardous waste charges, or taxes should be applied to encourage waste reduction, encourage recycling, and raise revenue for waste collection and waste processing. And steep fines and sanctions—high enough to enforce compliance and compensate for damage—should be levied for violating pollution control regulations.[34] For example, as shown in Table 4.1, in Latin America several market-based instruments have been used to maintain sustainable resource use.

SUMMARY

Some economists argue that economic development in the Third World countries depends on free-market operations. For example, the neoclassical counterrevolutionary economists generally argue that underdevelopment results from poor resource allocation and too much state intervention.

On the other hand, other ecodevelopment economists believe that since unrestricted markets could lead to environmental degradation, the state needs to mitigate negative externalities caused by market failures. In view of this, market-based environmental awareness programs (such as changing patterns of consumer demand, altering patterns of investments, changing production processes to reflect the environment, instituting environmental taxes, scrutinizing existing subsidies,

Table 4.1
Protecting the Environment:
Application of Market-based Instruments in Latin America

	Credit Subsidies	TAF/Tariff Relief	Deposit-Refund Schemes	Waste Fees and Levies	Forestry Taxation	Pollution Charges	Earmarked Renewable Resource Taxes	Earmarked Conventional Tax Levy	Tradable Permits	Eco-labeling (Environmental Awareness)	Liability Insurance
Barbados	X	X	X	X							
Bolivia			X	X	X				*	X	X
Brazil	X	X	X	X	X	X	X	X		X	X
Chile			X	X	X				X	X	X
Colombia	X	X	X	X	X	X	X	X			X
Ecuador	X	X	X	X			X			X	
Jamaica			X	X	X	*					
Mexico	X		X	X		X			X	*	X
Peru				X							
Trinidad and Tobago		X	X								X
Venezuela		X	X	X	X						

X   In place.
*   Under introduction.

Source: Richard M. Hube et al., *Market-Based Instruments for Environmental Policymaking in Latin America and the Caribbean* (Washington, D.C.: The World Bank, 1996).

etc.) are suggested to the developing countries to restructure their environments. But it needs to be mentioned that developing countries may lack the necessary infrastructure, legal system, training, and pricing mechanisms to adequately implement and enforce the suggested proposals.

REVIEW QUESTIONS

1. How can environmental policies be effectively incorporated into a market-oriented development strategy?
2. Which failures cause the most significant distortions with regard to sustainable development: market failures or policy failures?

CASE STUDY: MALAYSIA

The case study presented below illustrates Malaysia's attempts to incorporate environmental policies in its market-oriented developmental approach.

Since its independence in 1957, Malaysia has maintained a relatively open economy. The main guideline for its market-oriented and export-led industrialization, modeled after Japan and South Korea, was established in the New Economic Policy (NEP), adopted in 1976.

Further advancements toward a market-oriented economy were initiated as a result of the midterm review of the Fourth Malaysian Plan. Beginning in 1986, public utilities, telecommunications, and transportation were gradually privatized. Projects ranging from car parking lots to public housing schemes were sold to the private sector. In addition, wholly owned foreign enterprises were permitted to operate in the free trade zones. Foreign investors were allowed to hold more than 30 percent of equity in joint ventures and 30 to 70 percent in certain export companies.[35]

In 1991 the New Development Policy was announced to replace the NEP. The New Development Policy, along with the Second Outline Perspective Plan and the Sixth Malaysia Plan, formed the cornerstone of the 20/20 vision policy announced by Prime Minister Mahathir in March 1992 to transform Malaysia into an advanced nation by the year 2020.[36]

Malaysia's programs to privatize and restructure the industrial sector have had deleterious effects on timber, rubber, palm, oil, tin, petroleum, coca, and chemical-based agriculture. For instance, "although timber production has been buoyant, forest resources have been exploited at rates far in excess of the sustainable yield and considerable environmental degradation is evident."[37]

Up until 1981 forest reserves covered up to 60 percent of the total land area in Malaysia, containing one of the richest and most accessible sources of hardwood in the world.[38] Over the next decade, however, deforestation rates escalated to an average rate of two percent a year, and by the end of the 1980s, some 4 million hectares (16 million square miles) of forest had been cleared. In relative terms, Malaysia had chopped down more tropical trees in the 1980s than any other country except Indonesia and Brazil.[39]

This widespread loss of tropical forest cover has led to serious economic and ecological consequences for Malaysia. The loss of intact forests is critical, as they provide

- homeland of many indigenous peoples
- habitat for extensive fauna and flora with inherent educational and medicinal value
- supplies of hardwood timber
- supplies of other forest products such as nuts, oil, resins, and latex
- ecotourism
- storage of carbon dioxide
- protection of watersheds by retaining and regulating the flow of water.[40]

It can be argued that two primary forces have driven the devastating defor-estation rates in Malaysia: first, the country's drive to convert forestlands into plantations, building sites, and farmlands, and second, the booming external demand for timber.

The response of the Malaysian government has been to restrict logging in peninsular Malaysia. However, evidence shows that logging and clear-cutting concessions continue to be handed out in large portions in Sabah and Sarawak by corrupt officials. The practice of commissioning, contracting, and subcon-tracting licenses is but a ploy to obscure the identities of the concessions owners. Citing Sarawak, Mark A. McDowell points out that its "Minister of Tourism and Environment James Datuk Wong owns one hundred thousand acres of timber concessions."[41]

Furthermore, logging restrictions in the region have not been effective in solving the deforestation problem. In the hope of reducing the amount of deforestation and of increasing the government's share of export revenues, royalty rates were raised from a maximum 36 percent to a maximum of 57 percent of total export value. While this change in policy did manage to raise government revenues, it placed even more pressure on the forests. Because the royalty is an "ad valorem" charge based on the gross export value of the logs, the logging companies were induced to take only the best specimens of the most highly valued species. As a result, 72 percent of the uncut trees were damaged by the high grading practices, and this wasteful logging may have left Sabah's forests more susceptible to the fires that swept over millions of hectares in 1983.[42]

Similarly, rapid industrialization has given rise to zinc-, tin-, and chemical-based agriculture industries that have been largely responsible for depleting Malaysia's water quality. The Klang River in peninsular Malaysia is grossly polluted by heavy metals and toxic wastes.

The processing of rubber discharges an acidic effluent that has been tradi-tionally released untreated into nearby water sources. Equally damaging is palm oil processing, which creates a hot, thick oil waste that is disposed into the natural streams.[43] Soil exhaustion and depletion of poor tropical soils have been the side effects of poor farming methods. Runoff from toxic pesticides and chemical fer-tilizers have threatened the livelihood of inhabitants and wildlife.

The Malaysian government has been increasingly forced to deal with the harsh realities of environmental degradation. National plans have made it mandatory for larger developmental projects to include environmental impact assessments.[44] Although implementation has been slow, Malaysia has introduced the polluter-pays principle for discharge of polluting effluent by palm and rubber factories. Although maximum pollution discharge standards were set in 1978, compliance was not compulsory. This allowed lead time for factories to develop and com-mission waste treatment systems. However, some incentives were put into place: small fees for effluent discharges above a prescribed maximum, a licensing system as an incentive for waste discharge reduction, and fee waivers for factories involved in waste treatment research. Although it has made meaningful initial efforts, Malaysia has a long way to go before a comprehensive and enforceable envi-ronmental program is developed.

Discussion Questions

1. Assess and update the Malaysian case study.

2. What implications does the Malaysian case study have for economic development policies in other Asian NICS?

Notes

This chapter was prepared with the assistance of Laura van Galen, Amy Fisher, Joseph Kim, and Anthony Catinella, all of Dominican College, San Rafael, California.

1. United Nations Environmental Programme (UNEP), *Poverty and the Environment* (Nairobi, Kenya: UNEP, 1995): 11.

2. Vindo Thomas and Tamara Belt, "Growth and the environment: Allies or foes?" *Finance and Development* (June 1977).

3. The World Bank, *World Development Report 1992: Development and the Environment* (New York: Oxford University Press, 1992): 64.

4. Christopher Pass et al., *The HarperCollins Dictionary of Economics* (New York: HarperCollins, 1991): 518.

5. Harry G. Johnson, "The market mechanism as an instrument of development," in Gerald M. Meier (ed.), *Leading Issues in Economic Development* (New York: Oxford University Press, 1989): 517.

6. Ibid.

7. A. P. Thirwall, *Growth and Development* (Boulder, Colorado: Lynne Rienner, 1994): 214.

8. Gerald M. Meier, *Leading Issues in Economic Development* (New York: Oxford University Press, 1989): 517.

9. Ibid.

10. Ibid.

11. Ibid.

12. Malcolm Gillis et al., *Economics of Development* (New York: W. W. Norton, 1989): 119.

13. Ibid.

14. Thomas and Belt, "Growth and the environment: Allies or foes?": 22–24.

15. Michael P. Todaro, *Economic Development in the Third World,* 4th ed. (New York: Longman, 1989): 83.

16. Michael P. Todaro, *Economic Development,* 5th ed. (New York: Longman, 1994): 353.

17. Ibid., 589.

18. David W. Pearce and Jeremy J. Warford, *World without End: Economics, Environment and Sustainable Development* (Oxford: Oxford University Press, 1993): 195.

19. Ibid., 196.

20. Paul Ekins et al., *The GAIA Atlas of Green Economics* (New York: Doubleday, 1992): 35.

21. Ernesto M. Perina, "Aspects of urbanization and the environment in Southeast Asia," *Asian Development Review* (Fall 1989): 120.

22. Ibid., 114.

23. Ibid., 202.

24. United Nations, Economic and Social Commissions for Asia and the Pacific, *State of the Environment in Asia and the Pacific* (Bangkok, Thailand: United Nations, 1990): 218.

25. Thirlwall, *Growth and Development,* 215.

26. Pearce and Warford, *World without End*, 207.

27. Ibid.

28. Todaro, *Economic Development*, 355.

29. Morris Miller, *Debt and the Environment* (Geneva: United Nations Publications, 1991): 137.

30. Ibid.

31. Todaro, *Economic Development*, 353.

32. United Nations, *Guidelines on Integrated Environmental Management in Countries in Transition* (New York: United Nations, 1994): 4.

33. Ibid., 25.

34. Ibid.

35. The Hongkong and Shanghai Banking Corporation, *Business Profile Series: Malaysia* (Hong Kong: Hongkong and Shanghai Banking Corp., August 1985): 7.

36. *Far Eastern Economic Review* 156: *Malaysia in Asia 1992 Yearbook.*

37. World Bank, *Trends in Developing Economies 1989* (Washington, D.C.: The World Bank, 1989): 267.

38. World Resources Institute (WRI), *The Forest for the Trees? Government Policies and the Misuse of Forest Resources* (Washington, D.C.: WRI Publications, 1988): 52.

39. *The Economist* 331 (June 25, 1994): 39.

40. List adapted from Pearce and Warford, *World without End,* 116, 118.

41. Mark A. McDowell, "Development and the environment in ASEAN," *Pacific Affairs* (Fall 1989): 312.

42. World Resources Institute, *The Forest for the Trees? Government Policies and the Misuse of Forest Resources,* 54.

43. McDowell, "Development and the Environment in ASEAN," 317.

44. Ibid., 320.

chapter 5

Poverty and Environmental Degradation

Poor people may become trapped into short time-horizons with respect to resources over which they have little or no control because they lack assurances of future access to resources and because they lack other economic opportunities. To the extent that they are excluded from participation in the market economy, they also rely directly on non-marketed natural resources for their immediate survival.

—UN report, 1995[1]

The World Development Bank reports that in 1990 one-fifth of humanity was living in acute poverty. Generally, the lives of those living in poverty are "characterized by frequent death of children, lack of education, health care, and access to other basic necessities, and exploitation by a variety of forces including local politicians, major landowners, criminals, governments, transnational banks, and transnational corporations."[2]

Impoverished populations are the most likely victims of environmental degradation. People eking out a marginal existence and living at a bare subsistence level are often forced to scavenge in dump sites where they seek out wood and other organic fuels, food, clothing, and decent rubbish, both for consumption and for sale. They are most likely to live in depressed real estate areas near polluted waterways and highways, airports, nuclear facilities, and sewage plants. What type of national or global development strategy has the potential to eradicate this kind of poverty?

Answers to the above question are bleak when considering that the numbers of poor increased by approximately 100 million between 1985 and 1990 alone—close to the total population growth rate for the period.[3] This obvious social tragedy has challenged the theories of development economists for centuries. While classical economists expected that growth would automatically reduce income inequality, radical economists have focused on an income redistribution strategy, which contributed to a major drop in income growth, and the neoclassical economists have focused on providing basic needs to those below the poverty line.[4]

This chapter explores the historical evolution of these economic theories and attempts to discover how countries might tackle poverty and stimulate sustainable economic growth processes.

THE THEORETICAL FRAMEWORK OF POVERTY

According to the classical school of economics, poverty is seen as an individual problem. Attempts to help some groups of the poor, especially those who can participate in labor markets, will generally cause more social ills and magnify the problem of poverty.[5] According to Adam Smith, the father of classical economics, problems of poverty can best be solved not by government-mandated income transfers but by wages obtained in free markets. Thomas Robert Malthus advanced the notion that poverty is an inevitable punishment for overbreeding. For Malthus, overbreeding invariably results in poverty because population growth follows a geometric growth pattern, whereas food production follows an arithmetic growth pattern. David Ricardo developed the "iron law of wages," arguing that "increases in population with a fixed supply of land and diminishing returns in agriculture cause the rental share of national income to increase, benefiting the landowners. . . . [T]he owners of capital and laborers lose since they would share the remaining and smaller share of national income."[6]

Using an institutional approach to poverty, Joseph A. Schumpeter argued that the poor are poor "because they are exploited; the surplus they produce is appropriated by predatory landlords or capitalists. And this poverty persists because, since all goes to the owners of property anyway, there is no incentive to improve. Productivity remains stubbornly low."[7]

Though the above theoretical frameworks of poverty are instructive, prior to the 1970s there was little solid evidence on which theorists could base their assessment of poverty. Theoretical frameworks laid down before the 1970s were mainly speculative. A case in point is the trickle-down theory which gained momentum during World War II. This theory argues that if countries promote moderate to rapid rates of aggregate growth, eventually the economic benefits will filter down to the poor through multiplier effects.[8] Although this theory was strongly supported during the postwar period, recent evidence has shown that the Third World poverty rate, which declined 7.4 percent in the 1960s, fell a mere 2.4 percent in the 1980s.[9]

Responding to this deficiency in the trickle-down theory, Arthur Lewis in his dual-economy model focused on engaging the poor in the growth process. He "assumed a backward sector, usually (but not necessarily) identified with subsistence agriculture, which suffered from population pressure in that the maximum amount of labor which could be productively used was being supplied by too many hands putting in too few hours individually."[10] His solution to this problem was to recommend that developing countries with large agriculturally based, rural, poor sectors could benefit from transitioning to a higher wage-paying industrial sector.

Charting the changes in distribution of income of various countries in a time series analysis, Professor Simon Kuznets extended Lewis's work by proposing that the level of per capita GNP and inequality in the distribution of income may take the form of an inverted U. That is, in the early stages of economic growth, the distribution of income tends to worsen; only later does equality begin to improve.[11] Unfortunately, Kuznets based the inverted-U proposition on mere fragments of data. He was unable to gather accurate time-series information from the least-developed countries to effectively complete his analysis, and the trends of distribution were based on very few European countries.

To be acceptable, data on income distribution need to satisfy three factors.

1. The data should be based on nationally representative surveys rather than synthetic estimates built up from national accounts data, or general assumptions regarding the distribution of income (across occupations, or in other countries at a similar stage of economic development).

2. The data should cover the entire population rather than subsets, such as urban or rural dwellers. Partial coverage, which is often misleading, is particularly common in Latin America, where many countries collect information only for the urban population. In Peru, for example, the Gini coefficient for rural households is 32, compared with 42 for urban households. In South Africa, the Gini coefficient for the white population is 48, compared with 62 for the whole population.

3. The data should encompass all types of income, including nonwage income and income from household production. As tax records and labor force statistics are more commonly available than detailed data from household surveys, many of the figures used in the literature refer to wage or taxable income.[12]

Pari Kasliwal has pointed out that "recent studies have cast doubts on the reliability of the statistical evidence, with crucial implications for policy. The absence of a U-curve would imply that a transitory worsening of income distribution is not an essential feature of growth." This means trickle-down policies are "unacceptable because they are unnecessary."[13]

As was the case for the trickle-down theory, the Lewis- and Kuznets-type models were not easily incorporated into successful development strategies, especially in countries where accurate data and an information-gathering infrastructure for poverty analysis were unavailable. Also, because poverty is culturally specific and is affected by historical context, it needs to be clearly defined. As discussed by Gerald M. Meier,

> The perception of poverty has evolved historically and varies tremendously from culture to culture. Criteria for distinguishing poor from nonpoor tend to reflect specific national priorities and normative concepts of welfare and rights. In general, as countries become wealthier, their perception of the acceptable minimum level of consumption—the poverty line—changes.[14]

The materialists see poverty as a deficiency or deprivation of a material or nonmaterial nature. Others visualize poverty as a person's own perception of his or her condition. For the United Nations Educational, Scientific and Cultural Organization (UNESCO), a given percentage of illiteracy or a designated low level of distribution of radios or newspapers represents poverty. For the World Health Organization (WHO), criteria of poverty are expressed in terms of the ratio of physicians, nurses, and health centers to the population. For the Food and Agriculture Organization, poverty is evaluated in terms of per capita calorie or protein intake.

From an economic standpoint, the study and measurement of poverty depend upon on two factors: the average level of national income and the degree of inequality of income distribution. For any given level of national per capita income, the more unequal the distribution, the greater the incidence of poverty.[15] To distinguish the poor from the non-poor, in the 1970s development economists took a major step by establishing an international poverty line. Absolute poverty was defined as "income that secures the bare essentials of food, clothing, and shelter."[16]

Those who live in absolute poverty suffer the following deprivations.

- Four-fifths of income is spent on a monotonous diet.

- All such individuals are malnourished, and the physical and mental development of children is often impaired.

- Two out of every ten infants die within the first year of life and only five reach the age of 40.

- Only about one-third of adults are literate.[17]

Based on constant 1985 prices, a per capita income of $370 per year was used as a benchmark for the international poverty line. That is, those making an income below $370 per year were classified as living without basic physical needs, including clothing and shelter.

A study by Montek Anluwalia, N. Carter, and Hollis Chenery based on the above indicators concluded that 35 percent of the world's population is struggling at absolute poverty levels.[18] Though the study was instructive, the indicators (population figures, per capita GNP, and poverty estimates) used by the researchers were not reliable enough to reach a definite conclusion. As shown in Table 5.1, if distributional adjustments are made using each country's Gini Coefficient of Inequality, the results reverse. (Note: Distributional adjustments refer to intra- and intergenerational division of resources flow or per capita output.)

Table 5.1
Real GDP Per Capita, Gini Coefficient of Inequality, and Distribution-adjusted GDP per Capita in Four Countries, 1978

Country	Real GDP per Capita (PPP$) 1987	Gini Coefficient of Inequality	Distribution-adjusted GDP per Capita (PPP$)
Panama	$4,010	0.57	$1,724
Brazil	4,310	0.57	1,852
Malaysia	3,850	0.48	2,001
Costa Rica	3,760	0.42	2,180

Source: United Nations Development Programme, Human Development Report 1990 (New York: Oxford University Press, 1990): 22.

In response to the limitations of the above-mentioned methods of data collection, economists turned to using the Gini Coefficient of Inequality to estimate the extent of poverty. The Gini Coefficient of Inequality was crudely formulated by an Italian statistician, Corrodo Gini, in 1912. It was refined in the 1970s to provide a useful figure that reveals the degree of income inequality in any given country. Family percentages are recorded on the horizontal axis and the percentage of income is recorded on the vertical axis. The theoretical possibility of a completely equal distribution of income is represented by a diagonal line known as the 45-degree line or reference line. That is, if distribution were equal, observations would lie on the 45-degree line. Stated differently, 20 percent of all families would receive 20 percent of total income and 60 percent would receive 60 percent of income. The further the Lorenz curve bends away from the 45-degree line, the greater is the inequality of income distribution. The Gini coefficient (figure 5.1) is approximately defined as the numerical value of the area between the Lorenz curve and the 45-degree line (reference line), divided by the numerical value of the entire area beneath the reference line (45-degree line):

$$\text{Gini Coefficient of Inequality} = \frac{\text{Inequality area}}{\text{Triangular area}}$$

or

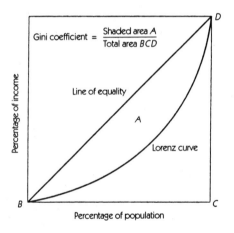

$$\text{Gini coefficient} = \frac{\text{Shaded area } A}{\text{Total area } BCD}$$

Figure 5.1
Estimating the Gini Coefficient

The coefficient lies between 0, which indicates perfect equality, and 1, which indicates perfect inequality. For example, Table 5.2 shows the relative share of total money income received by each fifth (quintile) of all families in India in 1983 and in 1989–1990. Based on the information given in Table 5.2, the income gap between the lowest 40 percent and the highest 20 percent has not significantly declined from 1983 to 1990. Even though the calculation of the Gini coefficient is generally instructive of a general idea of income inequality, it does not reveal all the facts because the data is based on very limited information.

Income distribution assumes that per capita income is a factor in poverty. For example,

> In the Philippines in 1970–71, the lowest 20 percent of the income distribution received only 5.2 percent of total income while the top 10% of households got 38.5 percent of total income. Taking 1 percent of total income from the richest group and giving it to the lowest 20 percent would raise the income of the poor by 19 percent, a meaningful increase. Yet it would lower the Gini concentration ratio only from .461 to .445, assuming that the redistributive gain is shared equally by the lowest two deciles.[19]

To expand the tools of measurement, national estimates of income inequality (that is, the Gini coefficient) are included with the HDI. As discussed in chapter 1, the HDI ranks countries according to their progress toward the maximum attainable values for life expectancy, literacy, and weighted real GDP indicators. "These factors are combined to provide a composite of diverse data. It is assumed that nutritional status and child mortality are reflected in life expectancy, and that employment rates are reflected in real income."[20]

As shown in Table 5.2, based on the aggregate calculation of the HDI, the situation in India showed little improvement in the years shown.

Table 5.2
Percentage of Aggregate Income Received by
Each One-Fifth of All Families in India

Income Rank	1983	Cumulative	1989–1990	Cumulative
Lowest fifth	8.1	8.1	8.8	8.8
Second fifth	12.3	20.4	12.5	21.3
Third fifth	16.3	36.7	16.2	37.5
Fourth fifth	22.0	58.7	21.3	58.8
Highest fifth	41.3	100.0	41.2	100.0
Income gap between the lowest 40% and the highest 20%		2.0		1.9
Gini Coefficient of Inequality		0.30		0.29
Human Development Index		(1990) = 0.31		(1992) = 0.38

Sources: Estimated from United Nations Development Programme, *World Development Report 1992* and *1993,* and *Human Development Report 1994* (New York: Oxford University Press).

The HDI also does not reflect information on environmental conditions.

> Life expectancy may reflect environmental conditions in a broad sense, but does not capture specific environmental quality aspects, certainly not in a prospective sense. And the income variable will not capture environmental change either, as the GDP statistics from which it is derived does not measure the depreciation of natural capital or environmental quality.[21]

But the link between poverty and the environment can be analyzed by investigating the geographic location of the poor. For example, as shown in Table 5.3, close to one-fourth of the population of the developing world lives in poverty. As indicated in the Human Development Report of 1990, "Poverty is growing fastest in Africa, with the number of absolute poor having increased by about two-thirds between 1970 and 1985."[22] The poor in the Third World countries are mainly "located either in ecologically fragile rural locations or in the peripheries of cities, which are also frequently fragile. Fragility means that the area is not resilient to stress or shocks such as climatic variations or population pressure."[23]

The Gini Coefficient of Inequality, the HDI, and the geographical location of the poor are rough estimates of the magnitude of poverty in a given country. But it is worth mentioning that the indigenous peoples are another group at great risk. For example, "in Bolivia, where the overall poverty rate is over 50%, almost three-quarters of the monolingual indigenous population are poor and two-thirds of the bilingual population are poor."[24]

Table 5.3
Poverty in the Developing World, 1985–2000

Region	Percentage of Population below Poverty Line			Number of Poor (millions)		
	1985	1990	2000	1985	1990	2000
South Asia	51.8	49.0	36.9	532	562	511
East Asia	13.2	11.3	4.2	182	169	73
Sub-Saharan Africa	47.6	47.8	49.7	184	216	204
Middle East and North Africa	30.6	33.1	30.6	60	73	89
Eastern Europe (excl. former USSR)	7.1	7.1	5.8	5	5	4
Latin America and the Caribbean	22.4	25.5	24.9	87	108	126
All developing countries	30.5	29.7	24.1	1,051	1,133	1,107

Source: Excerpted from World Bank, *World Development Report 1992: Development and the Environment* (New York: Oxford University Press, 1992), Table 1.1.

Note: The poverty line used here—$375 annual income per capita in 1985 purchasing power parity dollars— is based on estimates of poverty lines from a number of countries with low average incomes. Year 2000 figures are projections.

With the increase of available data in the 1970s came a wave of theories to guide countries in their efforts to tackle poverty and stimulate economic growth. For example, Milfred and Leet developed the trickle-up program in the Caribbean in 1979. These economists believed that "development must start from the bottom up, with even the smallest investments in individual or small projects and with total participation by the beneficiaries from conception to execution."[25] Their ideas were translated into the trickle-up theory, which was the core philosophy of the Caribbean project. Out of a budget of $700,000 (in 1989), about 70 to 75 percent of funds went directly to the poor. Rather than hoping that benefits from investments in large-scale physical infrastructures such as dams, ports, and highways would trickle down, Milfred and Leet focused on stimulating small-scale business in rural and urban areas by making $100 grants to small groups willing to commit at least 1,000 hours of their time to businesses they themselves planned. Also poverty alleviation programs were set up to build schools, latrines, clinics, and community shops, and to create fish ponds.

Irma Adelman favors a more radical approach to poverty alleviation in the LDCs. She argues that income redistribution should precede a concentrated effort towards growth, as opposed to the more common redistribution-with-growth strategy supported by Chenery and the World Bank. As she states: "Broadly, the more successful a country is in choosing efficient, labor-intensive patterns of products and production processes, the smaller its income inequalities."[26] Raising the income of the poor by increasing their employment, productivity, and access to productivity-enhancing assets will alleviate poverty. The two most promising strategies according to Adelman are reliance on export-oriented growth in labor-intensive manufactures and reliance on agricultural development-led industrialization.[27]

Adelman's analysis is very effective when looking at anti-poverty development strategies. However, when environmental protection policies are added to the equation, the theory becomes rather incomplete. Prior to a discussion of poverty and the environment, a brief review of some of the cardinal factors that contribute to poverty is given below.

CAUSES OF POVERTY

Major factors contributing to poverty are geographical location, cultural/institutional arrangements, and government policies. Because of their locations, some countries are more prone to natural disasters than others; the people living in these areas are generally very poor. A case in point is Bangladesh, which is periodically devastated by typhoons. Another example is chronic droughts associated with declining rainfall in the southern part of the Sudan.[28]

Some of the cultural and institutional factors of inequality are connected to racial and ethnic factors. For instance, as discussed by Kasliwal,

> In much of Latin America the poverty problem applies almost exclusively to
> the native Indian population in societies largely controlled by those of
> Spanish extraction and Mestizos. In South Africa income classes also divide

neatly along racial lines. Under the apartheid system, recently dismantled, the per capita income of Whites in Namibia was about $15,000; Black income (in the rural areas "reserved" for the majority) was about $120 [per year].[29]

Another cultural factor contributing to poverty, according to Kasliwal, is the prevalence of gender bias. Though women in Third World countries play the major role in food production and in nurturing families, they also tend to constitute the poorest group. Whereas traditionally the family structure itself provided security, dislocations have broken this structure down. "While many males migrate to find employment elsewhere, women are left to eke out a living as best they can."[30]

Even in households where an adult male is present, males more than females are favored in the distribution of food. In Africa, women generally produce 75 percent of the food, yet because of gender bias they suffer greater deprivation than men.[31]

Perhaps the most regrettable source of poverty in Third World countries is that caused by unintended government policies. Urban-biased development affects productivity and income in rural areas. Government-set prices for agricultural products are generally below market value. In addition, the rural poor have limited access to credit and capital markets. Poverty in Latin America and Africa is also a byproduct of dualism. As Kasliwal notes,

> This has deep historical roots in Latin America with its traditional division of large landholdings, "Latifundia," and a separate marginalized class of peasants. In many Latin American countries large-scale agricultural producers still control the bulk of land and labor resources. Africa traditionally has been much more egalitarian, but inequality arose from the colonial pattern of production in the agricultural sector and has expanded in the post-colonial period.[32]

POVERTY AND THE ENVIRONMENT

Does environmental degradation cause accentuated poverty, or does poverty contribute to the depletion of the environment? These questions have not yet been fully explored by development economists. As discussed by Partha Dasgupta and Karl-Goran Maler, some researchers "identify environmental problems with wrong sorts of economic growth, while others view them through the spectacles of poverty."[33] Although both visions are correct, sustainable development policies have been designed to eliminate poverty and maintain the economy at its optimal ecological size.

Lester Brown defines sustainable development as "development that can be kept up over time because it does not erode its natural resource base and the natural environment in which it must take place."[34] If human beings do not take the initiative to restructure present consumption patterns among the world's growing population, then resources will become scarce and eventually exhausted. Increasingly scarce resources lead to inflated prices; this renders many necessities of life unaffordable for vast numbers of people living at or below the poverty line.

Clean, less polluted neighborhoods will become enclaves for wealthy minorities. On the other hand, barren land, polluted waterways, and toxic air will be reserved for the proliferating squatter settlements of the poor.

Acknowledging this bleak situation, the World Development Report of 1992 suggests that permanent poverty reduction must be in harmony with a sustainable environment. Because the poor are both victims and perpetrators of environmental damage, they stand to benefit most from environmental policies and improvements.

> The economic activities stimulated by environmental policies—such as the use of agroforestry and windbreaks to slow soil erosion and the construction of infrastructure for water supply and sanitation—can provide employment. Targeted social safety nets make it less necessary for the poor to "mine" natural resources in time of crisis. Extension and credit programs and the allocation of land rights to squatters increase the ability of the poor to make environmental investments and to manage risk. Investments in water and sanitation and in pollution abatement will also benefit the poor by improving their health and productivity. But it is equitable economic growth, coupled with education and health services, that is most urgently needed.[35]

Furthermore, the report emphasizes the importance of equitable economic growth accompanied by education and health services. However, continued environmental degradation is inevitably a global concern which can lead not only the poor, but also the wealthy, toward extinction. Policies are required to clarify and improve the plight of the poor and must include the following.

- Improved property rights
- Improved water resource management
- Increased investments in sanitation
- Restructured institutional arrangements
- Reduced household energy pollution and over-consumption
- Increased use of renewable energy sources
- Enforced regulation and improvement of atmospheric emissions
- Additional incentives for communal and government management of resources[36]

Enactment of these policies is hindered by the high costs of implementing environmental protection and eradicating poverty.

SUMMARY

One-fifth of the world's population lives in acute poverty. What is more, poverty eradication has failed to keep pace with or surpass population growth. This obvious social tragedy has constantly challenged the theories of economic development.

Classical economics views poverty as an individual problem and suggests that if countries promote moderate to rapid rates of economic aggregate growth, eventually the economic benefits will filter down to the poor. On the other hand, psychologists and materialists view poverty as a person's own perception of his or her condition and the lack of material or nonmaterial benefits. But Irma Adelman favors the notion that income redistribution should *precede* a concentrated effort toward growth, as opposed to the more common redistribution-with-growth approach.

Although based on an inadequate theoretical framework, a per capita income of $370 per year (based on constant 1985 prices) was used by international organizations as a benchmark for measuring the international poverty line. Thus those making an income below $370 per year were classified as living without basic physical needs (including clothing and shelter) being satisfied. To expand the tools of measurement, national estimates of income inequality were further modified to include the HDI, composed of life expectancy, literacy, and real GDP.

Although it is very tough to estimate where environmental degradation causes accentuated poverty or poverty contributes to the depletion of the environment, the general purpose of sustainable development is to eliminate poverty and maintain the economy at its optimal ecological size. Because the poor are both victims and perpetrators of environmental damage, they stand to benefit most from environmental policies and improvements.

REVIEW QUESTIONS

1. What is the difference between absolute poverty and the international poverty line?
2. What are some of the characteristics of absolute poverty?
3. How might you distinguish the poverty theories prior to the 1970s from those in more recent years?
4. Discuss policy options available to LDC governments to transform income distribution. Which policies are most important, and why?
5. Why is economic growth alone ineffective in the eradication of poverty? Use examples from Third World countries and contrast with policies adopted by wealthier nations.

CASE STUDY: INDONESIA

Although its history goes back thousands of years, Indonesia's existence as a modern independent country began in 1945, when Sukarno declared it an independent republic after three years of Japanese occupation. However, for a long time after that, Indonesia was engaged in a protracted diplomatic and sometimes physical struggle with the Dutch, who were the dominant power in that area almost continuously from the early seventeenth century. Under UN pressure, an independent republic of Indonesia was created along with a new constitution in 1949.

The modern (post-World War II) history of Indonesia can be divided into three distinguishable periods: parliamentary democracy, democratic centralism, and the New Order period.

During the parliamentary democracy period (1945–1958), the political environment allowed freedom of expression and free elections. But during the era of democratic centralism that followed, President Sukarno attempted to suppress all opposing groups and effectively used the state apparatus to strengthen his own party. In foreign relations, he drew closer to China and North Korea. As argued by Leo Suryadinata: "The militant foreign policy of the Guided Democracy era drained Indonesia resources (especially foreign exchange reserves), and inflation became rampant."[37] As a result, Sukarno was deposed and General Suharto assumed power in 1965.

In 1966 the so-called New Order was proclaimed by the military regime in Indonesia. By 1973 Indonesia's nine political parties were forced to merge into two major parties (in addition to Golkar, the party of President Suharto): the Indonesian Democracy Party, which included the late Sukarno's Indonesian National Party and other Christian and nationalist parties, and the Development Unity Party (PPP), comprising the Islamic groups.

Although in name Indonesia is a multiparty state, in reality it is accurate to describe Indonesia as a one-party state, since party leaders are chosen under government supervision and must undergo government screening. Parliamentary democracy is used as window dressing to justify the continuance of the regime and its policies. The Indonesian army believes in its dual function as a defender and governor of the state. Although President Suharto's thirty-two-year grip on power ended on May 20, 1998 (in the wake of massive popular demonstrations against his regime's rampant corruption and inability to control the economy), the essential features of the Indonesian state remain unchanged under his "interim" replacement, B. J. Habibie. Unlike Suharto, however, President Habibie is a big hit among the pribumi, or indigenous Muslim leaders, who were cut off from the gravy train operated by Suharto and his cronies.[38]

Social Welfare

As Table 5.4 shows, the Golkar Party succeeded in reducing the number of people served by a single medical doctor, resulting in a significant improvement in life expectancy. This table also shows that Indonesia has effectively achieved universal primary education based on the participation rate of school-age children ages five to fourteen. In terms of poverty reduction,

> Indonesia started the 1970s with around 70 million people, or 60% of the population, in absolute poverty. By 1990, the number had dropped to about 27 million, or 15% of the population. Even during the difficult adjustment period in the 1980s, poverty reduction was sustained. The 1990 World Development Report found that, over the last two decades, Indonesia achieved the highest annual average reduction in the incidence of poverty among all the countries studied. Indonesia's success in reducing poverty is attributable to several elements of its development strategy: substantial investment in economic and social infrastructure that supported sustained, broad-based growth; strong emphasis on improving productivity in agriculture,

Table 5.4
Social Welfare Facilities in Indonesia

| | | | Year | | |
Indicator	1965	1975	1980	1985	1989
Population per physician	31,740	11,530	11,530	N/A	N/A
Life expectancy at birth (years)	44	51	54	55	N/A
Caloric intake, % of required	94	102	110	113	N/A
Infant mortality per 1,000 births	137	113	105	93	73
Primary school enrollment	72	83	112	118	119

Sources: World Bank, *World Tables: Social Data Vol. II; World Development Report 1987;* and *Human Development Report 1991.*

the source of livelihood to a majority of the population and the overwhelming bulk of the rural poor; structural reforms that induced a shift from inward-oriented, capital-intensive activities toward export-oriented, labor-intensive activities; and cushioning of the impact of adjustment in the 1980s on expenditure programs beneficial to the poor, notably social services.[39]

All of these successes, however, turned sour when the Asian financial crisis began in mid-1997 and the rupiah weakened after the Thai crisis. Suddenly, Indonesia's capacity to feed its 200 million people became strained, leading to the food and fuel riots that forced the resignation of President Suharto on May 20, 1998.[40]

The data on income distribution (Table 5.5) indicate that the income gap between the lowest 40 percent and the highest 20 percent declined significantly in Indonesia between 1976 and 1987. Also the Gini coefficient analysis indicates that income inequality had declined through 1987. However, the HDI, which combines indicators of national income, life expectancy and educational attainment, shows that socioeconomic disparities in Indonesia (0.491) are relatively high when compared to Thailand (0.685) and Malaysia (0.789), based on 1992 data.

[A] source of concern has been the emergence of a relatively high concentration of ownership and market power in the modern business sector, or conglomerates, and its implications for both the efficiency and equity of private sector growth. The operations of the top 200 such groups were estimated in 1990 at the equivalent of around one-third of GDP (excluding the small-holder and the oil extraction sectors), of which about a third was accounted for by the top 5 groups [mainly operated by President Suharto and his family, and the ethnic Chinese partners, who control about 70% of the economy].[41]

The conclusion reached from analyzing the nature of poverty in Indonesia is that about 27 million people remain below the absolute poverty level. The uneven geographical pattern of the incidence of poverty is highest in the Eastern Islands and parts of Java.

Table 5.5
Income Distribution in Indonesia

	1976	1987	1992
Lowest 40%	4.4	21.2	
Middle 40%	36.2	37.5	
Top 20%	49.4	41.3	
Income gap between lowest 40% and highest 20%	3.4	2.0	
Gini Coefficient of Inequality	0.41	0.30	
Human Development Index			0.49

Sources: Estimated from *World Development Report,* 1987–1990 data, and United Nations Development Programme (UNDP), *Human Development Report 1992.*

The incidence of poverty ranged from 45.6% in East Nusa Tenggara to 1.3% in DKI Jakarta in 1990. . . . The centerpiece strategy to reduce poverty will remain the promotion of a pattern of growth that expands opportunities for the productive use of the poor's most abundant asset—labor—and the widespread provision of basic social services (education and health) that enhance the poor's capacity to grasp those opportunities. However, finding ways to target these interventions to reach the disadvantaged groups and backward areas will be increasingly important.[42]

DISCUSSION QUESTIONS

1. What policies do you think can be effective in reducing absolute poverty and income inequality in Indonesia?
2. What makes alleviating poverty and protecting the environment difficult in Indonesia?
3. What are the strengths and weaknesses of the Indonesian case study?
4. What lessons did you learn from the Indonesian case study?

NOTES

This chapter was prepared with the assistance of Laura van Galen of Dominican College, San Rafael, California.

1. United Nations Environmental Programme (UNEP), *Poverty and the Environment* (Nairobi, Kenya: UNEP, 1995): 10.

2. Brian W. W. Welsh and Pavel Butorin, *Dictionary of Development: Third World Economy, Environment, Society* (New York: Garland Publishing, 1990): 1017.

3. The World Bank, *World Development Report 1992: Development and the Environment* (New York: Oxford University Press, 1992): 29.

4. Pari Kasliwal, *Development Economics* (Cincinnati, Ohio: South-Western College Publishing, 1992): 49–50.

5. Mwangi S. Kimenyi, *Economics of Poverty, Discrimination, and Public Policy* (Cincinnati, Ohio: South-Western College Publishing, 1995): 65.

6. Ibid., 68.

7. John Kenneth Galbraith, *The Nature of Mass Poverty* (Cambridge, Massachusetts: Harvard University Press, 1979): 5–6.

8. Ibid.

9. Gene Koretz, "Trickle-down economics may not help the poor . . ." *Business Week* (February 24, 1992): 26.

10. Cited by Deepak Lal in *The Poverty of Development Economics* (Boston, Massachusetts: Harvard University Press, 1985): 90.

11. Simon Kuznets, "Economic growth and income inequality," *American Economic Review* 45 (March 1955): 1–28.

12. Klaus Deininger and Lyn Squire, "Economic growth and income inequality," *Finance and Development,* 34(1) (1997): 38–41.

13. Kasliwal, *Development Economics* (Cincinatti, Ohio: South-Western College Publishing, 1995): 58.

14. Gerald M. Meier, *Leading Issues in Economic Development* (New York: Oxford University Press, 1995): 26.

15. Michael P. Todaro, *Economic Development,* 5th ed. (New York: Longman, 1994): 42.

16. E. Wayne Nafziger, *The Economics of Developing Countries* (Belmont, California: Wadsworth, 1984): 82.

17. Robert S. McNamara, "Presidential address to the World Bank, Washington, D.C., September 30, 1980," 20–21; and World Bank, *World Development Report 1980* (New York: Oxford University Press): 33.

18. Montek Ahluwalia, N. Carter, and Hollis Chenery, "Growth and poverty in developing countries," *Journal of Development Economics* (September 1979).

19. Malcolm Gillis et al., *Economics of Development* (New York: W. W. Norton, 1987): 77.

20. United Nations Environment Programme, *Poverty and the Environment,* 10.

21. Ibid., 17–21.

22. United Nations Development Programme, *Human Development Report 1990* (New York: Oxford University Press, 1990): 22.

23. David W. Pearce and Jeremy J. Warford, *World without End: Economics, Environment and Sustainable Development* (New York: Oxford University Press, 1993): 270.

24. United Nations Environment Programme, *Poverty and the Environment,* 25.

25. Brian W. W. Welsh and Pavel Butorin (eds.), *Dictionary of Development: Third World Economy, Environment, Society* (New York: Garland Publishing, 1990): 1017.

26. Irma Adelman, "A poverty-focused approach to development policy," in John P. Lewis and Valeriana Kallab (eds.), *Development Strategies Reconsidered* (New Brunswick, New Jersey: Transaction Books, 1986): 12.

27. Ibid., 65.

28. Kasliwal, *Development Economics,* 67.

29. Ibid.

30. Ibid.

31. United Nations Development Programme, *Human Development Report 1990,* 22.

32. Kasliwal, *Development Economics,* 66.

33. Partha Dasgupta and Karl-Goran Maler, "Poverty, institutions, and the environmental-resources base," *World Bank Environmental Paper Number 9* (Washington, D.C.: The World Bank, 1994): 5.

34. Welsh and Butorin (eds.), *Dictionary of Development,* 948.

35. The World Bank, *World Development Report 1992,* 31. See also Ismail Serageldin, "Poverty, adjustment, and growth in Africa" (Washington, D.C.: The World Bank, January 1989 report); and The World Bank, "Implementing the World Bank's Strategy to Reduce Poverty" (Washington, D.C.: The World Bank, 1993 report).

36. The World Bank, *World Development Report 1992,* 31.

37. Leo Suryadinata, "Indonesia," in Diane K. Mauzy (ed.), *Politics in the ASEAN State* (Kuala Lumpur, Malaysia: Marican & Sons, 1984): 117.

38. "Indonesia: From one gang of cronies to another?" *Business Week* (July 6, 1998): 57.

39. Zia Qureshi et al., *Indonesia: Sustaining Development.* A World Bank Country Study (Washington, D.C.: The World Bank, 1994): 4–5.

40. "Habibie's first hurdle: How to feed the country," *Business Week* (June 8, 1998): 58.

41. Qureshi et al., *Indonesia: Sustaining Development:* 5. Bracketed phrases added for clarification.

42. Ibid., 14.

Population and the Environment

[A] rapidly growing population can increase the pressure on resources and slow any rise in living standards; thus sustainable development can only be pursued if population size and growth are in harmony with the changing productive potential of the ecosystem.

—UN report, 1994[1]

A new framework should expand the definitions of issues—focusing not only on population size, density, rate of increase, age distribution and sex ratios, but also on access to resources, livelihoods, social dimensions of gender and structures of power. New models have to be explored in which population control is not simply a question of family planning but of economic, ecological, social and political planning, in which the wasteful use of resources is not simply a question of finding new substitutes but of reshaping affluent life-styles, and in which sustainability is seen not only as a global aggregate process, but also as one having to do with sustainable livelihoods for the majority of local peoples.

—UN report, 1995[2]

In 1992 the world population was 5.5 billion; by 2025 it is estimated to reach 8.2 billion, as 2,200 people are added to the world's population every fifteen minutes. It now takes less than forty-five years for a population to double, whereas before 1650 it took 35,000 years for the world's population to double.[3] According to demographic transition data, population grew at 0.05 percent from 8000 B.C. to 1650; 0.43 percent between 1650 and 1900; 0.91 percent between 1900 and 1950; and 1.93 percent between 1950 and 1980. This rate is predicted to decrease to 1.67 percent between 1980 and 2000.

In general, increase in population is associated with increases in favorable maternal health conditions and in technological development. In the developing countries growth in population is attributed to a rapid reduction in mortality rates due to improved health care, education, and sanitation.[4] While in the advanced regions the demographic transition seems to be over, in the developing countries the fertility transition has hardly started.[5]

Population problems are also viewed in terms of distribution. For example, "If food were equally distributed . . . less than half of the present world population could be fed on the record grain harvests of 1985 and 1986.[6] Essential resources such as favorable climate, breathable air, and deep, fertile soils took eons to develop. Now they are being depleted at an alarming rate. Global soil losses in excess of new soil formation have been estimated at 24 to 26 billion tons per year.[7]

There are two perspectives on the relationship between population and the environment. One school of thought assumes that population growth may actually increase the prospect for development. That is, the greater the increase in population, the better the chance that scientists and engineers will make discoveries, increasing human welfare in the long run. Other environmental economists argue that the environment is constantly degraded by the ever-increasing numbers of people depleting resources, eventually contributing to environmental degradation and poverty. These environmental economists argue that controlling population halts environmental devastation and may increase the rate of economic growth, particularly in the developing countries where 95 percent of the world's population increase takes place.

In his address to the Cairo conference, the late president of the World Bank, Lewis Preston, said:

> If we do not deal with rapid population growth, we will not reduce poverty —and development will not be sustainable. And yet, population in developing countries will increase more during this decade than before. South Asia's population will grow by two-thirds. Sub-Saharan Africa's will more than double. Who will feed and house the additional numbers? How will they be educated and employed? And what will be done to relieve the inevitable stresses on the environment?[8]

This chapter reviews the theories of population and analyzes the relationship between population and the environment. The case study looks at population trends and policies in China.

POPULATION THEORIES

From Table 6.1 we can interpolate that the world population currently stands at some 6 billion people. The largest concentration of people is in Asia, but the fastest rate of increase is in Africa. In this section of the chapter we briefly discuss the pessimistic, radical, pronatalist, and microeconomic population theories as well as the institutional theory of population growth and development.

The Views of the Pessimistic School of Thought

The first theory of population and economic growth was put forward by Reverend Thomas Malthus in 1798 in his book titled *Essays on the Principle of*

Table 6.1
World Population Trends (in millions), 1900–2100

Region	Year					
	1900	1950	1985	2000	2025	2100
Developing						
Africa	133	224	555	872	1,617	2,591
Asia	867	1,292	2,697	3,419	4,403	4,919
Latin America	70	165	405	546	779	1,238
Subtotal	**1,070**	**1,681**	**3,657**	**4,837**	**6,799**	**8,748**
Developed						
Europe, Japan, Oceania, (former) Soviet Union	478	669	917	987	1,062	1,055
North America	82	166	264	297	345	382
Subtotal	**560**	**835**	**1,181**	**1,284**	**1,407**	**1,437**
Total	**1,630**	**2,516**	**4,838**	**6,121**	**8,206**	**10,185**

Source: Thomas W. Merrick, "World Population in Transition," *Population Bulletin,* 42(2).

Population. In the so-called Malthusian population trap, Malthus proposed that unchecked population growth will inevitably lead to a subsistence level of living and to starvation. He postulated that while population grows at a geometric rate (multiplicative or 1, 2, 4, 8, 16 . . .), due to diminishing returns relating to fixed factors such as land, food supplies can expand only at an arithmetic rate (additive or 1, 2, 3, 4 . . .). As each member of the population holds on to less and less land, his contribution to food production begins to decline over time. Because the growth in food supplies cannot keep pace with the burgeoning population, the per capita income falls so low as to lead to a stable population existing barely above the subsistence level.

Malthus contended that the only way to avoid poverty as a result of population increase was for families to practice "moral restraint," such as delayed marriage and abstention, and thus to limit the number of offspring. Though Malthus's basic idea is the cornerstone for analyzing the relationship between population and development, Malthus failed to foresee the impact of technical progress on development. For example, from 1650 to 1980, while food production multiplied thirteen to fifteen times, population increased only eight times.[9] Also, it can be said that Malthus' theory failed to envision the power of education and industrialization to reduce fertility rates.[10]

David Ricardo, using the "iron law of wages," predicted a similarly bleak scenario. He asserted that population growth will act as a brake on wage increases. Even if wages rise, the increased population forces people to work for less wages.[11]

Similarly, Donna Meadows in the 1970s argued that population should be constrained to preserve the environment and the earth's fixed material resources, as well as to prevent massive food shortages.[12] In his book *The Population Bomb*, Paul Ehrlich warned that mass starvation awaits the world if the present rate of population growth does not slow down. Ehrlich was convinced "that the earth's resources are bound to run out, given the fast rate at which they are being depleted to serve the needs of the world's population."[13]

In a similar vein, the population-poverty cycle theory links population growth to the social, economic, and psychological problems of underdevelopment. According to the neoclassical growth model, resources are fixed, so savings must increase to enable output to grow. The poor, living on a subsistence level, cannot possibly manage to accumulate savings. In addition, high population rates limit government revenues needed to finance social and economic reforms. The neoclassical growth model states that population growth must be stabilized through the mechanism of family planning programs.[14]

The Radical View

The radical school of thought asserts that underdevelopment, not population, is the real culprit. These economists argue that overconsumption by the wealthy limits the living standards and prospects of the poor. They cite the fact that the rich nations consume almost 80 percent of the world's resources—nearly 16 times what Third World residents consume. For instance, the United States alone uses hundreds of times more energy fuel than developing countries and is one of the largest contributors to carbon dioxide emissions.[15]

Neo-Marxist economists fall within the radical school of thought. They argue that population control efforts are the rich pursuing their own self-interest at the expense of the poor. They go so far as to accuse population control programs of being racist, genocidal attempts to rid the world of the poor, who happen to be mostly nonwhite.[16] As pointed out by Gillis and colleagues:

> At the United Nations World Population Conference, held in Bucharest in 1974, a popular slogan was, "Take care of the people and the population will take care of itself." There and elsewhere, verbal wars have been waged between "family planners" and "developmentalists." Ideology often becomes entwined in the debate. Marxist spokesmen routinely contend that population pressure in capitalist countries is merely one more manifestation of class conflict. In a socialist society the problem will disappear because it will be possible to organize society "scientifically," thus providing full employment and satisfaction of everyone's basic needs. In the meantime, capitalist efforts to promote family planning are seen as just one more futile attempt to stave off the coming revolution.[17]

Stated in different terms, the radical school of thought is in opposition to birth control programs on the grounds that such programs will delay an inevitable economic revolution in society.

The Pronatalist (Optimistic) View

Pronatalists such as Julian Simon do not acknowledge a population explosion. Simon contends the free market will adjust to scarcities created by population pressures, and human ingenuity will solve any problems through technological innovation. Population growth brings about progress by stimulating innovation.[18] According to Simon's argument, the ultimate resource is people, who can exert their wills and imaginations primarily for their benefit and thus for the benefit of all. Initially, increased per capita income could be undesirable, but over time positive effects will prevail due to the interaction of population growth and technological progress. Rising population can only cause short-term problems, as more children must be fed and raised, but in the long term these children become productive adults.

Even for the LDCs, Simon suggests that growth in living standards is favored by moderate population growth, as opposed to either stationary or very rapid population growth. Technological change permits output to outpace population growth. Adding to the knowledge base through learning and economies of scale, per capita output grows faster. As A. P. Thirlwall argues:

> A society under pressure from population growth may be expected to respond by finding new and more efficient ways of meeting given needs. . . . Agricultural families may respond to the needs of additional children by changing methods, working harder and producing more. Studies suggest that the elasticity of output to increase in the number of children is about 0.5. Simon argues that population growth also has a large positive effect on agricultural saving, which tends to be overlooked because a large fraction is non-monetized.[19]

Though instructive, this theory doesn't stand up under scrutiny because the LDCs lack the level of capital and an educated labor force to take them to the plateau for economic takeoff.

The Microeconomic Theory of Fertility

Proponents of this theory argue that each individual possesses a set of tastes for a range of goods according to his or her economic capabilities and the relative prices of those goods. The microeconomic theory of fertility views children as a function of economic need, psychic factors, and explicit and implicit cost. Despite the existence of maternal depletion syndrome, multiple births are seen as supplementing family earnings (economic investment). When a family is poor, the implicit assumption is that more children will lead to more money and future security. Psychologically, children are seen as providing satisfaction to the family, notwithstanding the negatives: leisure time activities by family members with growing children, and the strains imposed by rapid population growth on the public health and public school systems.

Institutional Factors Relating to Fertility

In contrast with the above analysis of microeconomic factors, the macro factors that contribute to population growth are religious, social, and political. For example, numerous religions oppose the various available forms of population control. The Roman Catholic ban on all contraception and the opposition to artificial birth control by many Hindu priests as well as some fundamentalist Christians have contributed significantly to continuing population growth trends. Right-wing nationalists and conservatives often see a large population as necessary for both military and economic strength. Population control is often viewed by such individuals as an attempt to hold down the power of a nation or a people.[20]

LINKAGES BETWEEN POPULATION AND THE ENVIRONMENT

The linkages between population growth and the environment are very complex. "Citing population growth alone as the main cause of either poverty or environmental deterioration is therefore likely to misstate the problem. Environmental assets are also lost because of misguided government policies and the failure of market systems to account for external effects and the interests of future generations."[21]

One way of establishing the relationship between population and the environment can be explained using the concept of carrying capacity. As defined by ecologists, carrying capacity is "the maximum population size of a given species that an area can support without reducing its ability to support the same species in the future."[22] The carrying capacity is the maximum human population that can be steadily supported by the earth's resources. Stated differently, carrying capacity is the maximum number of people that can be sustained at the minimum standard of living necessary for survival.[23]

One consequence of population growth is the need for more land both for cultivation and for residential construction, leading to an increase in environmental deterioration. Similarly, population growth can lead to the decrease of per capita agricultural land soil productivity, and a decline in nonrenewable resources such as coal, oil, and metal ores. Population growth may be the main stimulus to technological change and to agricultural productivity, but, as observed in the developing countries, it also leads to a decline in agricultural products. Population growth can adversely affect the adequacy of schooling, health, and nutrition. A higher dependency burden can also reduce the savings ratio and thereby negatively affect capital investment. Finally, a rapid increase in population can exacerbate urban unemployment and underemployment in rural areas of developing countries.

Given the exponential nature of human population growth and our high consumption patterns, it can be said that sometime in the near future human beings will wipe out the productivity of the biosphere and cease to be sustained by the planet.[24] The central question is then, does the earth have a population growth problem or not? As stated by John Carey,

In particular, the question of just how much population control is necessary for sustainable development provokes a very nasty debate. On [one] side are the Malthusian pessimists like Stanford's Paul Ehrlich, who see teeming peoples as a malignant cancer that will grow to kill its planetary host. Unless the population bomb is defused, they say, no amount of development can save our priceless natural heritage. Nonsense, scoff the technological Panglossians, such as Ester Boserup, a Danish specialist in international development. They believe the additional people simply drive the engine of progress faster, raising standards of living for everyone. What keeps the disputes boiling is that plenty of evidence supports both positions.[25]

Given the dramatic increase in population, what kind of population policy should be followed to achieve sustainable development?

GLOBAL POPULATION POLICY FOR SUSTAINABLE DEVELOPMENT

In September 1994 a global policy concerning the dramatic increase in population growth, particularly in the LDCs, was issued by the United Nations International Conference on Population and Development in Cairo, Egypt. Some 20,000 government delegates, UN representatives, nongovernment organizations (NGOs), and media representatives met for nine days. The conference participants addressed a number of important issues such as immigration policy, reproductive health and reproductive rights, the empowerment of women, urbanization, and access to health care.[26] The Programme of Action states that the answer can be found in sustained economic growth in the context of sustainable development; education (especially for girls); gender equity and equality; and infant, child, and maternal mortality reduction. The provision of universal access to reproductive health services, including family planning and sexual health, is also critical to curtailing rising birthrates. Natis Sadik, secretary-general of the conference and head of the United Nations Population Fund, explained that the Programme of Action did not plan to use abortion as a means of birth control, but did intend that family planning services be provided to women.

It has been estimated that around 30 million women become pregnant each year as a result of contraceptive failure. Of these women, half seek an abortion, and some 250,000 to 300,000 women die annually from unsafe abortions.[27] Various population policies, such as family planning programs, access to contraceptives, population redistribution, sterilization, job opportunities for women, and increased education for girls are discussed below.

POPULATION CONTROL POLICIES

Government family planning programs involve any of four avenues of approach. They are:

- Raising the legal minimum age of marriage while utilizing skillful goal-oriented propaganda
- Legalizing abortion

- Promoting contraception
- Providing financial incentives for small families and penalties for large[28]

All these approaches deal with birth control as a means of family planning. Family planning has gained popularity among citizens of many developing nations with the increasing realization that as land becomes scarce, having more children in an effort to grow food is self-defeating.[29] Governments are learning to teach their citizens that family planning is the right thing to do. In Thailand Mechai Viravaidya has changed the traditional desire for having many children, in part by getting the country's most respected authorities—Buddhist monks—to bless condoms.[30] Thailand's National Population Policy was instituted in 1971, and in fifteen years the growth rate plummeted from 3.2 percent to 1.6 percent because contraceptive use rose from 15 percent to 70 percent.[31]

Similarly, the Family Welfare Project in Nepal, run by Shanti Basnet, has been very successful, partly because "one day Basnet even convinced the leader of Maguwa, a nearby village, to agree to voluntary sterilization. Then, five men followed his example, but today, half that village practices some sort of family planning."[32]

In Singapore new mothers in hospitals signed on for family planning programs. As stated by Jan S. Hogendorn, of those contacted in various hospitals, only 50 percent volunteer to participate in family planning programs.

> There is then a followup home visit by a Post Partum Contact Service (PPCS) to reinforce the decision and give further assistance. The midwives, planning assistants, and social workers who serve as motivators and staff the PPCS are given extensive family planning training. Contraceptives are thereafter made available at a price that includes a large subsidy.[33]

Government programs are not without problems. Many people are suspicious of the idea that "people are the problem and government is the solution."[34] For example, in India the sterilization campaign degenerated into use of coercive tactics, with men being dragged off for vasectomies in mobile clinics.[35] Other governments have used forced sterilization and forced abortion to keep their citizenry within accepted population quotas. However, the editors of the *Far Eastern Economic Review* suggest that the imposition of harsh quotas "feeds the appetite for big government when in fact the chief culprit keeping most of these nations poor is itself big government."[36]

Abortion is an extremely controversial topic among advocates of family planning. Muslims and Catholics alike find this topic very offensive; others believe it is the mother's free choice that should be given priority. Frances Kissling, president of Catholics for a Free Choice, has noted, "How come a country, a so-called country, that is in essence 800 acres of office space in the middle of Rome, that has a citizenry that excludes women and children, seems to attract the most attention when talking about public policy that deals with women and children?"[37]

Coercive governmental policies can lead to the favoring of male children, and are related to the low status of women in certain societies. Women are thought of as material gifts and are raised by their families to be given to their husbands' family, often with a large dowry. China's historical pattern of favoring male children has persisted into modern times, against the best efforts of the Chinese government. This has caused a crisis in demographics resulting from recent estimates that single men now outnumber single women by a ratio of 3:2. Experts predict that as a result of China's discrimination against female children and its single child policy, tens of millions of Chinese men will be lifelong bachelors.[38] In Jiekuang the government population control agencies have begun experimenting with policies designed to raise women's status, reasoning that if the value of girls is enhanced, girl children are less likely to be considered unfavorable.

> So now, girls with no brothers attend the local school for free, while the parents pay $7.50 a semester for boys. The girls' parents can enroll in a pension plan that will guarantee them nominal pensions in their old age. The parents also get preferential access to jobs in village enterprises such as the firecracker factory and the tea oil factory.[39]

THE FREE MARKET

Although free markets are volatile and unpredictable, they are seen as a powerful force to reign in the birth rate. As argued by the editors of the *Far Eastern Economic Review,* "if we want to empower people and not their governments, the way to do it is with free markets. . . . [S]ince Asia began opening its economies, economic growth has far outstripped population growth. In the process Asia has transformed itself from what only a generation ago was a poverty-stricken continent into what is today the most dynamic region on earth."[40]

Similarly, Malcolm S. Forbes believes that "poverty and malnutrition persist only in those areas where governments dominate and suffocate economic activity. Birthrates fall as a country's economy expands. Free people don't exhaust resources. They create them. Wealth comes from human imagination and innovation."[41]

A more explicit example of this can be seen in the new roles of women in China. When interviewed a young Chinese women felt that thanks to China's recent economic boom, she, like many Chinese women, can now look forward to gaining financial independence and social status through her career.[42]

Another example of a successful market mechanism to control population growth can be found in Taiwan, where the population growth rate has declined to 0.95 percent and is forecasted to achieve zero growth by 2035. As pointed out by *The Economist,*

> As prosperity has grown, income per person has risen from $145 in 1951 to $10,215 in 1992; the birth rate has fallen from about 50 per 1,000 in 1951 to just over 15 per 1,000 in 1992. Another effective way to increase the status of women and slow population growth is to create female entrepreneurs. The labor market has pulled women out of the home, and decent childcare is expensive. Good education is costly, too. Some parents say they can barely afford children.[43]

HEALTH CARE

Reproductive health goes hand in hand with issues of population control. In the LDCs, many women do not have access to reproductive health care services and almost half of the women die each year of pregnancy-related causes, while the rest are permanently maimed or made ill. As pointed out by Perita Huston, "This is a major public-health crisis that has gone unnoticed for far too long. . . . [P]roviding reproductive health services to the 300–500 million women who wish to plan their families would improve women's health and lower birth rates as well. . . . [I]t is simply a matter of allocating the needed resources."[44]

As pointed out by the United States Agency for International Development (USAID), day-to-day survival needs become the focus of national discourse in the LCDs to the detriment of rational environmental planning, even as population growth continues unchecked.[45]

When a woman has many children close together in age during her younger years there are drastic health risks to both her and her children; this limits her opportunities and diminishes her ability to invest in her children's education and health. As stated by USAID,

> More than 500,000 women die each year because of preventable complications from pregnancy, abortion, and childbirth; over 35,000 children die each day, mostly from preventable causes, and mostly in the developing world. The HIV/AIDS epidemic continues to spread at the rate of approximately 5,000 new infections per day. These conditions impede sustainable development and are tragedies for individuals, families, communities, and nations.[46]

Yet all of this is preventable. Lewis Preston estimates that a basic preventive health care package, covering maternal and child health, would only cost U.S.$8 per person in the poorest countries annually.[47]

THE ROLE OF WOMEN

The traditional role of women in Third World societies also factors heavily in the population/development/environment equation. Though half of the world's population is made up of women, many still do not have equal access to land, technology, education, employment, and political power. Particularly in the developing countries, women's daily experience gives them tremendous knowledge as well as an enormous stake in environmental issues. As Irene Dankelman and Joan Davidson point out:

> [T]he link between women and the environment is made in several ways. For example, women often farm the most fragile and poor lands and women are most adversely affected by the loss of environmental resources such as fuel and water, because they are responsible for using these resources. Thus, women are most concerned about preserving natural resources and could accomplish environmentally sound, sustainable development by working together if only outsiders would recognize this link and provide women with the resources to solve development problems.[48]

One method of improving the status of women is through education. As outlined by Lewis Preston at the Cairo conference, "An educated woman is more likely to delay marriage, space her pregnancies, and have fewer and healthier children . . . She is also likely to earn more if she works and to invest more in her children's education. Yet, nearly 100 million girls are denied education."[49]

Education is one of the most effective forms of birth control. "A woman in a developing country who has seven or more years of education has, on average, 2.2 fewer children than a woman who has no education."[50] Data gathered by the United Nations from ninety-three countries shows that for every year of schooling a woman receives, her fertility rate decreases by ten percent.[51] Raising the primary school enrollment rate of girls to match that of boys would cost just U.S.$1 billion.[52] Nafis Sadik has stated, "As many countries have now demonstrated, higher literacy, better health, and slower population growth are the best basis for economic development. . . . [N]one of these aims can be achieved without involving women as actors and agents as well as beneficiaries."[53]

With this in mind, the primary goal of the International Conference on Population and Development in Cairo was to curb population by enhancing the status of women around the world.

SUMMARY AND CONCLUSION

Every fifteen minutes, some 2,200 people are added to the world's population. At this rate, by 2025 the world's population will reach 8.2 billion. There are three major schools of thought on the association between population and the environment. The optimistic perspective assumes that population growth may actually increase the prospect for development. The pessimistic school argues that unchecked population growth will inevitably lead to social, economic, and psychological problems of underdevelopment. Environmental economists, on the other hand, argue a third point of view: that the environment is constantly degraded by the ever-increasing numbers of people depleting resources, eventually contributing to environmental degradation and poverty. Thus they view population control as a possible solution to the degradation of the environment.

But whether or not population control is needed to save the earth is a difficult question to answer. On the one hand, there are the dwindling resources and aesthetics of our environment, which may be due to out-of-control population growth. On the other hand, we may simply consume too much or consume in unstable ways. A larger population pool increases the likelihood of creative minds working on innovative solutions to modern problems, leading to such discoveries as the green revolution, which succeeded in increasing farm production. But can these innovations be sustained forever? And why should we take the chance of having to come up with some new way to feed people if we can simply cut down on the numbers of people to be fed? Whichever side a person takes in this argument, there is little doubt that fewer people will create less obstacles to overcome in the future.

A more convincing argument for population control is based on the causes as opposed to the effects of mass population growth. The world's population is growing at such a rapid rate because people in the developing countries believe they need their children's labor to be able to feed their families, knowing that not all of their children are going to survive. A reduction in the birthrate must take place at both the household and societal levels. This would reduce the dependency ratio and lead to increased savings; it would also lead to less of a drain on public resources.

We can assume that a main cause of the population problem in the LDCs is related to those societies' responses to their high mortality rates. However, we live in a dynamic world where there is no single cause and effect, but rather a complex interaction of many causes producing varied effects.

The common use of government-encouraged birth control is an example of the "Band-Aid" effect on population control. While there are some impressive statistics that show a slowdown of population growth, there is also a long list of human rights violations surrounding these programs. There are many stories of citizens being forced to use unsafe methods, to comply with mandatory sterilization requirements, and to submit to abortions. There are many instances where human health is damaged as a result of inappropriate government policies.

Another important part of developmental programs is the inclusion of women in both economic and education sectors. For example, women with a higher self-perceived value and higher education have fewer children than women with less education. If the population problem is to be solved, women need to be included in the development process. As people are encouraged to help themselves, population and consequently environmental problems can be solved. As suggested by Michael P. Todaro, ways to approach the population predicament in the developing countries are:

- Lowering birthrates among the poor by increased education leading to a higher status for women
- Providing nonagricultural job opportunities
- Raising the income levels of all
- Reducing infant mortality
- Developing an old-age support network outside of the immediate family[54]

REVIEW QUESTIONS

1. What theories account for the population explosion in the LDCs?
2. What is the relationship between population and the environment?
3. Critically assess the resolutions of the United Nations International Conference on Population and Development held in Cairo, Egypt, in 1994.

CASE STUDY: THE CHINESE POPULATION AND THE ENVIRONMENT

Until 1979 the People's Republic of China went through a period in which increased production and higher quality medical care received primary emphasis.

As a result, mortality rates decreased, birthrates increased, and China's population boomed. Today, almost one-fourth of the world's population lives in China, which comprises less than 7 percent of the world's arable land.[55] The current growth rate hovers at around 1.4 percent annually, or 16 million new people a year. Life expectancy continues to rise and the elderly population has surpassed 100 million.[56]

In 1979, as China's population approached one billion, a policy to control further growth was developed. China then implemented its single-child-family policy. Since then, the motto in China has become "late, sparse and few." Marry in the late twenties, have a large interval between children if there are more than one, but as a goal, only have one child.[57]

Government-sponsored family planning programs include the use of the intrauterine device, sterilization, and abortion, as well as the use of bribery, propaganda, a quota system, tracking women's menstrual cycles, and making door-to-door checks to make sure no one is concealing a pregnancy. Couples who stay within the one-child limit receive cash bonuses until the child is fourteen.[58] For one-child families, medical, nursery, and educational fees for the child are paid by the government, and the child is given priority placement in day care and schooling. As the child grows older, he or she is helped along with employment opportunities to enable the child to stay living within the parents' district.[59] This way parents are ensured a care provider for their elderly years.

Newlyweds who take the pledge to have only one child are given preferred housing, and a bonus is added to their yearly cash income. For an employed new mother, the normal leave of fifty-six days after birth is extended to seventy-two days off with pay.[60]

While childless families are not rewarded at all, families with more than one child are punished. Generally, the punishment includes the loss of housing rights, a reduced food ration or loss of subsidy on grain purchases, loss of educational priority, and job sanctions.

In China family planning is controlled by a "unit system." Each unit has a quota of allowable births per year. The official in charge of each unit must sign a document stating that no one in their unit will break the quota. If everyone in the unit stays within the quota, the official will receive a cash bonus.[61] In addition, the officials are allowed to add their own regulations, which could include orders for abortions and sterilizations. The official decides who gets land, who will receive bonuses and housing, who gets married, and who has children. In short, officials have the right and responsibility to maintain their quota using whatever means are necessary.[62]

As the officials carry out their duties, many illegal abortions are performed. "Although abortions are said to be illegal in China after the first trimester of pregnancy, this law is violated with impunity by officials under pressure to meet their quotas."[63]

There are many instances of concealed pregnancies being discovered in the second or third trimester leading to orders for an abortion. A punishment for not having an abortion could be boarding up the couple's house, leading to economic hardship and social humiliation.[64]

Although these policies seem stringent enough to effectively keep population growth to a minimum, enforcement of the 1980 one-child policy is very difficult. Children symbolize security and increased productivity. Many people in China still rely on sons to take care of them in old age, as the Chinese government provides no old-age benefits. A daughter, on the other hand, will marry away to care for her husband's family. This form of population control has led to increased female infanticide and mistreatment of women who have daughters.[65]

China's population growth continues to consume China's natural resources. There already exist extreme shortages of water, farmland, forests, and energy. China's forest resources are now only slightly larger per capita than Saharan and Sahelian countries.[66] In the 1950s 30 percent of the land in China was forested; in 1993 only 14 percent was forested.[67] In one province (Hainan) alone, "the forested areas fell from 867,000 hectares in 1950 to 247,000 hectares in 1983, a decline of 71%."[68] The loss of 500 hectares of land per year is causing food production to decline rapidly. The growing dependency on fertilizers and chemicals by farmers is adding to the pollution problem.[69]

While China ranks third in the world for energy production, its population of 1.2 billion constrains China's energy supply. In 1993 China was the world's sixth largest producer of oil; today the country is a net oil importer. Despite the high level of production, rationing is still required.

Water shortage is another environmental obstacle worsened by the growing population. At least 200 large cities now have an inadequate water supply, and the situation is getting worse in the north. For example, while Beijing's demand for water has been increasing by 7 percent per year, its supply has been declining by 5 percent per year.[70]

The government has recently attempted to address some of the environmental problems. For example, mass reforestation efforts are under way, and shelter belts are being established to mitigate desertification and conservation.

Increased family planning and birth control information is a major governmental priority that seeks to encourage voluntary and informed choices. Nonetheless, traditional religious and cultural traditions threaten the efficacy of these programs.[71] And the government has yet to provide the truly secure existence and benefits that would reduce the temptation to equate having children with ensuring the security and productivity of the family.

DISCUSSION QUESTIONS

1. Does the growing population level in China restrain its prospects for sustainable development?

2. What are the effects of China's governmental policies for controlling population growth? How effective are they?

3. What lessons did you learn from the Chinese case study?

NOTES

This chapter was prepared with the assistance of Amy Fisher, Shelley Alger, Sally Westfall, Johnny Sun, Chen Fen, and Chen Hui, all of Dominican College, San Rafael, California.

1. Quoted in United Nations, Department for Economic and Social Information and Policy Analysis, *Population, Environment and Development* (New York: United Nations, 1994): 23.

2. L. Arizpe et al., "Population and natural resources use" (1993), in United Nations Environment Programme (UNEP), *Poverty and the Environment* (Nairobi, Kenya: UNEP, 1995): 34.

3. Michael P. Todaro, *Economic Development,* 5th ed. (New York: Longman, 1994): 178–214.

4. David Pearce and Jeremy Warford, *World without End: Economics, Environment and Sustainable Development* (Oxford: Oxford University Press, 1993): 151.

5. United Nations Environment Programme, *Poverty and the Environment,* 30.

6. Paul Ehrlich and Anne Ehrlich, *The Population Explosion* (New York: Simon and Schuster): 28.

7. Ibid.

8. Lewis Preston, address to the International Conference on Population and Development seminar in Cairo, Egypt, September 5–13, 1994, quoted in Rahul Singh, "Agents of change," *Far Eastern Economic Review* (September 22, 1994): 21.

9. E. Wayne Nafziger, *The Economics of Developing Countries* (Belmont, California: Wadsworth, 1984): 208.

10. See, for example, Todaro, *Economic Development.*

11. Jacob Oser, *The Evolution of Economic Thought* (New York: Harcourt, Brace & World, 1963): 68.

12. Pearce and Warford, *World without End,* 43.

13. Paul Ehrlich, as quoted in Sarah C. De Mesa, "Copying in a finite world: Population growth and environmental ethics," *Economics and Society* (January 1992): 13–16.

14. Betsy Carpenter, "More People, More Pollution," *U.S. News and World Report* (September 12, 1994): 63.

15. Todaro, *Economic Development,* 150.

16. Ibid., 204.

17. Malcolm Gillis et al., *Economics of Development* (New York: W. W. Norton, 1987): 172.

18. Todaro, *Economic Development,* 204.

19. A. P. Thirlwall, *Growth and Development* (London: Lynne Rienner, 1994): 160.

20. Jan S. Hogendorn, *Economic Development* (New York: HarperCollins, 1992): 259–60.

21. Pearce and Warford, *World without End,* 149.

22. J. Roughgarden, *Theory of Population Genetics and Evolutionary Ecology* (New York: Macmillan, 1979).

23. See, for example, Pearce and Warford, *World without End,* 155.

24. Jenny Moon, "Population, consumption, and the environment" (unpublished paper, Dominican College, 1996): 1.

25. John Carey, "Will saving people save our planet?" *International Wildlife* (May–June 1992): 16–17.

26. Ibid.

27. Rahul Singh, "Growing pains," *Far Eastern Economic Review* (September 22, 1994): 21.

28. Hogendorn, *Economic Development,* 281.

29. Eugene Linden, "More power to women, fewer mouths to feed," *Time* (September 26, 1994): 64.

30. Carey, "Will saving people save our planet?" 23.

31. Daniel Chiras, *Environmental Science: Action for a Sustainable Future,* 4th ed. (Redwood City, California: Benjamin/Cummings, 1994): 107.

32. Don Hinrichsen, "Nepal's foothill: Mountain of change," *International Wildlife* (May/June 1992): 23.

33. Hogendorn, *Economic Development,* 282.

34. "The Cairo swindle" (editorial), *Far Eastern Economic Review* (September 22, 1994): 5.

35. Hamish McDonald, "Paying the price," *Far Eastern Economic Review* (December 26, 1991): 16.

36. "The Cairo swindle," 5.

37. Peter Waldman, "Abortion issue overshadows U.N. meeting," *The Wall Street Journal* (September 8, 1994): A–14.

38. Diane Brandy and Catherine Romano, "The world's most desired women," *Marie Claire* (March–April 1995): 49.

39. Susan V. Lawrence, "Family planning at a price," *U.S. News and World Report* (September 19, 1994): 57.

40. "The Cairo swindle," 5.

41. Malcolm S. Forbes, "People are an asset, not a liability," *Forbes* (September 12, 1994): 25.

42. Brady and Romano, "The world's most desired women," 5.

43. *The Economist* (June 5, 1993): 41.

44. Perita Huston, "Women and nature: an alliance for survival," *UNESCO Courier* (March 1992): 14.

45. United States Agency for International Development, "Stabilizing world population growth and protecting human health: USAID's strategy" (unpublished manuscript, 1994).

46. Ibid.

47. Singh, "Growing pains," 21.

48. Irene Dankelman and Joan Davidson, "Women and the environment in the Third World," in *Environment* (January–February 1990): 25.

49. Lewis Preston, president of the World Bank, as quoted by Singh, "Growing pains," 21.

50. Judy Mann, "Only the flexible move forward," *The Washington Post* (September 9, 1994): E–3.

51. Brad Knickerbocker, "Report on the environment," *Christian Science Monitor* (March 23, 1994): 7.

52. Singh, "Growing pains," 21.

53. Nafis Sadik, UN Population Chief Fund, as quoted by Rahul Singh in "Agents of Change," *Far Eastern Economic Review* (September 22, 1994): 28.

54. Todaro, *Economic Development,* 201.

55. "The future of China's environment," *New Statesman and Security* (January 8, 1993): 29.

56. Vaclav Smil, "China's environmental morass," *Current History* (September 1989): 277.

57. Howard G. Chen-Eoan, "Bringing up one by one," *Time* (December 7, 1987): 251.

58. Johnathon Mirsky, "The infanticide tragedy in China," *The Nation* (July 2, 1983): 12–14.

59. Joyce K. Kallgren, "Family planning in China," *Current History* (September 1986): 269–275.

60. Ibid., 271.

61. Steven Mosher, "Human rights in China," *Society* (January–February 1986): 28–35.

62. Ibid., 31.

63. Ibid., 33.

64. Steven Mosher, "Human rights in China," *Society* (September–October 1984): 4.

65. "The future of China's environment," 29.

66. Ibid.

67. Asuka-Zhang Shouchuan, "Fragile: China," *Japan Update* (May 1994): 17.

68. Smil, "China's environmental morass," 279.

69. Ibid., 277.

70. State Council of the People's Republic of China, *China's Environmental Preservation Yearbook* (Beijing: Chinese government publication, 1993): 33.

71. Emily MacFarquhar, "Population wars," *U.S. News and World Report* (September 12, 1994): 54.

chapter 7

Women and the Environment

Women will have to wait at least 450 years before they are represented in equal numbers with men in the higher echelons of economic power. At the current rate of progress, they will reach equality with men in decision-making positions only around the year 2465, reports the United States Fund for a Feminist Majority. A United Nations study puts the date even further away—around the year 2490! Should women wait that long to achieve equality in economic decision-making?

—Margaret Gallagher[1]

Investing in women is not a panacea. It will not put an end to poverty, remedy the gross inequalities between people and countries, slow the rate of population growth, rescue the environment, or guarantee peace. But it will make a critical contribution towards all those ends. It will have an immediate effect on some of the most vulnerable of the world's population. And it will help create the basis for future generations to make better use of both resources and opportunities.

—Nafis Sadik[2]

Domestic labor as the exclusive domain of women is almost universally recognized. That women also make significant contributions to national economies is generally not acknowledged. Women play a pivotal role in home-based production, food processing, and caregiving. They also play a major role in animal husbandry, marketing, and the gathering of water and fuel wood. Women care for their husbands, children, old people, the sick, the handicapped, and others who cannot look after themselves. As stated by the International Labour Organization, women

> often must assume a large share of the responsibility for the survival of their families, through direct production for consumption, income earning, providing health care, etc. Women constitute a substantial part—in some countries the majority—of the agricultural labour force, including workers

on plantations; they are engaged in home-based production of modern as well as traditional products, sometimes working for a contractor under the putting-out system; and many migrate from impoverished rural areas to work in the urban informal sector as traders, or in export processing zones as industrial workers.[3]

In the LDCs women's work is not monetized and therefore is undervalued and underestimated. Although women perform the bulk of agricultural work, they seldom have full title to property, but are allowed only land use rights. "Where rights are collectively held, it is almost invariably the male head of household who participates in the peasant association. In family farming systems, women have even less access to basic assets."[4]

Four global meetings to discuss the role of women in development took place within the auspice of the United Nations. These were in Mexico City (Decade for Women, 1975), Copenhagen (1980), Nairobi (1985), and Beijing (Fourth World Conference on Women, 1995). Generally, the division of labor between the sexes both within and outside the family and household accounts is the general explanation given for the origins and causes of gender inequality. In the 1970s and 1980s the "women in development" (WID) approach mainly focused on integrating women into development efforts through such measures as increasing their access to credit, land, and employment. Thus, following the integrationist ("add women and stir") approach, WID emphasized that growth and productivity would be better met if women were brought fully into the process.

On the other hand, the "gender and development" approach of the 1990s stressed that the key problem in gender relationships is women's subordinate status to men. Thus it calls for a fundamental reexamination of current social and political institutions, with the goal of giving women equality with men in both economic and political power.[5]

This chapter explores theories of gender inequality (defining gender as the social meaning given to biological sex differences[6]) and examines the relationship between women and the environment. The case study at the end of the chapter presents an explication of the complex interdependencies between women and the environment.

THEORIES OF GENDER INEQUALITY

There are two theoretical approaches to gender issues. The first perspective stresses the "coercive" aspects of the gender system—how male control of economic, political, ideological, and physical resources perpetuates a substantial male advantage over women. The second perspective stresses "voluntaristic" aspects of the gender system and examines how women make choices that inadvertently contribute to their own disadvantage.

Coercive Theories

The coercive theories tend to stress structural variables and are distinguished into Marxist-feminist, mezostructural, and microstructural theories.

Marxist-Feminist Theory. The Marxist-feminist theory of coercion emphasizes the mutually reinforcing nature of capitalism and patriarchy as they contribute to female oppression. Using class analysis, the Marxist-feminist argues that capitalism requires the production of surplus value by male labor-force workers (in modern times workers are increasingly female as well). The maintenance and reproduction of a relatively docile labor force, where the work is accomplished primarily in the unpaid domestic sphere by women, is also a fundamental aspect of capitalism as defined by this school of thought. Because capitalism seeks inexpensive labor to maximize profits, women are increasingly employed outside the home, but in low-wage jobs.

Marxist-feminists argue that female oppression in the contemporary world is sustained by the power of capitalists to protect and enhance their interests, which include low-wage employment for women and unpaid domestic and familial work. This system is sustained by the working class because of inherent accrued advantages both in the formal economy and at home. For Marxist-feminists, the elimination of female oppression requires the demise of both capitalism and patriarchy, as an ideology and as a form of husband-wife relationship.[7]

Mezostructural Theory. This theory focuses on organizational structure. Stated simply, the differences in male and female attitudes and behaviors are produced by different and unequal social roles. Women are generally in a disadvantaged position because they are blocked by men from upward mobility.[8]

Microstructural Theory. The microstructural approach focuses on gender inequality resulting from male-female interactions, especially those that occur between husbands and wives. Based on exchange theory, the microstructuralists assume that power asymmetries in society permit males to exercise dominance over women.

Voluntaristic Theories

The voluntaristic theories are centered at the micro level and focus on the processes by which males and females internalize gender-normative ways of being and behaving. Included in this category are feminist neo-Freudian theory and socialization theory.

Feminist Neo-Freudian Theory. The current division of labor places child-rearing practices overwhelmingly in the hands of women. Child-rearing practices may have vastly different, gender-differentiated outcomes, especially in the relational capacities of each gender. Nancy Chodorow argues that by becoming deeply embedded in the unconscious personality structure of each gender, the division of labor and gender inequality are therefore the automatic results and reinforcement mechanisms of the very system that produces them.[9]

Socialization Theory. The socialization theory is based on the assumption that gender-appropriate ways of thinking, feeling, and acting are taught to children by adults. To the extent that children are successfully socialized, they will mature into adults who will make choices consistent with their gender self-identity. For men, this socialization process requires a demonstration of strength and competence. For women the socialization process perpetuates a sense of weakness.

Thus, through the socialization process, the gender system is replicated from one generation to the next.

WOMEN AND THE ENVIRONMENT

Recognizing the different roles of males and females in society, it is necessary to disaggregate environmental issues on the basis of gender. Therefore, to discuss the role of women in relation to the environment, it is essential to frame women as managers of the traditional environment. Many areas typical of women's work require maintenance of the environment as it already exists. Second, women must be seen as rehabilitators of the natural environment—repairing and taking preventive action to ensure sustainable development. Finally, women need to be seen as innovators in the use of new and more appropriate technology.

The role of providing and securing shelter is generally assumed by women.

> To empower women in this role, we are concerned about the collaborative resources that women have in working together to challenge authorities, to mobilize, to get access to infrastructure and to basic services. Often it's not so much a matter of them going out and finding resources for themselves, but of them challenging government and authorities to get those resources.[10]

Women have a vested interest in improving the environment, as that is their traditional domain. As Irene Dankelman and Joan Davidson point out, the link between women and the environment is made in several ways. For example, women often farm the most fragile and poor lands and are most adversely affected by the loss of environmental resources such as fuel and water, because they are responsible for using these resources. Thus women are most concerned about preserving natural resources and could accomplish environmentally sound, sustainable development by working together if outsiders would recognize this link and provide women with the resources to solve development problems.[11]

EMPIRICAL RESULTS

It is very difficult to fully and exhaustively test the above theories because there have been a limited number of studies in this area. However, it is safe to assume that women generally comprise a large percentage of the world's labor force. By and large, women are making a vast and unacknowledged contribution to the economic welfare of their communities, mainly in unpaid work and in small-scale businesses. As stated in the *State of the World Women's Report, 1985,* "Just as society undervalues the work women do in the home, so their skills are undervalued when applied to work outside in the world of employment."[12]

According to a 1990 UN survey, if unpaid house and family care work were counted as productive output in national income accounts, global output would increase by 20 to 30 percent.[13] For instance, when broken by countries, women's unpaid labor equaled 28 percent of Norway's GDP; 23 percent of the United States' GDP; 11 percent of the Philippines' GDP; and 22 percent of Venezuela's GDP.[14] Thus, it could be argued that the gender income gap mainly reflects gender differences in family roles which constrain the allocation of time between the labor market and the household.

However, the adverse economic conditions in the LDCs in the early 1980s prompted many poor women to participate both in formal and informal economic sectors to compensate for losses in real family income. Even so, because of gender bias and being involved in marginal productivity, their incomes did not increase. "In rural Africa, poorer women farmers and nearly landless women have responded to economic contraction and food insecurity by increasing the time they devote to farming marginal lands and to low-productivity informal sector activities."[15]

Women's earnings are frequently about 70 percent of men's. For instance, in Mali and Afghanistan, "89 and 97 percent respectively of all formal employment goes to men. Women's wages are usually lower than men's even when they do similar work."[16]

Because of socialization processes, parents invest heavily in male children and place greater expectations on boys than on girls. "This discrimination begins very early in life. Research in Bangladesh found that boys under the age of five were given 16 percent more food than girls and that girls were likely to be malnourished in times of famine. A study in India found that boys were given far more fatty and milky foods than girls."[17]

Similarly, because of structural adjustments in many developing countries during this period, women were negatively affected because the main burden of adjustment falls on women and children. As stated by Jeanne Vickers, "When we speak of the poorest of the poor, we are almost always speaking about women. Poor men in the developing world have even poorer wives and children. And there is no doubt that recession, the debt crisis and structural adjustment policies have placed the heaviest burden on poor women, who earn less, own less, control less."[18]

Export-led development has increased women's participation in cash crop production and other foreign exchange activities, but, as Vickers points out, it has devalued the traditional areas of women's work. "Micro-level income-generating programmes for women have often, inadvertently, reinforced women's marginalization from the wider economic process."[19]

Even though women provide more than 50 percent of the world's agricultural products, they represent very few of the agricultural advisors because they are regarded as not having formal education. Job discrimination reinforces the male perception that women are incompetent.

Women's daily experience gives them a unique environmental perspective, which gives rise to tremendous knowledge as well as a recognition of the enormous stakes involved. Women have long been the backbone of grassroots environmental projects, from garbage collection in Mexico to tree planting in Africa.[20] Joanna de Groot argues:

> Women's disadvantaged position in production and reproduction should be understood as the outcome of complex interactions between economic needs, family interest, state interventions and male power, whether in post-1949

China or apartheid South Africa; the sexualization and domestication of
women in both ideology and practice in Iran or Latin America can only be
grasped as an equally complex interaction of male and socioeconomic con-
flicts over resources, status and autonomy. Women themselves have to deal
with these complex realities, according to the priorities which seem relevant
to them. Discussions of women and development need to take account of the
dialectics of choice and circumstance, and to treat Third World women not
as passive, exotic victims either of external forces or local conditions, but
rather as active participants in such dialectics.[21]

POLICY IMPLICATIONS

If policymakers hope to make faster progress in improving economic performance, reducing poverty, slowing down population growth, and stopping environmental degradation, they will have to go much further in their efforts to
involve women in economic development.[22]

In addition to the need for population control, the status of women must be
raised to enable them to exert some control over the environment that affects
them. Worsening environmental conditions have a significant impact on women.

> Women have learned that their breast milk is contaminated with dioxin, that
> pesticides and herbicides are present in ground water. They are told that the
> life-giving Sun is becoming dangerous due to a weakened ozone layer, that
> children everywhere are vulnerable to genetic disorders caused by contaminated
> environments. Women have observed these phenomena and feel alienated
> from a society which has lost touch with the beauty and power of nature.
> They fear that future generations will be deprived of the diversity of Nature's
> creatures and the music of bird song.[23]

To improve the status of women in society requires a substantial social investment in education and the creation of female entrepreneurs. But, as pointed out
by Nafis Sadik, "Investing in women must go beyond such services, and remove
the barriers preventing them from exploring their full potential. . . . [T]hat means
granting them equal access to land, to credit, to rewarding employment—as well
as establishing their effective personal and political rights."[24]

WOMEN AND EDUCATION

Bella Abzug has noted that "86 million girls—43 million more than boys—
have no access to primary-school education. Approximately 500 million children
start primary school, but more than 100 million children, two thirds of them
girls, drop out before completing four years of primary school. Of the world's 1
billion illiterate adults, two thirds are women."[25]

The literature on human capital theory indicates the importance of schooling
and experience.[26] Schooling is one the most important means for women to acquire
knowledge and skills that enable them to fully participate in the labor market. For
example, as shown in Table 7.1, the illiteracy rate among females in developing
countries tends to be far higher than among males.

Table 7.1
Adult Illiteracy Rate (%), 1980 and 1995

	—— 1980 ——		—— 1995 ——	
	Female	Male	Female	Male
Developed regions	5	2	2	2
Developing countries:				
Sub-Saharan Africa	71	48	53	33
Latin America and the Caribbean	23	18	15	12
North Africa and Western Asia	74	45	56	32
Eastern and Southeast Asia and Oceania	42	20	24	9
Southern Asia	76	47	63	37

Source: The World's Women, 1995: Trends and Statistics (New York: United Nations): Chart 4.1.

Given these illiteracy rates, gender differences in human capital stock may arise from investments in formal schooling and on-the-job training. But investment in schooling is perhaps the single strongest influence on women's control of their own future. Every large-scale survey in developing countries has discovered that the education women receive is one of the most universal and reliable predictors both of their own fertility and of their children's health. This effect holds regardless of school curricula and different cultures, even when other factors such as income and employment opportunities come into play.[27]

By and large, women in LDCs often experience oppression under the existing patriarchal political, social, and religious structures. Many countries deny women the right to education because religious tradition defines the role of women in society as wives and mothers. Despite stated national policies of equal access to educational opportunities, social dogma is often so strong that women find themselves ostracized as a result of their education. Those fortunate enough to graduate from high school or college frequently find themselves denied opportunities of employment commensurate with their training.

As shown in Table 7.2, females receive less education than males in almost every developing country. In Sub-Saharan Africa, northern Africa, and southern Asia, enrollments for boys in primary and secondary levels generally far exceed those for girls.[28]

As rightly argued by Michael P. Todaro, "The existence of an educational gender gap is important to recognize because it is proven that educational discrimination limits economic development while sustaining social inequality."[29] In addition, Wadi D. Haddad concludes that reducing the educational gender gap is essential for the following reasons.

- The education of women brings higher rates of return than that of men in LDCs.
- Improving women's accessibility to education increases productivity in rural areas but also results in delayed marriage, lower fertility rates, and improved child health.
- Healthier conditions for children (because of healthier and informed mothers) leads to multiplier effects for many generations.
- Any improvement in women's status has a large impact on breaking the cycle of poverty within a nation.[30]

In analyzing the requisite adjustments necessary in an economy to create better educational opportunities for women, it is vital to consider both the external and internal policies of a nation's educational system. External policies modify the economic and social signals outside the system that determine the demand for education and the political treatment of women in those systems. On the other hand, internal policies concentrate on effectiveness and accessibility by making changes in public finance as well as contents and methods of promotion.[31]

Traditionally, external policies seek to remove the distortions in an economy that discourage investment in women in the labor force. They do this by removing incentive distortions, such as artificially high wages; increasing job opportunities; and slowing the rate of rural-urban migration. Distortions affect the upward mobility of women because high wages lead to a more capital-intensive economy and a less worker-dependent economy. Increasing the demand for workers is

Table 7.2
Primary and Secondary Enrollment per 100
School-Age Population (%)

	1980 Girls	1980 Boys	1990 Girls	1990 Boys
Developed regions	92	92	99	98
Eastern Europe	91	92	90	89
North Africa	50	74	67	82
Sub-Saharan Africa	38	52	44	55
Latin America and the Caribbean	77	78	83	81
Eastern Asia	86	89	91	92
Southeast Asia	72	77	74	77
Southern Asia	32	55	43	59
Western Asia	71	82	84	89
Oceania	61	65	59	66

Source: The World's Women, 1995: Trends and Statistics (New York: United Nations), Chart 4.5.

important because employers in turn spend more in investment for their employees in terms of training, skills, and education.[32]

However, the creation of a more labor-intensive economy does not necessarily guarantee the hiring and promotion of women. If anything, it can provide an incentive for employers to exploit women by paying them lower wages. Unless the investment created by removing distortionary policies is guided by government rewards for investment programs that benefit women, there is the danger of net losses to women rather than net gains.

An increase in revenue allocations to educational systems for human development is necessary to accomplish these gains.[33] By shifting the focus toward the development of primary education, self-education and better work experiences are promoted. Furthermore, it is essential that the money allocated be earmarked toward development of women's literacy programs. Many times LDCs spend exorbitant revenues on facilities and higher education without investing for the long-term benefits that accrue from improving the condition of women.

There should also be incentives such as gender scholarships that encourage attendance of women in higher institutions of learning. Subsidies cut from higher income brackets should be redirected to women, especially those who have never attended school. However, it needs to be stated that "the social returns to female education—notably better health for future generations and slower population growth—far exceed the private benefits to the parents who pay, creating a strong case for special measures, including subsidies."[34]

An issue of crucial importance is transformation of rural systems, which can only come about through increased efficiency in agriculture. Permitting women to own property will lead to increased mastery of agricultural concepts, particularly how to use certain inputs and how to expand small lots into cash crops.[35] To accomplish this, more women need to be trained and hired as teachers. Modification of curricula to relate more directly to local production activities, removal of gender bias in books, and helping young women to enter the labor force[36] are also extremely important.

WOMEN AND THE MARKET

As mentioned earlier, traditional economic analysis tended to make a large portion of women's work invisible, together with the gendered views of the proper role of men and women in society, because economic activity was largely associated with the market.

> Income-earning activities were conceptualized as work; so was agricultural "family labor" that produced market-oriented goods. . . . A wide range of unpaid activities, however, [that] produced goods and services for . . . family consumption were not, economically speaking, considered work. This included domestic production as well as voluntary work in institutions and communities. Given that a high proportion of women concentrate in these activities, the result was the economic invisibility and statistical underestimation of women's work.[37]

In modern economics, one way to increase the status of women is to include women in the marketplace, that is, to create female entrepreneurs. Generally speaking, female entrepreneurs are the engineers of change and can be viewed as having at least four characteristics.

1. Women are coordinators of other productive resources.
2. Women are the decision makers in times of uncertainty.
3. Women are innovators.
4. Women often fill gaps within an economy.

To create female entrepreneurs in the LDCs requires major changes in social-ization processes and child-rearing practices. As socialization changes, women then need to be trained and encouraged to be entrepreneurs. For example, female productivity and income can be increased by improving access to credit, providing training for and administrative support to women in accounting and economic planning, and minimizing bureaucratic requirements.[38] In Bangladesh a policy of reserving 10 to 15 percent of government jobs for women resulted in an increased women's share of all government jobs from less than 3 percent in the early 1970s to 8 percent in 1990.[39]

As shown in Table 7.3, in spite of increasing public attention to the impor-tance of women in the economies of the developing countries, progress toward increasing their participation in the job market has been less than satisfactory.[40]

Table 7.3
Women's Share in the Adult Labor Force (%)

	1970	1990
Developed countries	33	42
Eastern Europe	44	47
North Africa	9	21
Sub-Saharan Africa	39	38
Latin America	20	34
Caribbean	32	43
Eastern Asia	40	41
Southeast Asia	35	40
Southern Asia	20	35
Central Asia	45	44
Western Asia	19	25
Oceania	31	36

Source: *The World's Women, 1995: Trends and Statistics* (New York: United Nations), Chart 5.4A.

This analysis demonstrates that women's position in the LDCs, as reflected in their legal rights, education, health, employment, and decision-making power, has been less than desirable. According to the radical perspective, female oppression in the contemporary world is sustained by the power of the capitalist system and by the existence of a patriarchal ideology. But it can also be said that gender inequality is due to the socialization process. That is, gender-appropriate ways of thinking and acting are taught to children by adults. Given these contrasting views, it can be said that more accurate gender-sensitive approaches will be useful not only to generate quantitative measurements of women's work but also allow accurate analysis of

> (a) the inequality in the distribution of leisure and domestic work; (b) productivity changes in unpaid production; (c) shifts in domestic work and family welfare as a result of changes in family income and employment status of household members; and (d) the extent to which fictitious measurements of GDP growth can be avoided, as in the case of shifts of production from the households to the market sphere.[41]

In recognition of the importance of women's contribution to sustainable development, and the need to improve the status and role of women, many Asian countries have begun to formulate policies and implement programs. Some of the recommendations include:

- Adoption and implementation of national policies and programs to ensure equal opportunities for females in all sectors of social and economic development as well as political participation
- Intensive efforts to improve the status of women's health, and to ensure all girls and women equal access to education and employment as well as credit and other supportive services for promoting self-employment
- Access to increased decision-making authority and the management of resources and protection of the environment
- Less restriction to participation in the labor market [which] leads to modifications in demographic policy or cultural traditions
- Abolishment of discrimination against women, legislative and otherwise[42]

Many governments are willing to make the necessary changes to allow women in their countries to be not only mothers and wives, but valuable members of the larger society. But it is necessary that women themselves take power into their own hands to shape the direction of their lives.[43]

SUMMARY

Domestic labor as the exclusive domain of women is almost universally recognized. Particularly in the LDCs women make a vast and unacknowledged contribution to the economic welfare of their communities, mainly in unpaid work.

There are two broad theoretical approaches to the issue of gender inequality. The first approach focuses on the perpetuation and continued acceptance of male control over women in the economic, political, ideological, and physical resource arenas. The second perspective focuses on how women make voluntary choices that inadvertently work to their own disadvantage.

But when recognizing the different roles of males and females in society, it is necessary to disaggregate environmental issues on the basis of gender. First, women have a vested interest in maintenance of the environment, as that is their traditional domain. Second, women act as rehabilitators of the natural environment to ensure sustainable development. Finally, women need to be seen as innovators in the use of new and appropriate technology.

Thus, if policymakers want to make faster progress in sustainable development, they must enable women to exert control over the environment that affects them. To improve the status of women in society, among other things, requires a substantial social investment in education, the creation of female entrepreneurs, and most especially granting them equal access to land, credit, rewarding employment, and personal and political rights.

REVIEW QUESTIONS

1. What is gender inequality? Assess the various theories that seek to explain the existence of gender inequality in developing countries.

2. Give empirical evidence to show the relationship between women and the environment in LDCs.

3. Assess the five policies suggested by Asian governments to improve the condition of the women in their countries.

CASE STUDY: WOMEN, THE GRAMEEN BANK OF BANGLADESH, AND THE INTERNATIONAL DEVELOPMENT EXCHANGE

Many programs have been initiated to help women in their development efforts. The Grameen Bank in Bangladesh has initiated one of the most successful such experiments. It was created in 1976 by economist Dr. Muhammad Yunus in an effort to improve the dismal repayment rate (about 10 percent) to the Industrial Bank of Bangladesh.[44]

The program was conceived when Professor Yunus noted that a number of poor women living near his university were trying to earn a living constructing bamboo stools, but they had no money to purchase materials. After relating their plight to his graduate students, he and his students designed an experimental credit program to assist the women.

He provided them with a small amount of credit (about $69 each), without normal bank collateral, from his own pocket. But he found that the repayment rate on the credit was above 99 percent, since the credit was deemed nonessential (i.e., was not used for purposes predetermined by government officials or other countries' NGOs).

This project became a full-fledged bank, known as the Grameen Bank, in 1983. Apropos of the bank's name—"Grameen" comes from the Bangla word for "village"—the Grameen Bank works only in villages, which is one of many ways that it reimagined the idea of a bank.[45]

The unique operating procedures of the Grameen Bank grew out of several earlier attempts to reach the rural poor in particular, and were a sharp departure from traditional banking practices.[46] "To qualify for a loan, the woman must show that her family's assets fall below the bank's threshold. She is not required to furnish collateral, have a credit history, or a guarantor. Instead, she must join a five member group and a forty member center and attend a meeting every week."[47]

Each person was asked to guarantee the repayment of a loan to any of the other four members. The bank's most significant innovation is that "[t]he chair of each group has a weekly review meeting with a staff member of the bank. . . . This combination of collective collateral, close supervision and peer group pressure has resulted in very high repayment rates."[48]

Grameen experienced a very high loan recovery. As of February 1987 about 97 percent of loans had been recovered within one year after disbursement, and almost 99 percent within two years. Its good performance is reportedly attributable to a combination of factors: close supervision of field operations, dedicated service by bank staff, borrowing for purposes that generate regular income, solidarity within groups, and repayment in weekly installments. Another factor that encourages repayment is the borrower's knowledge that the availability of future loans depends on the repayment of borrowed funds. Bank staff meet weekly with groups to disburse loans, collect savings deposits and loan payments, and provide training in financial responsibility. This means high operating costs. The ratio of expenses to loans rose from nine percent in 1984 to 18 percent in 1986; these high costs were partially offset by low-cost funds from international agencies.[49]

When the bank was originally developed, the Bangladesh government contributed 60 percent of the initial paid-up capital, and the rest came from the savings of the borrowers themselves. Although international support has been considerable, dependence on foreign funding declined from 83 percent to 60 percent in a recent ten-year period.[50] The Grameen bank of Bangladesh has been successfully defying the conventional laws of lending. According to a recent report, the bank is 75 percent owned by borrowers, of whom 91 percent are women.[51] Not only are the women borrowers improving their economic status, they are having fewer children than nonborrowers. And these families took it upon themselves to plant 6 million trees over several years' time as they got title to land.[52]

The bank had extended its services to more than 35,000 villages through its nearly 60,000 centers. Around 1 million households have received credit. What is more, the loans have generated a great deal of employment, especially for rural women.[53] For instance,

> Up to 1994, the bank has revolved its loan capital more than five times. It has helped millions of villagers to move from one or two meals a day to three, and from one or two sets of clothing to three or four. Grameen members

have borrowed money to pay for their children's education, to buy medicine, to build houses, and to accumulate assets for old age. Today there are fifty six countries around the world who have introduced Grameen methodology.[54]

An innovative development organization called Trickle-Up is attempting the same thing.

> The philanthropists loaned $100 to a woman named Grace Mbakwa to launch a clothing business. Before the aid, Mbakwa had been living hand-to-mouth with her husband and eight children. Now business is thriving, and bringing new resources to Tugi (her village). An added plus to this program is that each bit of profit lessens the need for overgrazing (the main environmental problem in the village).[55]

Some of the long-term objectives of the Grameen Bank include:

- making their members creative, disciplined, united, and courageous
- giving families good living standards
- repairing and building new houses
- cultivating vegetables year-round and selling the surplus
- picking out as many seedlings as possible during the season for planting
- having small families and taking care of their health
- educating their children and making them earn enough money to finance their training
- seeing to it that their children and homes are clean
- building latrines and using them
- drinking water from a well
- standing against the practice of accepting or giving dowry
- causing harm to no one
- increasing their income and making important investments in common
- helping each other and giving a helping hand to someone in difficulty
- restoring order
- taking part in all social events

Prosperity among Grameen members has brought economic growth and development. The upkeep and construction of new houses has given villagers a sense of security and it has also given women the opportunity to own land. Land is the most important asset in Bangladesh, and women have never had any rights to own land under Muslim law.[56]

The International Development Exchange (IDEX) is another organization that helps to improve the lives of many people, particularly women. IDEX "builds partnerships to overcome economic and social injustice, working towards people's greater control over the resources, political structure, and economic processes that affect their lives."[57] IDEX works with grassroots development projects in Bangladesh, Ghana, Guatemala, India, Mexico, Mozambique, Nicaragua, the

Philippines, and Zimbabwe, and educates North Americans about the challenges and successes of marginalized people around the world. Their projects are often very small and are based on helping many local women to create small business enterprises, women's groups, agriculture development, and social services.

An example of one of their projects is in Damankunyili, Ghana, where IDEX helped forty women further develop their communal farming project and build a mill. After learning accounting skills the group has become quite successful. According to IDEX, the participants say that the project taught them to develop a school for their community.[58]

Another very successful IDEX project is in rural Canton Xantun, Guatemala, where IDEX along with Aj Quen helped indigenous women weavers form co-operatives. These women had formed the Buen Hogar or the Good Home Club to organize themselves to help their community. One of their decisions included creating a weaving cooperative so that they could increase their incomes and still be available for their husbands and children. They joined Aj Quen, a group of artisans who helped others find fair market prices for their Guatemalan crafts. Aj Quen gave additional help by providing educational training. These women worked with IDEX to acquire manual sewing machines and initial materials so that they could sell high priced finished goods, and eventually build a community room so that all the women could work together. An example of how this project changed the women's lives can be found in the story of Maria.

> Maria got her husband's reluctant permission to leave home for one hour to attend her first women's group meeting in Canton Xantun. When the meeting ran long she was locked out of her home by her husband—for an entire week. She remained an active member of the group and today has gained more voice within her household, is seen as a leader of her community, and serves on the board of her Aj Quen group.[59]

The project is a huge success. All of the women enjoy higher incomes and higher levels of education, and are still able to be with their families. They were able to save money for their children's education and for building a water system.[60] This Canton Xantun project illustrates why all of IDEX's projects work so well: IDEX works directly with the local communities to achieve the communities' own objectives.

The causes of population growth are rooted in complex human decisions. Thus the results of programs are not always those intended. "Government programs that subsidize jobs or housing can spur population growth by giving people false confidence in the future, while a tiny loan that enables a woman in Bangladesh to buy a sewing machine to start a business may give her an incentive to limit the number of children she bears."[61]

These projects illustrate that when people take responsibility for their own development, they do what is in their own best interest—and for women in developing countries that includes reducing the number of children they have. Development must embrace women both economically and educationally, because studies show that women with a higher self-perceived value have fewer children when compared with less self-confident women. Ultimately women's participation in development is necessary so that their perceived value improves, but out of this advantage comes a bonus: sustainable development is fostered.

DISCUSSION QUESTIONS

1. What are the effects of the Grameen bank and the IDEX programs on women and how do they relate to sustainable development?
2. What is unique about the IDEX program, and what distinguishes it from other types of foreign aid or assistance? What implications for policymaking can be extrapolated from this case study?

NOTES

This chapter was prepared with the assistance of Jaquilin Ang, Kitipong Muttamara, Tripetch Wongniwatkajorn, Amy Foster, Sergio Parra, and Nancy Commins, all of Dominican College, San Rafael, California.

1. Margaret Gallagher, "Work and power," in United Nations Department of Public Information (ed.), *Women: Looking Beyond 2000* (New York: United Nations, 1995): 41.

2. Nafis Sadik, "Investing in women: The focus of the '90s," in Laurie Ann Mazur (ed.), *Beyond the Numbers* (Washington, D.C.: Island Press, 1994): 210.

3. International Labour Office, *World Labour Report* (Oxford: Oxford University Press, 1987): 251–255.

4. Gerald M. Meier, *Leading Issues in Economic Development* (New York: Oxford University Press, 1995): 288.

5. Ann Thrupp et al., "Women and development," *World Resources 1994–95* (Washington, D.C.: World Resources Institute): 44.

6. N. Cagatay, D. Elson, and C. Grown, "Introduction," *World Development,* 23(11): 1827–36.

7. See, for example, Oliver Sacks, *The Man Who Mistook His Wife for a Hat and Other Clinical Tales* (New York: HarperPerennial, 1990).

8. See, for example, Rosabeth Moss Kantor, *Men and Women of the Corporation* (New York: Basic Books, 1977).

9. Nancy Chodorow, *The Reproduction of Mothering: Psychoanalysis and Sociology of Gender* (Berkeley, California: University of California Press, 1978).

10. Sally Sotheimer, *Crisis and Development in the Third World* (New York: Monthly Review Press, 1991): 136–37.

11. Irene Dankelman and Joan Davidson, quoted in *Women and Environment in the Third World Environment* (January–February 1990): 25.

12. Quoted in Jeanne Vickers, *Women and the World Economic Crisis* (London: Zed Books Ltd., 1991): 19.

13. Quoted in United Nations Development Programme (UNDP), *Human Development Report 1993* (New York: Oxford University Press, 1993): 45.

14. Ann Thrupp et al., "Women and development," 46.

15. Meier, *Leading Issues in Economic Development,* 298.

16. Sadik, "Investing in women: The focus of the '90s," 212.

17. Ibid.

18. Jeanne Vickers, *Women and the World Economic Crisis,* 15.

19. Ibid., 22.

20. Jay R. Hair, "Women's voices must be heard at Summit," *International Wildlife* (May–June 1992): 26.

21. Joanna de Groot, "Conceptions and misconceptions: The historical and cultural context of discussion on women and development," in Haleh Afsar (ed.), *Women, Development, and Survival in the Third World* (New York: Longman, 1991): 123.

22. Barbara Herz, "Bringing women into the economic mainstream," *Finance and Development* (December 1989): 22–25.

23. Perita Huston, "Women and nature: An alliance for survival," *UNESCO Courier* (March 1992): 14.

24. Sadik, "Investing in women: The focus of the '90s," 209.

25. Bella Abzug, "Health and education," *Women: Looking Beyond 2000* (New York: United Nations, 1995): 11.

26. See, for example, G. S. Becker, "Human capital, effort, and the sexual division of labor," *Journal of Labor Economics* 3 (January 1985): 33–58.

27. Sadik, "Investing in women: The focus of the '90s," 220.

28. See, for example, Herz, "Bringing women into the economic mainstream."

29. Michael P. Todaro, *Economic Development,* 5th ed. (New York: Longman, 1994): 387.

30. Wadi D. Haddad et al., *Education and Development: Evidence for New Priorities,* World Bank Discussion Paper No. 95 (Washington, D.C.: World Bank, 1990).

31. Todaro, *Economic Development,* 471.

32. Ibid., 389.

33. Ibid., 390–91.

34. Herz, "Bringing women into the economic mainstream," 24.

35. Todaro, *Economic Development,* 302–5.

36. Herz, "Bringing women into the economic mainstream," 24.

37. Lourdes Beneria, "Toward a greater integration of gender in economics," *World Development* 23(11): 1843.

38. See, for example, Herz, "Bringing women into the economic mainstream," 24.

39. United Nations Development Program, *Human Development Report 1993,* 45.

40. "Women in the workplace in developing countries," *Finance and Development* (June 1992): 44.

41. Beneria, "Toward a greater integration of gender in economics," 1844.

42. "Bali Declaration on Population and Sustainable Development," *Fourth Asian and Pacific Population Conference,* Bali, Indonesia, August 19–27, 1992 (New York: United Nations, 1992): 14–15.

43. Sadik, "Investing in women: The focus of the '90s," 226.

44. Alexander Counts and Rachel David, "Credit for the poor: Garmeen Bank success spread," *Why* (Fall–Winter 1992): 22.

45. David Bornstein, *The Price of a Dream* (New York: Simon & Schuster, 1996): 20.

46. World Bank, *World Development Report 1989* (New York: Oxford University Press, 1989): 117.

47. Bornstein, *The Price of a Dream,* 20.

48. United Nations Development Programme, *Human Development Report 1993,* 95.

49. World Bank, *World Development Report 1989,* 117.

50. United Nations Development Programme, *Human Development Report 1993*, 95.

51. Counts and David, "Credit for the poor: Garmeen Bank success spread," 22.

52. Ibid., 24.

53. United Nations Development Program, *Human Development Report 1993*, 95.

54. Bornstein, *The Price of a Dream*, 20.

55. John Carey, "Will saving people save our planet?" *International Wildlife* (May–June 1992): 14.

56. Nancy Commins, in "Social development in Bangladesh" (unpublished paper, Dominican College, 1996): 8.

57. International Development Exchange (IDEX), *Linking Communities in Development* (San Francisco: IDEX, 1995).

58. International Development Exchange (IDEX), "Year in review: IDEX portfolio of projects," *IDEX Update* (San Francisco: IDEX, 1995): 3.

59. International Development Exchange (IDEX), *Weaving a Pattern for Partnership* (San Francisco, IDEX, 1994).

60. International Development Exchange (IDEX), *Lesson #2: Worksheet for Weaving Cooperative Projects* (San Francisco: IDEX, 1994).

61. Eugene Linden, "Population: The awkward truth," *Time* (June 20, 1996): 20.

Rural Development and the Environment

 gricultural employment accounts for a large percentage of the labor force in less developed countries and constitutes a large share of GDP as well. Rather than a poverty trap to be escaped, rural economic development is a key to improving income and welfare in the LDCs and can be a driving force in sustainable economic development. A rural-based strategy should maximize labor force participation in the rural sector. Many developing countries in the post-World War II era ignored the importance of rural development, concentrating instead on industrialization as the path to rapid economic growth. It is clear now that, lacking adequate policies for rural development, there will be no improvement in the developing countries in income inequality, poverty, population growth, or adequate food supplies. It needs to be stressed that without a strong rural base, economic growth can collapse despite gains in the industrial and urban sectors.

This chapter discusses the theoretical foundation for rural development in the first section. Subsequent sections examine policy implications and the relationship between rural development and the environment. The two case studies explore agricultural development in China and Cuba, with particular emphasis on environmental impact and present-day measures taken to offset environmental degradation.

RURAL DEVELOPMENT: A THEORETICAL FRAMEWORK

The classic economic paradigm assumes that the LDCs are organized as a dual economy. That is, higher wages exist in the modern, urban sector parallel with low earnings in the traditional, rural agricultural sector. Classical economist Arthur Lewis developed a theory based on a two-sector model (rural and urban). According to Lewis, a structural transformation occurs as a country proceeds through economic development stages, with a gradual transference of labor from the rural sector to the modern urban industrial sector. Workers from the rural sector transition to dynamic capitalist sector occupations, because in the stagnant rural areas the margin of worker productivity is very low. Lewis suggested that workers with marginal productivity could shift out of the rural sector into the more productive capitalist sector without sacrificing agricultural output.[1]

Thus Lewis' model assumed that rural laborers would respond to the economic boom in the urban area, making a rational decision to move to the capitalist sector based on the potential for increased future earnings. As pointed out by Michael P. Todaro, workers migrate to cities with the expectation of finding higher-paying jobs. The actual earnings of those living in the city are inconsequential and there is a powerful belief that within a period of time their income will increase. That is, the rational rural laborer migrates to a city if the present discount value of an expected lifetime earnings stream in an urban location exceeds the stream for a rural location.[2] Todaro gives the following example: If the average rural income is 60 units and the average urban income is 120 units, the unemployment rate would have to be 50 percent for migration not to be profitable.[3]

Gustav Ranis and John C. H. Fei extended Lewis's model and argued that the rural sector is characterized by the existence of stagnant subsistence agriculture in which institutional forces determine the wage rate. In the commercial industrial sector, on the other hand, market forces determine the wage rates.[4]

As played out over the years, economic policies based on the above theory have been a prescription for increased displacement of rural farmers into urban slums, where they struggle to survive on the margins of an industrial sector incapable of absorbing the masses of unemployed and underemployed. This new group of migrants in the cities places an enormous strain on infrastructure, housing, and social welfare systems, and has led to the development of an informal or underground economy. Unemployment and underemployment are not necessarily confined to the rural areas; comparable problems exist in the urban sectors of developing countries. To be successful, economic development must gradually increase the output of the urban sector; this can only be accomplished by reinvestment of profits. While this is standard practice in the capitalist industrialized nations, it is not the case in the LDCs. Foreign investors typically repatriate profits through legal channels or practice capital flight to home countries, where investments are generally safer. The LDCs are economically dependent on foreign investment and are vulnerable to the above practices, which seriously constrain investment-based growth.

The urban sector cannot efficiently absorb the flows of migrant workers from the rural sector. Instead, the industrial sector may consume a larger share of its output in feeding the labor force, leaving a smaller surplus for capital accumulation for further employment.[5] In the 1960s and 1970s Third World nations witnessed a massive migration of rural populations into urban areas despite rising levels of urban unemployment and underemployment; this reduced the validity of the Lewis two-sector development model.[6]

The dual economy pattern within urban areas during the 1960s and 1970s was matched by a dual economy between the rural and urban segments of society. Government policy focused on urban and industrial development as the driving force for economic growth, to the neglect of agriculture. Policies supported below-market prices for food crops for urban dwellers. Social services in rural areas were rarely expanded, and health services and educational opportunities were not developed for rural dwellers. These factors perpetuated the cycle of poverty in the countryside, making it impossible to eliminate economic stagnation in rural regions. Given these realities, what policy implications can be drawn to enhance rural development in the developing countries?

RURAL DEVELOPMENT POLICY

Failure to address rural development in the LDCs led Todaro to outline policies aimed at curbing the rate of migration from the rural areas to the cities. The first element calls for a balance to be struck between rural and urban economic opportunities with an initial emphasis on rural development to correct past distortions. Higher rural incomes will reduce urban migration. The second element states that policies to reduce urban unemployment through increased job creation actually induce migration, leading to even higher percentages of unemployment.

Todaro's third point is that indiscriminate expansion of educational opportunities can actually increase unemployment in the urban sector. One would think that increasing the level of education of the population is desirable; however, it is only good if it parallels a growing urban sector. When profits are not reinvested to increase growth, more education increases the amount of idle human resources. Workers labor under the misconception that more education will lead to expanding job opportunities, when in reality this policy can create more competition for the same jobs. Understandably, workers may feel a strong sense of alienation from a government that stresses the importance of education but fails to provide subsequent employment. Education tracks should be directed toward enhancing rural development rather than those tracks which foster continued migration to overcrowded cities.

Todaro notes that wage subsidies and factor price distortions do nothing to constrain migration. Subsidized wages do not reflect real wages. Increased supplies of cheaper food will attract poor rural residents to urban areas. In addition, wage subsidies do not increase the number of available jobs, and factor price distortions alter prices for the purpose of increasing labor-intensive modes of production. Once again this can further induce migration.

Todaro's final point is that rather than instituting a means to increase employment in the urban sector, developing countries would be better served by finding ways to keep people in the rural sector.[7] Substantial improvement in the welfare of the rural population depends on structural changes. Reduction in the absolute size of the rural population, large increases in commercial demand for farm products, and large increases in the capital-labor ratio in agriculture[8] are some of the indicated structural changes. Moreover, rural works programs can improve the welfare of the poorest segments of the farm population. Such programs provide supplemental employment and income to the rural population and at the same time build important infrastructure for agriculture and other sectors.

There is also the need for a broad-based focus on employment within the agricultural sector. More efficient utilization of the relatively abundant resource of human labor facilitates the expansion of output; at the same time, it generates the income that enables the poor to raise their levels of consumption.[9] Likewise, programs designed to strengthen institutional infrastructure and to build managerial skills are also needed for rural development. The neglect of these problems is in part a consequence of the tendency for economists to focus on what to do while neglecting the details of how to do it.[10]

Past failures of the development process in LDCs, which ignored the rural sector, have led to more comprehensive theories of rural development. The goals of rural development in these models are more balance between rural and urban areas, creation of a rural industrial base, more equal distribution of wealth, and improved levels of education and health care in rural areas.

Other structural changes include reform in landholding patterns, in farm size, in methods of debt collection and extension of credit, and in production processes. Success of these structural reforms depends on cultural sensitivity and acceptance by the peasants, and on a wider distribution of agricultural benefits resulting from increased agricultural production. Not only must land be redistributed in many cases, but new systems of incentives, economic opportunities, and access to inputs must be put in place.[11]

Agricultural productivity must increase to benefit individual small farmers and to provide food surpluses for cities. Price reforms allowing for reinvestment of profits by farmers in agricultural production will maintain growth in this sector that will be responsive to the increasing needs of a country as it develops. If little return is generated for rural producers, over the long run the investment necessary to continue expanding agricultural production (and productivity) will not occur, subverting the goal of sustainable development. If investment in agriculture does not bring returns comparable to investment in industry, over time agricultural profits will be reinvested in the industrial sector, and not for continued agricultural development.[12]

Development of a rural industrial base can aid the LDCs in producing labor-intensive trade exports. This is vital in the early stages of industrial development in garnering foreign exchange reserves to fund further capital development. Rural development can go beyond cottage industries and handicrafts; when properly utilized these modes of production can diminish the urban pull and rural push. The rural industrial sector as described here is often more capable of utilizing the LDCs' comparative advantage over larger-scale enterprises in the cities, and thus is a valuable component of early-stage industrialization for a developing nation.

Successful rural development must also include the creation of increased opportunities for nonagricultural employment in rural areas. Often, this involves the creation of small- to medium-size labor-intensive industries, serving to broaden the economic base of those regions where a large part of the population resides. Surplus agricultural laborers remain in local areas, avoiding mass migrations to urban regions and associated strains on social structures.

Finally, sustainable development depends upon population control and improvements in gender equality and opportunities for women. Since poverty and inequality are rooted in the rural sectors of many developing countries, they must be attacked structurally to facilitate a strong relationship between rural development and the environment.

RURAL DEVELOPMENT AND THE ENVIRONMENT

Where once environment-friendly policies were considered a luxury the developing world could not afford, they are now factors that must be addressed to achieve sustainable development. Environmental degradation in the rural areas of developing nations is of dire importance because it has a direct effect on the food and fuel supplies of the rural poor. Starvation, higher infant mortality rates, and death resulting from disease will increase when food is in short supply.

The constraints on sustainable development in rural areas are soil erosion, nutrient depletion, and harmful salinization. There are many examples where soil erosion has severely impacted the ability of farmers to produce food. "In Guatemala, 40% of soil productive capacity has been lost due to erosion. In Haiti, top-quality soil is non-existent, and in Africa, 16% of the cropland . . . will be lost by the year 2000 if no conservation measures are taken."[13]

This creates a vicious cycle because as soil erosion becomes more extensive, there is increasing pressure to exploit remaining resources. Degradation can only increase in the absence of measures to prevent these destructive practices. Soil erosion in the developed countries is combated by the use of fertilizers. However, in the developing countries fertilizers are too expensive for farmers to afford.[14]

A major hindrance to improved environmental outcomes is the lack of consensus around a concrete definition of sustainability. The building of dams to harness hydroelectric power highlights various conflicting perspectives. Environmentalists tend to believe this technology destroys the productive potential of ecosystems. Furthermore, perceived benefits such as irrigation and additional hydroelectric power do not outweigh the costs: inundation of productive land, displacement of people, increased prevalence of disease, reduced downstream productivity resulting from salinization, delta erosion, and drying of downstream lakes and channels. The lifetime operations of dams often do not meet expectations because inadequate watershed management causes high rates of sedimentation. Improper irrigation can lead to salinization and reduced productivity, destroying the potential of the land that the dams brought under cultivation.[15]

Proponents of dam projects point out important advantages. Many more rural workers can be gainfully employed when agricultural economies experience the boost that often accompanies access to modern methods of irrigation. There is also the potential for both expansion and intensification. Land previously thought to be unusable can be brought under cultivation. Proponents of dam technology say its opponents are too militant in their conservation efforts.[16]

Deforestation practices are used to bring additional land under cultivation and are generally carried out by agricultural corporations. Forests are cleared to grow quick cash crops such as bananas, cocoa, cotton, palm oil, sugar, or tobacco, or to raise beef. Often corporate interests promote slash-and-burn techniques among local farmers. Corporate deforestation is far more detrimental than slash-and-burn techniques because it completely uproots trees and ruins the natural contouring of the land.[17] Both methods destroy the natural capacity of the forest to provide and protect the gene pool, absorb rainwater, retain soil, protect fisheries, stabilize the climate, and to offer direct recreation for people.[18] Neither of these agricultural practices is environmentally sound; generally land that is deforested loses its agricultural productivity within three years.[19]

Pesticides continue to wreak havoc with the environment in developing countries. Misguided policies of development agencies have promoted the improper use of pesticides. Despite the obvious deleterious consequences, the use of pesticides is rapidly increasing in developing countries, which account for 10 to 25 percent of all pesticides used in the world. From 1967 to 1974 pesticide use in Africa increased by a factor of ten. Between 1972 and 1978 it increased fivefold in the Philippines. One of Central America's most pressing problems is acute pesticide poisoning.[20]

An important factor in the continued use of pesticides is the resulting high-yield crops which alleviate food shortages. This is very important considering that thirty-seven of the world's countries are unable to feed their people.[21]

Sustainable development methods in the LDCs are very difficult to implement, with many solutions creating unexpected problems. One effective example is the stove project in Kenya. A new stove design results in an annual fuel savings of 1.5 million tons of wood. This translates into a savings of U.S.$2 million per year. It benefits both the agricultural and industrial sectors of the society.[22]

It is also possible to establish water and soil preservation techniques, intercropping, agroforestry, and organic fertilization at low cost, particularly in the LDCs. Building windbreaks can reduce soil erosion and increase soil moisture retention. This stopped the decline of crop yields in the Majjia Valley in Niger. Land terracing helped deter soil erosion in Kenya, where 33 percent of the farms were prone to erosion. The building of stone walls along land contours slows water runoff and increases crop yields by an average of 50 percent. This was the case in the Yatuega plateau of Burkina Faso. Land contouring and organic fertilizers increased crop yields by up to 400 percent in the Guinope area of Honduras.[23]

The measures described above are relatively simple and are particularly effective in developing countries because they are labor intensive rather than capital intensive. Adoption of such measures does not automatically solve the problems of environmental degradation in rural areas, but instituting these practices can help to forestall continued damage and can have the added benefit of helping a nation to feed its hungry people.

SUMMARY

In the LDCs, agricultural employment accounts for a substantial percentage of the labor force and constitutes a large share of the GDP. Thus to foster rural economic development a rural-based strategy should maximize labor force participation rather than concentrating on industrialization as a path to rapid economic development.

Since poverty and inequality are to a large extent rooted in the rural sectors of many developing countries, they need to be attacked structurally to facilitate sustainable development.

Sustainable development methods in the LDCs are very difficult to implement, with many solutions creating unexpected problems. For example, the building of dams to harness hydroelectric power highlights various conflicting perspectives. Environmentalists tend to believe this technology destroys the productive potential of ecosystems. The proponents of the dam project, on the other hand, claim that many of the rural workers can be gainfully employed. Instituting such measures does not automatically solve the problems of environmental degradation in the rural areas, but it can help a nation to feed its hungry people.

REVIEW QUESTIONS

1. Outline Arthur Lewis's dual-development strategy. What are the strengths and weaknesses of Lewis's dual model of development for the LDCs?
2. Assess Michael P. Todaro's strategy for curbing worker migration from the rural areas to the cities in the developing countries. Why is it that government policies designed to increase urban employment may actually exacerbate population pressures in urban areas?
3. Research alternative environmentally sound methods of economic development and discuss these in the context of the North-South debate over economic justice.

CASE STUDY: THE CHINESE RURAL DEVELOPMENT STRATEGY

Chinese leaders were especially sensitive to rural development as they began implementing policies of economic reform in the late 1970s and early 1980s. With a population of 1 billion people, 80 percent of whom were living in the countryside, the specter of mass migrations to already-crowded Chinese cities was certainly a situation to be avoided if economic development was to have any chance of success. Government restrictions on area of residence and migration would not have been able to withstand the economic pressure created by neglect of the rural sector. The Chinese Communist Party had, since the founding of the People's Republic of China in 1949, concentrated on rural development as the basis for economic development in China. Conditions were ripe for implementation of a rural-based model of economic development as China began its economic reform program in 1978. Chinese leaders initiated economic development in the countryside, and it was not until large gains in rural income and production had been achieved that the economic development plan expanded to include reform of the urban sector in 1984. By establishing rural development first, the Chinese government avoided mass migrations to urban areas.

Experiments were carried out in Sichuan and Anhui provinces in 1977 and 1978 to test a new agricultural system.[24] Successes in those areas led to the spread of the "contract responsibility system" nationwide in 1978. Production teams of the old commune system were broken up, and land was divided into family plots. Farmers worked the land as their own and paid "rent" in the form of grain quotas to the central government and the village government. Any surplus crops could be consumed or sold to the government at a higher price (or later sold in free markets). Thus there was motivation to produce more and to farm more efficiently. Even the care and cultivation of orchards and fishponds were contracted out to village families.

The new system led to great increases in agricultural production, ranging from 6.6 to 10.5 percent in the period from 1980 to 1988 (as compared with growth rates of 2.2 percent in the period from 1954 to 1980).[25] Competition among individual farmers selling in free markets led to better quality produce and more variety of crops grown.

Under this new system, farmers had other incentives to produce more efficiently and productively. Mechanization, the use of chemical fertilizers, and the use of pesticides all increased, with benefits in crop yields but to the ultimate detriment of the environment. With the shift from collective to individual production, projects completed in the past by production teams under the commune system now were often neglected. Irrigation systems were not maintained and production of organic fertilizer from human wastes was curtailed, and even stopped completely in some areas. State investment in agriculture also was reduced, from 10.6 percent of total state investment in 1978 to only 3.3 percent of total state investments in 1986. What were some of the side effects of pesticides and chemical fertilizer use?

Environmental Impact of Intensive Development Policies

Pesticides and chemical fertilizers effectively raise agricultural output, improve the existing land by raising yields per hectare, and indirectly increase output per worker. The increasing use of fertilizers, pesticides, and herbicides are equally effective on both large and small farms because they do not necessarily require large capital inputs or mechanized equipment. Because the Chinese government was only concerned with higher agricultural development, there was no consideration of long-term environmental impact and there were no measures to limit pesticide and fertilizer contamination of the soil and water. Overuse of chemical pesticides and fertilizers is causing environmental damage at an alarming rate.

The widespread use of pesticides and chemical fertilizers to increase production in China can be traced back to the period of the Great Leap Forward, when the slogan of "all store food to prepare for war" encouraged greater agricultural production in preparation for a possible conflict with the Soviet Union. Moreover, the three-year plague of locusts that damaged rural areas and destroyed crops caused serious food shortages and starvation, prompting the government to encourage these chemical means of increasing crop yields among the peasant farmers.

In the years that followed, farmers habitually used pesticides and chemical fertilizers in combination with traditional organic fertilizers (stressed as part of the self-sufficiency movement during the commune period); their use has never been prohibited by the government. Intensive farming practices (no fallow periods) deplete nutrients in the soil year after year. Thus, farmers cannot end the cycle of fertilizer use to improve the nutrient content of the soil. Overuse and a lack of knowledge of beneficial farming methods among rural peasants are main sources of environmental pollution.

Pesticide Pollution

Using pesticides to protect crops from damage from insects is a method to increase production in agriculture. But only 20 percent of pesticides stay on the crops, with the remainder leaching into the soil, the atmosphere, and into rivers, or absorbed by the roots of plants. At present the main pesticides polluting the environment in China include chlorinated organic pesticides and toxic chemical elements such as mercury, arsenic, and aluminum fluoride. Problems similar to those created by PCBs and DDT have been caused by other chlorinated organic compounds, including kepone and mirex. Most of the offending organic compounds are chlorinated hydrocarbons, which are both toxic and persistent in the environment.[26]

The episodes of pollution by chlorinated hydrocarbons serve to emphasize the need for a national toxic substances control act that would prevent potentially catastrophic pollution resulting from chemical wastes. Testing of all new chemical agents for human toxicity and for ecological effects should be mandated by law; only if shown to be safe should such agents be approved for use. Such a law is long overdue, and if wisely administered, can greatly reduce, if not eliminate entirely, the danger that a new chemical will damage human health or the natural environment. However, if such a law is administered too zealously, the world may be denied the use of new chemicals that could be of great benefit to humans. Administrative wisdom is needed to provide the kind of balance that will give protection while at the same time assuring that incentives to produce beneficial new chemicals will not be destroyed. The amount of pesticide use has increased year by year. A study of the Shanghai Agricultural Department estimated in the 1950s the average annual amount applied was 564 metric tons; in the 1960s it was 2,100 metric tons—much more than the amounts in European countries or America.[27] All these toxic chemicals are distributed persistently and widely in the agricultural environment.

Chemical Fertilizer Pollution

Overuse of chemical fertilizers over a long period, or neglecting the specific condition of the soil and weather and applying inappropriate chemical fertilizers blindly, will result in soil pollution or a decline in the quality of farmland. Overuse of chemical fertilizers makes most nutrients, such as nitrogen, phosphate, and potassium, penetrate the soil and flow out of the soil in runoff water. Different classes of organic toxins are metabolized and transformed in different ways by aquatic organisms.

The amount of chemical fertilizers applied in Shanghai suburbs in 1950 was only 0.6 kg per mu field. By 1980 the amount increased to 161 kg per mu field. In 1987 it was 185 kg, an increase of 8.2 percent over 1986, and in 1991 it was 250 kg,[28] the highest levels in the country.

The percentage of nitrogen, phosphate, and potassium applied is often inappropriate, with nitrogen surpassing the total of phosphate and potassium fertilizers. Nitrogen fertilizer goes into farmland and accumulates in the soil so that the amount of nitric acid in crops increases constantly. Once released into the environment, it can be transformed into nitrite, which is harmful to humans and animals.

Sewage Pollution

Prior to economic reforms, farmers relied most heavily on organic materials for their fertilizer needs. This provided a relatively environmentally sound way to increase crop yields while at the same time creating a system for disposal of large amounts of human waste products from nearby urban areas. With the dismantling of collective farming, the system of collection of sewage waste and transformation into organic fertilizer has broken down, forcing individual farmers to rely on chemical fertilizers.

Chemical fertilizer use is part of the technological progress in Chinese rural development, but its use has created chemical runoff problems as well as eliminating an efficient means of sewage disposal. In many areas there is no infrastructure for sewage disposal to replace this traditional system, so human wastes build up in areas bordering villages and towns, as well as urban areas. Use of human and animal waste in Shanghai suburbs is now lower. Shanghai's population of 13 million in 1991 produced 4.745 million metric tons of excrement; the annual excrement from cattle was 8.9 million tons.[29] But because peasants no longer like to use organic fertilizer, excrement from urban and rural areas piled up around villages, polluting the atmosphere, attracting flies and mosquitoes, and fouling local rivers. So far the organic compounds as major pollution sources in these suburbs are up to more than four thousand tons. Thus controlling these sources has become very urgent.

Rural Industry

As farming efficiency improved, agricultural employment dropped below its previous levels. It was estimated that agriculture would employ only 60 percent of the population by 1991 and 30 percent by the year 2000, as opposed to 80 percent when the reforms began.[30] Surplus rural labor by the year 2000 is estimated to be around 250 million workers.[31] The employment of these people in factories in the rural area potentially will create huge pollution problems.

To provide additional employment in rural areas for surplus agricultural laborers, the package of economic reforms includes provisions for establishing small and medium-scale enterprises in rural areas. Local governments and farmers' collectives are encouraged to start such enterprises. These enterprises have increased rapidly, growing at a rate of 100,000 yearly during the 1980s, creating jobs for

120 million people.[32] These factories have contributed greatly to the recent increases in industrial output in China. For the most part consisting of low-technology, low-cost production facilities, these enterprises often lack the awareness and capacity to address environmental pollutants created by their manufacturing processes. The largest source of pollution in the Shanghai rural area is rural industry. Low technology, poor working conditions, and bad management have led to the heavy release of pollutants from factories. Electroplating, chemical production, textile dyes, and the paper industry are major sources of rural pollution. Wastes coming from the electroplating, chemical, dye, and paper industries make up 87 percent of the total pollutants from township industries in the Shanghai rural areas.[33] Consider solvent-borne inks, for example, which are widely used in the printing industry. As these inks dry, large amounts of solvent vapor enter the air or drain into the ground. During their production, use, and disposal, many of these chemicals are released into the environment, taken up by the food chain, and transferred to humans via ingestion.

It is clear from the above analysis that the Chinese economy, fueled by rural development, has grown at a very rapid rate. Though there have been some attempts to regulate pollutants and industrial emissions in China, government enforcement has not been stringent or standardized. Given the current state of processing facilities and the lack of funds by enterprises and the government to put toward environmental control systems, there likely will be little progress in this area in the near future.

Rural agents lack the information to curb pollution, and there is little understanding of the consequences for the environment and public health to motivate a willingness to change. The government has established a responsibility system for control of the environment among local authorities to address local environmental problems, and the provincial government oversees local actions. It remains to be seen whether or not these measures will be effective.

Thus rural development in China is successful but unsustainable if the present course is followed. More action is needed to deal with environmental degradation before the loss of natural capital threatens future economic development. Without improvements in infrastructure, education, health care, and social services, sustainable development over time will not be achieved.

DISCUSSION QUESTIONS

1. Discuss the strengths and weaknesses of the Chinese rural development strategy.
2. What lessons can be drawn from the Chinese case study?

NOTES

This chapter was developed with the assistance of Zhao Xiaomei, Tsai Weihsin, Greg Caressi, Susan Schultz, and Glomelyn E. Rosario, all of Dominican College, San Rafael, California.

1. W. Arthur Lewis, *The Theory of Economic Growth* (Homewood, Illinois: Richard Irwin, 1955).

2. See, for example, Michael P. Todaro, "A model of labor migration and urban unemployment in the less developed countries," *American Economic Review* 59 (March 1969): 138–48.

3. Michael P. Todaro, *Economic Development,* 5th ed. (New York: Longman, 1994): 267.

4. Gustav Ranis and John C. H. Fei, *Development of the Labor Surplus Economy* (Homewood, Illinois: Richard Irwin, 1964).

5. Jan S. Hogendorn, *Economic Development* (New York: HarperCollins, 1992): 356–60.

6. Todaro, *Economic Development,* 265.

7. Ibid., 270–72.

8. Gerald M. Meier, *Leading Issues in Economic Development* (New York: Oxford University Press, 1984): 458.

9. Ibid., 466.

10. Ibid., 464.

11. Todaro, *Economic Development,* 314–15.

12. See, for example, William E. James et al., *Asian Development* (Madison, Wisconsin: University of Wisconsin Press, 1989).

13. Walter V. C. Reid, "Sustainable development: Lessons from success," *Environment* (May 1989): 8.

14. Ibid.

15. Ibid.

16. Thayer Scudder, "River basin projects in Africa," *Environment* (March 1989): 6.

17. Conrad B. MacKerron, *Business in the Rainforests: Corporation, Deforestation and Sustainability* (Washington, D.C.: Investor Responsibility Research Center, 1993): 147.

18. Alan Thein Durning, "Saving the forests: What will it take?" *Worldwatch Paper* (December 1993): 21.

19. Reid, "Sustainable development: Lessons in success," 8.

20. Ibid., 9.

21. Ibid.

22. Ibid.

23. Ibid., 29.

24. Nina Halparin, Lectures on Chinese economic development at Stanford University, June 1988.

25. Harry Harding, *China's Second Revolution: Reform after Mao* (Washington, D.C.: Brookings Institution, 1987): 107.

26. Chen Ming Fan, "Agricultural environment suffering from heavy pollution," *Chinese Environmental Protection* 3 (Spring 1994).

27. Ibid.

28. Ibid.

29. Ibid. (See Appendix.)

30. Yi Wei Qi, as quoted in Harding, *China's Second Revolution: Reform after Mao,* 102.

31. Vaclav Smil, "China's environmental morass," *Current History* (September 1989): 288.

32. *The Economist* (August 1, 1987): 10.

33. Chen Ming Fan, "Agricultural environment suffering from heavy pollution."

Education and the Environment

In their 1987 report, the World Commission on Environment and Development (the Brundtland Commission) predicted that over the course of the following forty to fifty years the world's population would double, and economic output would increase to four or five times the then-current level. While these levels of growth are possible, they cannot produce sustained improvement in the standard of living without incurring a strong negative environmental impact.

There are many approaches to improving the environment, but in the long run people throughout the world must increase their awareness of the impact they have on the environment and change their behavior to improve the quality of life in a sustainable manner. This can only be accomplished by raising environmental awareness in the population. As one environmental biologist puts it, "Environmental education must . . . be made generally available in schools and other educational institutions, so that citizens and officials can introduce an ecological dimension into decision-making."[1]

The environmentally responsible citizen has:

- environmental awareness and sensitivity
- a basic understanding of the environment and its related problems
- feelings of concern for the environment and motivation to actively participate in environmental improvement and protection
- skills to identify and solve environmental problems
- active involvement at all levels in working toward resolution of environmental problems[2]

This chapter explores general theories of education and linkages between education and the environment. The first section of the chapter examines educational theories and economic growth; the second portion of the chapter explores the relationship between education and the environment; and the case study describes a conservation education program in three developing countries.

THEORETICAL FRAMEWORK

Generally speaking, there are four major theoretical perspectives on the relationship between educational expansion and economic growth. These are the manpower-planning approach, human capital theory, status allocation theory, and class reproduction theory.

During the 1950s the discussion of education centered on the need for a trained workforce, and the development of human resources through the educational system was regarded as an important prerequisite for economic growth and a good investment of scarce resources. The manpower-planning approach "presumes that the economy's need for educated labor can be predicted, making it possible to plan the growth of the educational system to avoid both manpower shortages, which may slow down economic growth, and manpower surpluses, which waste educational resources and may lead to educated unemployment or 'brain drain.'"[3]

The manpower-planning approach may be based on the surveys of employers to obtain hiring projections for specified time periods (say, how many workers they expect to hire in the next five or ten years); or it may use extrapolations of historical data. A more sophisticated method developed by Jan Tinbergen and Herbert Parnes involves deducing the future employment pattern from a projection of GNP. Malcolm Gillis and colleagues have noted the following.

> The Tinbergen-Parnes methodology predicts manpower needs through the following steps. (1) It starts from a target growth rate of GNP during the planning period, which must be at least several years long, since the training of middle- and high-level manpower takes time. (2) It then estimates the structural changes in output by sector of origin needed to achieve that overall growth rate. (3) Employment by sector is estimated, using some set of assumptions about labor productivity growth, or about the elasticity of employment growth relative to output growth, which is its inverse. (4) Next, employment by industry is divided into occupational categories using assumptions about the "required" structure in each industry; these are then summed across industries to get the economy's required occupation mix. (5) Occupational requirements are then translated into educational terms via assumptions about what sorts of education are appropriate for each occupational group.[4]

This line of reasoning was taken to its logical conclusion by the Tanzanian government in the early 1960s, when it chose to limit the attendance rate at its primary schools to about 50 percent in order to give temporary priority to the higher levels of schooling most directly tied to economic manpower needs.[5]

Logical as the broad outlines of the manpower-planning approach seemed, this approach had several flaws. First, the art of manpower planning is based on projections, but data in the less developed countries are extremely limited and unreliable because of structural changes undergone by a number of the less developed countries over the years. Second, even in those countries without structural changes and with available data, projection of past trends was of little value because the stagnation of the past has often yielded to periods of sustained growth.

Third, most manpower studies confined their attention to high-level manpower needed by the modern sectors (that is, mostly urban employment). Fourth, the employment classifications and manpower ratios (e.g., the desirable ratio of engineers to technicians, doctors to nurses) were often based on manpower studies in developed countries. Moreover, the educational qualifications corresponded to each category of job in industrialized economies and did not fit the realities of the LDCs.[6]

Thus disillusionment with the manpower approach followed in the 1960s.

> Many governments found their budgets overstrained by the attempt to expand all levels of schooling simultaneously. Demand seemed unquenchable; expansion of capacity at one level of schooling only increased the demand for places at the next higher level. Paradoxically, the continuing boom demand for schooling was accompanied by an apparent decline in some of its benefits to the individual. The rise of unemployment among the educated caused politicians and officials to wonder whether more and more resources should be devoted to expanding the school system, just so people could be unemployed.[7]

Unlike the manpower-planning approach which emphasizes the benefits of education, human capital theory came out of neoclassical economics, which is based on cost-benefit (the rate of return) analysis. It argued:

> The "cost-benefit" principle is what a rational individual roughly applies when deciding how best to spend his money when his desires exceed his means. He examines his alternative, weighs the cost of each and the corresponding satisfaction or utility he feels it will bring him, and then chooses those particular options within his means that promise the highest ratio of benefits to costs.[8]

Following the same logic, human capital theorists further assumed that people with more years of education are highly paid because they are more productive than people with fewer years of schooling. If earnings are a reflection of worker productivity, a nation with more educated people should achieve greater economic productivity than a nation with fewer educated people.[9] For example, Harbison argues:

> Human beings are the active agents who accumulate capital, exploit natural resources, build social, economic, political organizations and carry forward national development. The principal institutional mechanism for developing human skills and knowledge is the formal educational system. Clearly, a country which is unable to develop the skills and knowledge of its people and utilize them effectively in the national economy will be unable to develop anything else.[10]

Thus, according to the human capital theory, investment in the formal education and training of the labor force can result in economic development. Empirical evidence also clearly indicates that expenditures on education contribute positively to labor productivity (measured as the ratio of total output to

labor input). The economic payoff on investment in education—from both a
private and public standpoint—is high in absolute terms and as compared to
other investments.

As discussed by Wadi D. Haddad and colleagues, empirical evidence linking
education and development can be seen in three forms.

1. *Growth accounting studies*, which estimate the contribution to economic growth of
   investment in the education of the labor force during a specific period of time
2. *Productivity studies*, which estimate the contribution of additional education to the
   physical productivity of workers and farmers
3. *Cost-benefit studies*, which evaluate the economic contribution of formal education
   and training in terms of their private costs (earnings foregone and other expenses incurred by students while in school) and public costs, and the additional income earned
   by those who take the education and training[11]

Growth accounting does not provide criteria for educational investment policy
but can only indicate that economic growth can occur when a nation simultaneously invests in education. However, as shown in Table 9.1, there is enough evidence
to show that workers and farmers with more education and training are more
productive than those with less education.

Table 9.1
The Relationship between Education and Productivity

Study	Database	Results
Patrick & Kehrberg (1973)	Five agricultural regions in Brazil, individual farmers (1969)	Education has a positive and significant effect
Lockheed, Jamison & Lau (1980)	Survey of 18 studies; meta-analysis	A farmer with 4 years of education; average productivity 8.7% higher than with no education
Jamison & Lau (1982)	Survey data on types of farms; farmer education; physical inputs/physical outputs, Malaysia, Korea, Thailand	Positive, significant effect on output; also qualitatively important
Jamison & Moock (1984)	Survey of 683 rural households, 2 districts in Nepal	Education only affected; 75-farmer efficiency in wheat production
Fuller (1970)	Worker survey, two electrical machinery factories, Bangalore, India	In-plant vocational training yields higher productivity than institutional vocational education
Min (1987)	Worker survey, auto factory, Beijing	Vocational education yields 7% higher productivity than academic education. Additional years of education not significant

Source: Compiled from Wadi Haddad et al., *Education and Development 95.* World Bank Discussion Papers: 5.

Based on calculations of the net present value of projects and also on calculations of the rate of return, cost-benefit analysis also establishes that economic payoff to education is high and remains high with economic growth. As shown in Table 9.2, among various levels and types of schooling, primary education appears to offer the highest rate of return in low-income countries.

Table 9.2
Rates of Return to Males' Education, by Level of Development

Level of Development	Social Rates			Private Rates		
	Primary	Secondary	Higher	Primary	Secondary	Higher
Primary product, Low-income	26	17	12	40	20	32
Marginal industrial, Middle-income	28	17	13	46	29	26
Industrializing, Middle-income, High education	28	13	13	24	15	19
Newly industrialized	16	16	12	24	18	20
Industrialized	n/a	10	10	n/a	13	12

Source: Wadi Haddad et al., *Education and Development 95* (World Bank Discussion Papers): 10.

The rate-of-return approach had various limitations in estimating costs (e.g., income forgone by students, especially in countries where unemployment is endemic) and the calculation of future benefits (e.g., discounting superior intelligence, motivation, family background, and connections). But human capital theory began to come under heavy attack during the 1970s. For example, a number of political sociologists objected strongly to the argument that the central goals of schooling are to build character and to assist in the development process. Instead, they argued that, though unintentional, schooling may also impart values and attitudes that may not be in alignment with the developmental aspirations of the nation. For instance, many schools are not producing passive students thoroughly socialized to accept the reproduction of the existing social relations of production, but rather are producing nondevelopment-oriented students.[12] In addition, as discussed by Pari Kasliwal, "Ever since slavery was abolished, investors cannot bind returns from human capital investments—that would amount to bondage. Corporations have tried to do it, as have whole nations, but no foolproof institutional means have been found for investors—outside of the individual and his or her family—to gain from a human capital investment."[13]

The status allocation theory of education (the screening hypothesis) claims that higher education has no direct effect on productivity of workers but rather acts only as a method to enable employers to select people of higher ability in the hiring process. Stated differently, the status allocation theory views schooling as a means of distributing positions according to educational credentials. That is, the long process of grading and selection by the school system serves to identify those individuals with the highest innate intelligence. According to the "diploma disease" argument, individuals with more schooling enjoy a larger share of the economic pie than those with less schooling. This is the reason why many sons and daughters of middle- and upper-class families in the LDCs are disproportionately represented in secondary and higher education; it is also why a large proportion of education budgets are generally allocated to secondary and higher education. Ironically, in many LDCs the cost of higher education is heavily subsidized by the government.[14]

More recently, a whole new social category, the educated unemployed, has developed. The supply-demand equation for graduates is distorted because the market cannot absorb the large number of graduates. Eventually, college graduates will displace those originally qualified for certain positions; this displacement forces these workers to accept employment for which they are overqualified. This in turn causes those displaced to seek additional education or in turn to displace those at lower levels. The "overeducation" problem was evident in Kenya and Ghana, where both countries have experienced a sizable "aspiration-opportunity" gap that has led its educational base to grow beyond its economic base.[15]

Class reproduction theory, or the "radical" school of thought, argues that schools do not necessarily contribute to economic growth. Being elitist, these theorists emphasize classical studies and humanities, which are irrelevant to the economic needs of the society. In addition, proponents of the class reproduction theory argue that schools mainly replicate the existing class structure (serving the interests of the dominant class) and fail to serve the interest of the economic needs of society.[16] Stated differently, the class reproduction theory assumes that the means of production determine conditions and practices in the superstructure, which in turn react to the needs of the economic base. The superstructure refers to the state, school, church, ideology, and communication apparatus. It embraces those conscious social relations and those social ideas and sociopsychological attitudes that are necessary for the existence of a given mode of production, which make possible the continuation of the existing production relations and which, in particular, consolidate the established system of ownership of the means of production.[17] When the economic base changes, incompatible factors within the superstructure change with it.[18] Hence educational institutions generally receive their purpose from the economic base. Schools mirror the economy, and when the economy changes, the instructional content, social relations between staff members and students, and the quality of school graduates change accordingly. Expansion of schools coincides with the growth of the economy.

> [I]n some circumstances, schools might over-expand to accommodate popular demands or factors such as sudden increases in technology, energy resources, recession or depression, and this may negatively affect the absorptive capacity of the economy. In such situations, schools can produce unemployable labor resources. The over-supply creates a contradiction between the economic base and the superstructure.[19]

It should also be pointed out that the radical or Marxist school of thought is of little help in terms of direct policy guidance, but offers merely general condemnation of economic power and class structure.[20]

EDUCATION AND ENVIRONMENTAL ISSUES

The need for comprehensive environmental education has been well known for decades. For instance, the UN conference on the Human Environment in Stockholm issued the recommendation that an international program in environmental education be established which is "interdisciplinary in approach, in-school and out-of-school, encompassing all levels of education and directed toward the general public."[21] Though real progress will require a long term international commitment, initially the UNESCO-UN Environmental Programme (UNEP) begins to address the need for environmental education.

The *World Development Report 1992* suggested a threefold approach to improving environmental knowledge and understanding. The first step is to establish the facts. Many decisions in developing countries are made out of ignorance resulting from a lack of accurate environmental data. While the rewards of environmental data collection are high, it is also expensive and underfunded in developing countries. The solution called for in the report suggests that countries concentrate on monitoring only the most harmful pollutants.

The second step is to value resources and conduct cost-benefit analyses. This essentially means assigning value to resources, including the less tangible benefits of an undamaged environment, and determining the trade-offs between economic growth and the costs of environmental policies.[22]

The third step improves information and education. While no specific suggestions are provided for this mammoth undertaking, the report does assert that behavioral change is the most important result of improved access to information and environmental education. Not only are well-informed citizens more likely to put pressure on governments, but polluters will more likely accept the costs and other inconveniences of environmental policies.

Fortunately, some individuals have clear ideas of what is needed and they are active in bringing about changes. For example, Anthony Cortese of Tufts University describes the need for a steady supply of interdisciplinary professionals and specialists in the areas of environment and population, including demographers, attorneys, scientists, health specialists, engineers, economists, and planners. There is currently a severe shortage of all types of environmental professionals. Continuing education is also essential in this rapidly changing area as new information becomes available.[23]

Environmental education needs to be offered in more institutions and locations. It must become an integral part of the curriculum from kindergarten to professional school. Where programs are in place, there must be a shift in emphasis from an educational approach based on controlling, remediation, and cleaning up pollution to an approach based on preventing pollution and maintaining existing ecosystems. It is estimated that of the 400 engineering schools in the United States, only ten to fifteen offer significant courses in pollution prevention. Only twenty-five of the 700 business schools offer courses on business and the environment.[24]

Thus comprehensive worldwide environmental education is a must if there is to be continued improvement in the global standard of living during population and economic activity expansions. Innovative programs and solutions are being developed and implemented. As individuals, we can take the initiative to educate ourselves and those close to us, changing our own behavior; to support those exerting leadership in the field of environmental education; and to call upon all educational institutions to make the environment a top priority.

Traditionally, environmental education has emphasized the notion that behavior can change as we become more knowledgeable about the environment and its associated issues.[25] This is linked to the assumption that if human beings are more knowledgeable they will become more aware of the environment and its problems and thus be more motivated to act in responsible ways.

Recent studies show that before a person can intentionally act on a particular environmental problem, that individual must be cognizant of the underlying ecological and human issues.[26] In addition, there must be knowledge of the available courses of action and their comparative effectiveness. Understanding gives human beings a sense that they can make a critical difference. These environmental action strategies have been labeled as the cornerstone of training in environmental education.[27]

Skills and knowledge in this area allow learners to investigate environmental issues and evaluate alternative solutions. Once these investigative and evaluative skills are in place, students are better able to take positive environmental action to achieve and/or maintain a dynamic equilibrium between quality of life and quality of the environment. Perhaps a good place to begin in the LDCs would be the creation of programs to introduce primary school-age children to their national park systems. This could be accomplished in the context of awareness of and sensitivity toward the natural world.

SUMMARY

The four major theoretical approaches that explain the relationship between schooling and economic development are manpower-planning, human capital, status allocation, and class reproduction theories. The manpower theory focused on the need for trained workforce. The human capital theory is based on the calculation of the present value of educational investments. The status allocation theory, or the "screening hypothesis," claims that higher education has no direct effect on productivity, but only enables employers to select better-educated individuals in the hiring process. The class reproduction theory mainly argues that schools instead of serving the needs of the society mainly replicate the existing class structure.

To create awareness and improve the quality of life in a sustainable manner, environmental education must be available in schools and other educational institutions. According to the World Development Report of the World Bank, threefold approaches are needed to improve environmental knowledge and understanding. The first approach is to establish the facts. The second step is to value resources and conduct cost-benefit analyses. The third step should concentrate on improving information and making education an integral part of the curriculum so that there could be changes in the behavior of the participants. Perhaps a good place to begin in the LDCs would be the creation of programs to introduce primary-school-age children to their forests or national park systems.

REVIEW QUESTIONS

1. Discuss the theoretical framework of educational expansion and economic growth.

2. Evaluate the assumptions of the manpower-training approach.

3. What are the strengths and weaknesses of the human capital approach?

4. Compare the underlying assumptions of allocative (screening) educational theory and class reproduction theory.

5. What makes a good environmental education? Discuss two ways of effectively implementing environmental education.

CASE STUDY: PUPILS AND PARKS IN MALAYSIA, BORNEO, AND CENTRAL BRAZIL

Environmental education is a recent phenomenon in developing countries. The relatively new park systems in some of the developing countries foster more favorable attitudes toward conservation, augment limited school curricula, promote sustainable natural resources, and increase a park system's flow of benefits to the public by serving as an educational resource.

The case study presented here describes the results of a conservation education program in Malaysia, Borneo, and central Brazil by targeting local primary schools in national parks.[28] The program's emphasis was to encourage visits of primary students to the national parks. This in turn would prompt the students to interact on a personal level with nature. The children could experience nature through all their senses, rather than sitting in a classroom receiving information from a lecture and a chalkboard.

Three goals were developed for the program.

1. Introduce students to the parks and to their value and benefit.

2. Introduce students to basic ecological principles while in the nature setting to complement their school curricula.

3. Increase student interest in the natural world.

These goals go beyond the traditional behavior model and begin to change behavior from the earliest level of education.[29]

To assess whether the programs were successful, measurable aims and objectives were identified. Students were required to accomplish the following four tasks after attending the program.

1. List benefits of the park.

2. Explain several ecological principles.

3. Identify several common plants and animals in the park and their adaptation to the environment.

4. Stimulate enough interest in the environment so as to continue their activities at their schools and homes.[30]

Once in the park the students went on a guided walk in which they identified local plant and animal species. Students were given tasks that allowed them to use all five senses. Students were also asked to broaden their thinking beyond simple observation and to expand what was seen into different areas of science. For example, a study of decaying logs led to an investigation into decomposition, soil formation, and nutrient cycling.[31]

At the end of every program, teachers and students were asked to fill out questionnaires, commenting on each activity and suggesting improvements for the future. Students were further encouraged to explore the natural world and to share information with their families. A ten-item activity list was developed. Upon completion of nine activities, students became "Junior Rangers" and received a certificate and badge.[32]

Has this program been a success? Yes, if one considers that 72 percent of the students completed the Junior Ranger activity book. This shows that the students were continually applying what they learned after the program. Furthermore, the students showed positive cognitive gains in their comprehension of environmental issues. Most important, these students serve as carriers of information to their families and other community members.[33]

As shown in the case study, a developing country's road to economic success will to a large extent depend on its educational system. In part, those developing countries that have done well economically have failed to consider the environmental impact of their development strategies. As indicated before, simply creating awareness about known environmental problems will not change behavior. If schools are to contribute to worthwhile sustainability, behavioral changes through relevant activities must start at the primary level.

Discussion Questions

1. What are the strengths and weaknesses of the case study?

2. Given the goals of the "pupils-and-parks" program, do you think that adequate evaluation techniques were devised to assess the program?

3. What lessons can we learn from the case study?

NOTES

This chapter was written with the assistance of John Stayton, Jihong Liu, James Knight, and Lakkrin Taepaisitpong, all of Dominican College, San Rafael, California.

1. Claude Villeneuve, "The citizen and the environment," *UNESCO Courier* (November 1991): 18.

2. Harold R. Hungerford and Trudi L. Volk, "Changing learner behavior through environmental education," *Journal of Environmental Education*, 21(3) (1991): 9.

3. Malcolm Gillis et al., *Economics of Development*, 2d ed. (New York: W. W. Norton, 1987), 216.

4. Ibid.

5. Philip H. Coombs, *What Is Educational Planning?* (Paris: UNESCO-International Institute for Educational Planning, 1970): 40.

6. Ibid.

7. Gillis et al., *Economics of Development*, 216.

8. Coombs, *What Is Educational Planning?*, 43.

9. See, for example, Lester Thurow, *Generating Inequality: Mechanisms of Distribution in the U.S. Economy* (New York: Basic, 1974).

10. Frederick H. Harbison, *Human Resources as the Wealth of a Nation* (New York: Oxford University Press, 1973): 3.

11. Wadi D. Haddad et al., *Education and Development*. World Bank Discussion Papers 95 (Washington, D.C.: The World Bank, 1991): 3.

12. Asayehgn Desta, *Schooling for Alienation: the Ethiopian Experience* (Paris: UNESCO, International Institute for Educational Planning, 1979): 7.

13. Pari Kasliwal, *Development Economics* (Cincinatti, Ohio: South-Western Educational Publishing, 1995): 152.

14. See, for example, John Meyer, "The effects of education as an institution," *American Journal of Sociology* 83 (1977): 55–77.

15. Philip H. Coombs, *The World Crisis in Education* (London: Oxford University Press, 1985): 196.

16. See, for example, Thurow, *Generating Inequality.*

17. Ibid.

18. Oscar Lange, *Political Economy,* vol. 1 (New York: Macmillan, 1962): 26.

19. See, for example, Asayehgn Desta, "A socioeconomic analysis of schooling in Ethiopia," *Northeast African Studies* 4(2) (1982): 27–46.

20. Kasliwal, *Development Economics,* 153.

21. F. R. Thibodeau and H. H. Field, *Sustaining Tomorrow* (London: University Press of New England, 1984): 89.

22. Ibid., 87.

23. Anthony Cortese, "Education for an environmentally sustainable future," *Environmental Science and Technology* 26(6) (1992): 1109–10.

24. Ibid., 1110–11.

25. Harold R. Hungerford and Trudi L. Volk, "Changing learner behavior through environmental education," *Journal of Environmental Education* 18(2) (1986–1987): 9.

26. J. M. Hines, "Analysis and synthesis of research on responsible environmental behavior: A meta-analysis," *Journal of Environmental Education* 18(2) (1986–1987): 1–8.

27. A. P. Sia, "Selected predictors of responsible environmental behavior," *Journal of Environmental Education* 17(2) (1985–1986): 31–40.

28. "Pupils and parks: Environmental education in national parks of developing countries," *Childhood Education* (annual theme, 1992): 290.

29. Ibid.

30. Ibid.

31. Ibid.

32. Ibid.

33. Ibid.

Health Services and the Environment

Arguably the most important and immediate consequences of environmental degradation in the developing world take the form of damage to human health. Not only is health an end in itself, but a healthy work force is essential to the development process as a whole.

—David W. Pearce and Jeremy J. Warford[1]

he health status of populations in developing countries has improved remarkably during recent decades. In 1975 life expectancy in developing countries averaged fifty-six years; by 1990 it increased to sixty-three years. In 1975 152 out of 1,000 infants died before reaching their fifth birthday; by 1990 the number had fallen to 106 (see Table 10.1). Despite this improvement, many people in Third World countries fight a constant battle against malnutrition, disease, and ill health owing to scarce food supplies, insufficient food production, mass poverty, polluted drinking water, poor sanitation, and limited affordable medical care.[2]

> If death rates among children in poor countries were reduced to levels prevailing in the rich countries, 11 million fewer children would die each year. Almost half of these preventable deaths are a result of diarrheal and respiratory illness exacerbated by malnutrition. In addition, every year 7 million adults die of conditions that could be inexpensively prevented or cured; tuberculosis alone caused two million of these deaths. About 400,000 women die each year from the direct complications of pregnancy and childbirth. Maternal mortality ratios are, on average, thirty times as high in developing countries as in high-income countries.[3]

The persistence of poor health (morbidity and mortality) has not necessarily contributed to a decline in human capital, but it has made economic development in many of the developing countries a very slow process. Poor health reduces worker productivity. Malnourished and ill children find it difficult to concentrate on schoolwork. In fact, it is argued that "in poor countries with a high burden

Table 10.1
Progress in Health by Demographic Region, 1975–1990

Region	Population 1990 (millions)	Deaths 1990 (millions)	Child Mortality 1975	Child Mortality 1990	Life Expectancy at Birth (years) 1975	Life Expectancy at Birth (years) 1990
Sub-Saharan Africa	510	7.9	212	175	48	52
India	850	9.3	195	127	53	58
China	1,134	8.9	85	43	56	69
Other Asia and islands	683	5.5	135	97	56	62
Latin America and the Caribbean	444	3.0	104	60	62	70
Middle Eastern crescent	503	4.4	174	111	52	61
Former Socialist Economy of Europe (ESE)	346	3.8	36	22	70	72
Established market Economy (EME)	798	7.1	21	11	73	76
Developing countries	4,123	39.1	152	106	56	63
World	5,267	50.0	135	96	60	65

Source: The World Bank, *World Development Report, 1993* (New York: Oxford University Press, 1993): 2.

of disease, measures that cut childhood mortality by a modest 15 percent could increase the rate of income growth by nearly 25 percent."[4]

This chapter examines economic development theories of health service and analyzes the relationship between health and economic development. It then explores the ways in which environmental factors affect health service. Finally, a case study is presented reflecting the experience of Thailand with regard to a major public health crisis and its environmental etiology.

THEORETICAL FRAMEWORK

Health services were first studied and measured in relation to economic development from the standpoint of the provision of public health care. Health service provision was quantified by the ratio of doctors and hospital beds to total population. The flaw with this approach to health services is that it caused investment to be directed toward curative rather than preventive services. Over the years this approach has broadened to include preventive measures such as immunization, vaccination, cancer screening, family planning, mental health and harmony, and environmental protection.

Better health is regarded as a basic human need, and most theories dealing with health services and development fall under the umbrella of welfare economics, which is defined as "a normative branch of economics concerned with the way economic activity ought to be arranged so as to maximize economic output and social justice."[5] Its components include income, health, the quality and quantity of work and leisure, environmental quality, personal and social security, and an individual's emotional and spiritual life.[6]

Milton I. Roemer and Ruth Roemer developed a model that is a clear example of welfare economics at work. The Roemers studied the period from 1950 to 1980 and identified trends showing a substantial improvement in overall health conditions, in spite of the extreme differences in health status between the developed and underdeveloped world. The contributing factors are:

- social and economic development with decolonization, increased industrialization, growth of gross domestic product, urbanization, the gains of women, and enhanced education
- cross-national influences due to international trade, the spread of technology, and widespread affirmation of human rights
- national health system development through expanded governmental health programs.[7]

Efforts in the public sector are responsible for the overall improvement in health conditions. The Roemers conclude that public action is the best catalyst of equitable health services, both preventive and curative, and that when the role of the private sector increases in health services, there is a tendency towards lower standards of living, deindustrialization, poor health, and falling educational standards.[8] Based on their research, the Roemers suggest the following steps to bring about equitable health services in developing countries.

- adequate financial support for national health systems, through progressive taxation, social security, and other measures of equitable economic policy
- political commitment prioritizing health, education, and human well-being as a surer path to security and peace than military expansion
- trained health personnel to provide comprehensive health services and to administer those services effectively in communities, provinces, and nations
- consumer involvement in the planning, policymaking, and operation of health systems at all levels
- strong ministries and departments of health to direct, integrate, and assure high quality preventive and curative services for all people
- attention to environmental hazards such as tobacco, addictive drugs, toxic occupations, trauma, and violence, and undertaking social action to minimize and eliminate these risks
- maximum international collaboration for overall socioeconomic development in countries, essential for creating the fundamental conditions for healthful life[9]

The major problem with this argument is the inescapable reality of health service costs. Most developing nations do not have the capital for improved health services.

Interestingly enough, the four-capital model (manufactured capital, ecological capital, human capital, and social and organizational capital) assumes that human welfare will eventually decline, regardless of any strides made toward economic development and health services. That is, as the flow of future production increases, a rise in GDP inevitably results in a decrease in human welfare. In the long run, problems such as environmental pollution and degradation will incur exorbitant human and monetary costs, canceling out strides made in GDP.[10] Rapid industrialization often leads to a propensity for negative spillovers such as polluted drinking water, cardiovascular diseases, and unsafe work sites. Medication and hospitalization costs rise as the human capital stock deteriorates, which will eventually outpace any rise in GDP. Paula Ekins and colleagues state that to create sustainable economic development, "authorities need to place the prevention of disease and the promotion of health at the heart of policy planning."[11] In addition, they suggest a shift in emphasis from simply providing medical services to dynamic collaboration between agencies to directly affect the availability of:

- safe drinking water
- adequate housing
- a healthy diet, emphasizing fresh, locally grown food wherever possible
- an environment where excessive alcohol, tobacco, and drug abuse are discouraged
- jobs with a wide range of skill requirements, leading to lower unemployment
- a safe, clean, and quiet environment
- adequate income and opportunities through the redistributive effects of taxation and international economic reform
- health care education, including community involvement and public information
- primary health care for all[12]

On the other hand, Dean T. Jamison argues that in the developing countries where income and education are constrained, it should be the government's responsibility to improve the health status of its citizens. Governments could both strengthen the household capacity to improve health and increase spending on health. Governments strengthen household capacity to improve health when they:

- pursue economic growth policies that will benefit the poor (including, where necessary, adjustment policies that preserve cost-effective health expenditures)
- expand investment in schooling, particularly for girls
- promote the rights and status of women through political and economic empowerment and legal protection against abuse[13]

Jamison suggests the following actions to improve the effectiveness of essential health services to needy populations.

- Reduction in government expenditures on tertiary facilities, specialist training, and interventions that provide little health gain for the money spent
- Financing and implementation of a package of public health interventions to deal with the substantial spillover effects surrounding infectious disease control, prevention of AIDS, environmental pollution, and behaviors that put others at risk (e.g., drunk driving)

- Financing and ensuring delivery of a package of essential clinical services. The comprehensiveness and composition of such a package can be defined only by each country, taking into account epidemiological conditions, local preferences, and income. In most countries publicly mandated funding of essential clinical services is an acceptable mechanism for redistribution of welfare improvements.

- Improving management of government health services through such measures as decentralization of administrative and budgetary authority and contracting out of services.[14]

Robert Hecht and Philip Musgrove recommend four policies to overcome the existing weaknesses of health systems in the LDCs.

- Government financing of a nationally defined package of essential public health and clinical care, especially for the poor. Widespread and efficient delivery of such a package.

- Reduced allocation of resources aimed at funding health services outside the parameters of the essential package. This would be far more cost-effective.

- Health insurance that not only achieves broad coverage of the population but also has built-in payment mechanisms to control the cost of health services.

- Diversity and competition in the supply of health inputs, particularly drugs, supplies, and equipment, as a means of improving quality and driving down costs. A competitive private sector can provide the full range of health services, including those financed publicly.[15]

Governments in the developing countries could reduce their current burden of disease by 25 percent if they were to make a national package of health services available to everyone.[16]

HEALTH AND THE ENVIRONMENT

WHO acknowledges the urgency required to meet the needs of present and future world populations for food, water, and energy without depleting the global resource base. In addition, WHO stresses that sustainable development can only be achieved if adverse health and environmental consequences of industrialization and urbanization are avoided. WHO calls for the following changes:

- reform of government plans and management of economic development

- research into the needs of poor farmers

- development of partnerships between local authorities and community organizations

- involvement of those dependent on natural resources in decisions regarding resource use and protection[17]

WHO and the World Bank stress reform and community involvement as a means for achieving better health. This is particularly important with regard to the specific environmental conditions outlined below.

ACCESS TO SAFE WATER VERSUS MORTALITY RATES

Generally, diseases associated with water in developing countries can be grouped into four categories.

1. *Waterborne diseases*—associated with water contaminated by human and animal waste which, if ingested, may lead to cholera, typhoid, and diarrhoeal diseases

2. *Water-washed diseases*—associated with water scarcity or inaccessibility, which makes it difficult to maintain personal cleanliness, and leads to diarrhoeal diseases and contagious skin and eye infections, as well as waterborne diseases and infestation with lice or mites that may also be vectors of typhus

3. *Water-based diseases*—associated with parasites that pass part of their life-cycle in water, such as schistosomiasis

4. *Water-related diseases*—associated with insect vectors of disease for which water provides habitat. These may vary according to the type of habitat. For example, mosquitoes that transmit malaria breed in clean water, while those that transmit filariasis breed in flooded pit latrines and polluted water. *Simulium* blackflies that spread river blindness breed in moving water, and *Chrysops* deerflies that transmit eyeworm breed in muddy swamps.[18]

As shown in Table 10.2, improvement in access to safe water can increase a country's HDI. For example, in Hong Kong, Kuwait, Mexico, Thailand, and Sri Lanka, where the 1990 HDI is above 0.60 and safe water is available to between 60 and 100 percent of the population, the mortality rate for children under five years of age is between 7 and 49 per 1,000 live births. On the other hand, in countries with a low HDI, access to safe water is very limited and the mortality rate is very high. Safe water also includes a sanitation component. In India and Bangladesh the percentage of the population with access to safe water is high (75 percent and 78 percent, respectively), but infant mortality is also high because of limited access to sanitation. The water supply is often contaminated in the distribution process because of faulty or nonexistent sewage systems. In India only 13 percent of the population have access to efficient sanitation conditions. WHO documents that of India's 3,119 towns, only 209 have partial sewerage and only eight have full facilities. Along the Ganges River 114 cities (each with a population greater than 50,000) dump untreated sewage in the river each day.[19] Similarly, in Pakistan only half the population has access to safe water conditions, and as little as 22 percent have proper sanitation conditions.[20] What implications can we draw from the public health information (limited as it is) that we have about LDCs?

Several LDCs have initiated water management and primary environmental rehabilitation projects. Although still in the experimental stage, the projects employ strategies that, if properly developed, may contribute to sustainable development.

Table 10.2
**Relationship between Human Development Index, Infant Mortality,
and Access to Safe Water and Sanitation**

Country (and HDI rank among all countries)	HDI (1990)	Access to Safe Water and Sanitation (% of population, 1988–1990)		Mortality (per 1,000 live births)	
		Safe Water	Sanitation	Infant (1991)	Under 5 yrs. (1990)
Hong Kong (24)	0.913	100	—	6	7
Kuwait (52)	0.815	100	98	14	19
Mexico (53)	0.805	78	74	37	49
Thailand (74)	0.715	72	62	28	34
Sri Lanka (86)	0.663	60	50	25	35
Peru (95)	0.592	58	49	80	116
Guatemala (113)	0.489	60	57	51	94
Vietnam (115)	0.472	50	53	39	65
Kenya (127)	0.369	28	46	68	108
Pakistan (132)	0.311	50	22	101	158
India (134)	0.309	75	13	90	142
Bangladesh (147)	0.189	78	12	111	180
Ethiopia (151)	0.172	19	17	125	220
Somalia (166)	0.087	56	12	125	215
Guinea (173)	0.045	33	—	137	237

Source: United Nations Development Programme, *Human Development Report 1993* (New York: Oxford University Press, 1993): 135–39, 156–57—extracted from Tables 1, 2, and 11.

WATER MANAGEMENT STRATEGIES

The key to improving water and sanitation lies in development and reform of water management techniques. Sound water management must recognize the importance of safe and sufficient supplies of water in achieving optimal health as well as the fact that fresh water is a scarce and finite resource. WHO suggests the following strategies to improve water management.

- Increase quality by revising the allocation of water to different users.
- Safeguard quality with clear and enforceable pollution control policies.
- Encourage techniques and technologies promoting economical use of fresh water, recycling of water, and reduction of water pollution.
- Manage water distribution and waste water collection and treatment on a more equal basis.
- Involve all sectors and groups in the community in the decision-making process.[21]

Sound financial practices also play an important part in achieving better water management. They include a price structure that reflects real costs and encourages efficient usage. The aim of sound financial practice should be to ensure that revenues from water sales are sufficient to maintain the water supply and management system.

PRIMARY ENVIRONMENTAL CARE

Primary Environmental Care (PEC) was developed to promote sustainable development at the community level. PEC is a cooperative of local groups or communities that, with varying degrees of outside support, applies its skills and knowledge to the care of its natural resources and environment. There are three integral elements to PEC: satisfaction of basic needs, protection and optimal utilization of the environment, and empowerment of groups and communities. In addition to water supply and sanitation projects, more than eighty additional endeavors that follow PEC guidelines have taken into account the needs of consumers in planning the development of better management systems. PEC members tend to promote alliances between public and private groups. PEC must adhere to the following nine guidelines in order to be successful.

1. Build on local knowledge and resources.
2. Build on and work with local social organizations and management systems.
3. Build on locally available resources and technologies.
4. Practice participatory methods in the planning, implementation, monitoring, and evaluation of projects.
5. Create consensus as to the correct entry points for initiating projects.
6. Foster flexibility in implementing projects.
7. Maintain an open-ended approach for the duration of the project.
8. Encourage multiplication strategies.
9. Encourage the appropriate attitude among project professionals.[22]

Although returns on investment in the health care sector are difficult to quantify, involvement of local consumers and communities, improved management, and public and private partnerships are essential for better health, which leads to sustainable development. Use of existing resources and recognition of the key role of women enable community leaders and other groups to achieve success.

SUMMARY

During recent years, the health status of populations in developing countries has improved substantially. Nonetheless, it could be said that the persistence of poor health in the developing countries has contributed to poor economic development.

To analyze the relationship of health to economic development, health services were first studied in terms of the ratio of doctors and hospital beds to total population. The emphasis was on curative rather than preventive services.

Since an ounce of prevention is worth a pound of cure, sustainable economic development can be realistically achieved only if governments of developing countries place the prevention of disease and the promotion of health at the heart of policy planning. In addition, adverse health and environmental consequences of industrialization must be avoided, and full community involvement should be encouraged.

REVIEW QUESTIONS

1. How can better health contribute to economic development?
2. Why are returns to education higher than returns to health expenditures?
3. What is the difference between morbidity and mortality?
4. Define welfare economics.
5. What are strengths and weaknesses of Milton I. Roemer and Ruth Roemer's model?
6. Apply the four-capital model to forecast economic development in an LDC.
7. Discuss how environmental protection can be included in the development strategies of a Third World country.

CASE STUDY: AIDS IN THAILAND

The East Asian countries hit hardest by the financial crisis that commenced in 1997 and 1998 were for years admired as some of the most successful emerging market economies, owing to their rapid growth and the striking gains in their populations' living standards.[23] For example, between 1975 and 1993, Thailand's GDP grew at an average of 11.42 percent per year—a rate unmatched anywhere in the world—and its savings rate increased from 20 percent to 37 percent.[24] But though Thailand was regarded as one of the world's leading economies among developing countries, it was already apparent to many that a potential major catastrophe was on the horizon. In Thailand's case, the connection between prostitution and its economic and cultural life, and its association with AIDS, were major contributing factors to the ensuing tragedy.

AIDS initially appeared in Thailand in 1984 and has been traced back to a gay man who reportedly traveled to the United States.[25] In just a few years Thailand's AIDS epidemic was at the forefront of the developing world, and dire warnings were made by the United Nations that the Thai Ministry of Public Health was greatly underestimating its extent.[26]

The progression of HIV infection in Thailand can be divided into four well-documented stages. Between 1984 (when the first case of HIV was documented) and 1987, HIV infection was almost exclusively contained within the Thai homosexual population. The second stage of transmission was the rapid spread among intravenous drug users. The HIV rate soared from 1 percent of drug users in 1987 to 43 percent in 1988.[27] A number of factors were identified that resulted in this dramatic increase: needle sharing, better HIV detection, prison drug smuggling, and an unusual release of prisoners back into society in December 1987.[28] In the early 1990s the HIV infection rate for two high-risk groups, drug users and prisoners, plateaued at about 40 percent and 10 percent, respectively.

However, much more alarming is what epidemiologists and other public health officials are observing in the third and fourth stages of transmission. The third stage represents an epidemic spread of HIV transmission among prostitutes. In June 1989 a survey showed that an amazing 44 percent of female prostitutes in the city of Chiang Mai (the second largest city in Thailand) were HIV positive.[29] The less-populated north showed an especially significant rate of HIV infection among prostitutes, with Thai male customers making up the primary source of infection, since the north has a low rate of tourism. The ultimate severity of the economic impact of AIDS within Thailand depends largely on northern Thailand, and much less so on the central and southern sections.

A follow-up to the initial study in Chiang Mai, made two months later, confirmed a 36.5 percent prevalence rate among the female prostitutes. Thirty-five of the fifty-six women who were seronegative were retested, and seven tested positive (a new incidence rate of 20 percent within a two-month period).[30] In studies in the early 1990s, it was concluded that low-income or lower-class prostitutes throughout Thailand had an overall rate of 23 percent seropositivity.[31] This data indicates that, unlike epidemiological trends for intravenous drug users, overall HIV incidence rates are indeed increasing.

Thailand's prostitutes can be classified into three very different categories: low-income, high-income, and commercial sex workers. The low-income prostitutes work in brothels or tea houses. They have either been sold by their families or kidnapped by sex brokers, possess very low education, tend to be in their early teen years, and have a low awareness level of AIDS. The high-income prostitutes are older than their counterparts, possess some knowledge of AIDS education, and have voluntarily chosen this type of work.[32] And high-income commercial sex workers are employed by a massage parlor, coffee house, or bar where there might be HIV testing available.[33]

High-income prostitutes' customers consist of foreigners and wealthy Thais, while low-income prostitutes cater strictly to the Thai population. Thailand has been estimated to house between 800,000 and 2 million prostitutes,[34] the vast majority of whom are low income and come mainly from the north and northeast areas of Thailand.

The fourth and most recent stage of the HIV epidemic involves the heterosexual population. Heterosexual transmission is now the predominant mode through which HIV is spread.[35] The behavior of Thai heterosexual males is a major factor in this transmission. Unlike the case in the West, among Thai heterosexual males the use of prostitutes is an open and group-sanctioned expression of Thai manhood that can continue throughout the male's life. One study indicated that 26 percent of Thai males had sex with multiple sex partners within the most recent six months, and 75 percent of Thai males had at least one prostitution experience.[36] The type of prostitute with whom contact is made greatly affects risk. While studies show a 4 percent HIV rate for massage parlor working girls, those in northern brothels or low-income brothels have HIV rates ranging from 72 percent to 100 percent.[37]

Another factor in the heterosexual transition stage is the changing male-to-female ratio of HIV infection. In 1986 the ratio was 17:1 and narrowed to 5:1 by 1989. By the end of the next decade, it is projected to reverse to 1:2.[38] Not only will women become the largest HIV infected group, children are also becoming infected.[39] Overall, 95 percent of all new HIV cases in Thailand can be linked to heterosexual contact.[40]

While the majority of Thai prostitutes are having sexual relations with Thai men, the "sex tourist" business continues to be of great importance. Tourism became big business in Thailand in the mid-1980s, and by the early 1990s accounted for 7 percent of Thailand's GDP, with 5 million tourists generating over $5 billion to the Thai economy annually.[41] It is estimated that 20 percent of all tourists to Thailand can be labeled as sex tourists.[42]

In the early 1990s Thailand public officials were faced with a dilemma. Do they ignore HIV signs and symptoms of a fast-spreading infectious disease and hope the tourists keep coming, or do they actively develop educational and preventive programs to preserve the supply of prostitutes? Initially, Thai's public stance was to completely ignore the epidemiological evidence because of the fear of losing tourists and their dollars, but that is exactly what happened anyway. All facets of the tourist industry (transportation, accommodations, sightseeing, retail and prostitutes) felt fewer dollars flowing into their economy. So in 1991 Thailand did a complete about-face and aggressively and actively promoted an AIDS awareness and prevention program.[43] The program was so successful in 1991 and 1992 that in 1992 the Thai government claimed that the previous government's HIV campaign had "seriously affected tourism," and the AIDS awareness campaign would be toned down.[44] This statement was met with tremendous opposition, led by a former minister and currently the best-known AIDS expert in Thailand, Mechai Viravaidya.[45] AIDS was kept in the political spotlight by Mechai and others, and its economic impact was used as leverage to garner financial support from the Thai government and NGOs. However, combined with the recent economic crises, the ability of such organizations to continue functioning effectively against such an overwhelming epidemic is increasingly questionable.

With the number of HIV cases approaching a projected 4 million at the turn of the century, the effect of this epidemic on Thailand's economy is becoming overwhelmingly devastating. With only about 90,000 hospital beds in the entire country,[46] Thailand is caught in the horns of a dilemma. On the one hand, this developing country cannot afford to divert dollars away from other health care needs of the rest of the population. On the other hand, the indirect costs associated with AIDS are enormous. It is estimated that Thailand could potentially lose $8.7 billion in income from AIDS-infected individuals who would have been in their most productive years.[47] When one looks at the aggregate cost of all the factors involved (labor shortages, declining tourism, lost income, increasing health care expenditure, and the sheer human toll combined with present day Thai cultural

attitudes, behaviors, and religious beliefs), the picture is bleak.[48] One must conclude that the AIDS epidemic will cause ever-increasing damage to the already
severely threatened economic development of Thailand for the foreseeable future.
The only hope will be a fundamental shift away from the widely accepted Thai
proverb, "If you don't see the coffin, you shed no tears."[49]

DISCUSSION QUESTIONS

1. Discuss the impacts of AIDS on the economic development of Thailand.

2. What are the strengths and weaknesses of the case study?

3. What lessons did you learn from the Thailand experience?

NOTES

This chapter was prepared with the assistance of Laura van Galen, Juliet Meehan, and Brad
Sturr, all of Dominican College, San Rafael, California.

1. David W. Pearce and Jeremy J. Warford, *World without End: Economics, Environment
and Sustainable Development* (New York: Oxford University Press, 1993): 133.

2. Michael P. Todaro, *Economic Development in the Third World,* 4th ed. (New York:
Longman, 1989): 20.

3. The World Bank, *World Development Report 1993* (New York: Oxford University
Press, 1993): 2.

4. Dean T. Jamison, "Investing in health," *Finance and Development* (September 1993): 3.

5. Christopher Pass *et al., The HarperCollins Dictionary of Economics* (New York:
HarperCollins, 1991): 553.

6. Ibid., 46.

7. Milton I. Roemer and Ruth Roemer, "Global health, national development, and the
role of government," *American Journal of Public Health* 80(10) (1980): 1188.

8. Ibid., 1191.

9. Ibid.

10. Ibid.

11. Paula Ekins et al., *The GAIA Atlas of Green Economics* (New York: Doubleday, 1992): 693.

12. Ibid.

13. Dean T. Jamison, "Investing in health," *Finance and Development* (September 1993): 3.

14. Ibid.

15. Robert Hecht and Philip Musgrove, "Rethinking the government's role in health,"
Finance and Development (September 1993): 7.

16. Jose-Luis Babadilla and Helen Saxenian, "Designing an essential national health package,"
Finance and Development (September 1993): 10.

17. World Health Organization, *Our Planet, Our Health: Report of the WHO Commission
on Health and Environment* (Geneva, 1992): xiv.

18. World Health Organization 1992 report *(Our Planet, Our Health)* as cited in United
Nations Environmental Programme (UNEP), *Poverty and the Environment* (Nairobi, Kenya:
United Nations Environmental Programme, 1995): 46–47.

19. Ibid., 113.

20. Ibid.

21. Ibid.

22. Ibid., 132.

23. International Monetary Fund staff, "The Asia Crisis," *Finance and Development* (June 1998): 18–21.

24. John M. Leger, "The Boom: How Asians started the Pacific Century early," *Far Eastern Economic Review* (November 24, 1994): 43–49.

25. S. Dinkerton, "A second South Korea?" *Forbes* (December 21, 1992): 149–58.

26. A. Clements, "Thailand stifles AIDS campaign," *British Medical Journal* 304 (1992): 1264.

27. K. Choopanya, "Risk factors and HIV seropositivity among injecting drug users in Bangkok," *AIDS* 5 (1991): 1513.

28. Ibid.

29. T. Siraprapasiri, "Risk factors for HIV among prostitutes in Chiang Mai, Thailand," *AIDS* 5 (1991): 579–82.

30. Ibid.

31. Division of Epidemiology, Ministry of Public Health, "Thailand—Update," *AIDS* (January 19, 1993).

32. Siraprapasiri, "Risk factors for HIV among prostitutes in Chiang Mai, Thailand."

33. Ibid.

34. *The Economist* (September 21, 1991): 21.

35. M. P. Ryan, "AIDS in Thailand," *Medical Journal of Australia* 154 (1991): 282–84.

36. B. Weniger, "The epidemiology of HIV infection and AIDS in Thailand," *AIDS* 5(Supp. 2) (1991): 571–85.

37. See, for example, Division of Epidemiology, Ministry of Public Health, "Thailand—Update," *AIDS* (January 19, 1993); and C. A. Kammerer, "Hill tribes endangered at Thailand's periphery," *Cultural Survival Quarterly* (Fall 1992): 23–25.

38. Ryan, "AIDS in Thailand."

39. Ibid.

40. S. Nitayapan, "Development of the AIDS vaccine," Chiang Mai University Conference on AIDS, March 26, 1993.

41. A. Clements, "Thailand stifles AIDS campaign," *British Medical Journal* 304 (May 16, 1992): 1264.

42. R. Moreau, "Sex and death in Thailand," *Newsweek* (July 30, 1992): 50–51.

43. "Thailand tries again to tackle AIDS," *British Medical Journal* 305 (December 5, 1992): 1385.

44. Clements, "Thailand stifles AIDS campaign," 1264.

45. Ibid.

46. Ibid.

47. *U.S. News and World Report* (July 27, 1992): 49–59.

48. *Business Week* (February 22, 1993): 52–53.

49. S. Erlanger, "A plague awaits," *New York Times Magazine* (July 14, 1991): 4.

Multinational Enterprises and the Environment

 host of serious environmental problems face the world today, ranging from the threat of global warming owing to the emission of greenhouse gases to the problems posed by acid rain, deforestation, hazardous and nuclear wastes, urban smog, and even ordinary garbage disposal.

Transnational corporations (TNCs) are key players in the international arena and they represent some of the most powerful economic forces in the modern world. Annual sales of the larger TNCs are on the order of $100 billion. Thus they have a significant portion of the resources that will be needed to address environmental problems. But it is clear that TNCs have merely adjusted their own standards of production downward, instead of helping to improve host country conditions. They have made use of more lax environmental laws to produce more cheaply, creating more pollution than they otherwise would. For example, German cars built in Brazil for Brazilian consumers have lower standards than those built in the Federal Republic of Germany for the United States.[1]

Enterprises conducting and controlling productive activities in more than one country are multinational enterprises (MNEs). Under neoclassical economic assumptions MNEs are conduits for the introduction of capital, technology, management, and marketing techniques to host countries. Their presence in host countries is assumed to increase competition, improve efficiency, create jobs, and improve the distribution of income (by lowering the returns to capital while bidding up wages).[2]

Although their presence in the LDCs (only 25 percent of foreign direct investment is predominantly in the higher-income countries of Asia and Latin America) is extremely limited, there is an ongoing effort to attract them through trade and investment liberalization policies. Acquisition of capital, technology, and know-how as a result of strategic alliances with MNEs is an essential element in the development strategy of many countries. For example, multinationals may bring savings from abroad, generate needed foreign exchange, alleviate shortages of managerial and technical skills, and increase government revenues through taxation.

Though multinationals are frequently viewed as an important component of economic development, there is also a fear among governments of LDCs that they may come to dominate economic life and impose excessive environmental costs.[3] Economists outside the mainstream of economic thought write that

> [f]oreign companies might capture the commanding heights of the host economy, soak up indigenous sources of capital as they drive local firms out of business, create a small labor elite for themselves while transferring the bulk of the workers into the ranks of the unemployed, and siphon off oligopoly profits for repatriation to corporate headquarters. This could hardly be favorable for the rate of growth or the structure of the development process.[4]

Similarly, Isaiah Frank argues that multinationals tend to

> reinforce a pattern of development that over the long run would trap countries in their poverty because of inevitable decline in the price of exports of primary commodities as compared with the price of imports of manufactured goods. At the same time, rich countries would gain both from high financial returns to their investors and from a flow of cheap raw materials for their own industries.[5]

Some policymakers in developing countries have seriously questioned the contribution that MNEs make to economic development. The reasons for their skepticism begin with political opposition to control of national resources from abroad. In addition, critics charge that multinational companies use inappropriate technologies and that their centralized management structures prevent the development of local initiative.

MNEs often fund themselves in the local market, crowding out potential domestic borrowers, royalty and interest payments, management fees, and other means of avoiding price controls, foreign exchange regulations, local taxes, and limits on profit remittances.[6]

Similarly, a study by the United Nations Center on Transnational Corporations (UNCTC) indicates that MNEs significantly contribute to environmental problems and account for roughly 80 percent of human-generated greenhouse gases. Also, "[t]hey are the primary producers and intermediate consumers of chlorofluorocarbons, which are the principal cause of stratospheric ozone depletion and account for at least 15 percent of greenhouse-gas emissions."[7]

This chapter maps out the theories explaining why multinational enterprises invest in developing countries and, using a case study, tries to assess their impact on the environment of host countries.

THEORETICAL FRAMEWORK

Many theories exist to explain which factors contribute to the decision of firms to set up production facilities overseas. A central organizing principle is foreign direct investment (FDI). FDI involves partial ownership and an effective voice in the management of an enterprise. From a strategic point of view, firms invest abroad for the following reasons.

- to gain access to domestic and foreign markets
- to gain access to raw materials
- to increase production efficiency
- to take advantage of technology or managerial expertise
- to ensure political safety[8]

However, the underlying theoretical framework for decisions to invest abroad includes location-specific factors, firm-specific factors, eclectic theory, and home country factors.

Location-specific factors prompt MNEs to establish facilities abroad in order to take advantage of host government investment incentives. These include reduced operating costs (the costs of labor, resources, transportation, economies of scale, and benefits from weaker currencies), circumvention of rising protectionist sentiments in host countries (such as defensive and offensive marketing strategies), and the ability to prolong the life expectancy of their products.[9]

The internationalization theory of foreign direct investment views firm-specific assets as a primary incentive. Based on this theory, multinational enterprises invest abroad when they can obtain oligopoly power over production, marketing, and distribution, and when resources can be controlled through backward vertical integration strategies. The market imperfection theory says the control of inelastic firm-specific advantages, such as marketing, technology, and management know-how, may secure monopoly rents on a global scale for MNEs when compared with domestic entrepreneurs.[10]

Industry-specific factors examine the role of knowledge.

> Knowledge provides a monopoly advantage which can best be exploited through discriminatory pricing by the firm itself, rather than, for example, by licensing. Secondly, the production of knowledge requires long-term research and development, and at any stage before projects are completed the value of the knowledge obtained may be difficult to establish, if the firm were contemplating selling.[11]

The market imperfection theory was further elaborated by Richard Cave's theory of sector-specific capital and Raymond Vernon's product cycle model. Vernon argued that multinationals in the innovating countries use exporting in the early stages of the product life cycle, followed by licensing and then FDI, as an entry mode to other countries in order to take advantage of locational factors.[12]

Drawing on relevant theories from organizational behavior, corporate strategy, and economics, the eclectic theory views international production as a function of a firm's locational advantages, ownership-specific advantages, and internationalization advantages.[13]

Locational advantages from FDI are derived when a firm benefits from lower costs in the foreign country. These include cheap labor, a supply of natural resources, and lower transportation costs.[14] Ownership advantages allow the foreign firm to appropriate rents as a result of innovation and differentiated products, giving the firm some monopoly element or proprietary knowledge that others cannot duplicate.[15]

Internationalization advantages arise because markets for human capital, knowledge, marketing, and management expertise have high information and transaction costs. It is therefore administratively better to remove those transactions that the market performs imperfectly and to use internal administrative methods of allocation within the firms, instead of relying on the open market.[16]

The home-country perspective views the country of origin as the source of encouragement for multinational corporations. Home governments may offer tax benefits and other incentives for home-based multinationals investing overseas because home-based GNP is positively affected by profits, royalties, and fees and by preferential access to raw materials.

As shown in Table 11.1, the nominal percentage of global foreign direct investment decreased from 25 percent at the beginning of the 1980s to 17 percent at the end of the decade. A disproportionate share of foreign direct investment is going to the ten listed countries and their regions. Note in particular the large share received by Asian countries, the sharp drop-off in Latin America, and the minuscule share going to Africa and to the LDCs. This is not surprising given the fact that private capital gravitates toward countries and regions with the highest financial returns and the greatest perceived safety.[17]

Table 11.1
Foreign Direct Investment (FDI)
in Developing Regions and Countries, 1980–1989

Host Region and Economy	—Percentage Share of Global FDI—	
	1980–1984	1988–1989
Developing countries	25.2	16.9
Africa	2.4	1.9
Latin America and the Caribbean	12.3	5.8
East, South, and Southeast Asia	9.4	8.8
Least-developed countries	0.4	0.1
Ten largest host countries	18.1	11.1
Argentina	0.9	0.6
Brazil	4.2	1.5
China	1.1	1.9
Colombia	0.8	0.2
Egypt	1.1	0.8
Hong Kong	1.4	1.2
Malaysia	2.3	0.7
Mexico	3.0	1.4
Singapore	2.8	2.0
Thailand	0.6	0.8

Source: Michael P. Todaro, *Economic Development,* 5th ed. (New York: Longman, 1994): 528.

CORPORATE ENVIRONMENTAL MANAGEMENT

Following the Earth Summit in Rio de Janeiro in 1992, many MNEs introduced a proactive management policy of greening the investment environment in a number of developing countries.

> We have already begun the transition to a new era in which environmental issues will increasingly drive our economic life. The transition to economically sound and sustainable development is as imperative for the continued viability of our economy as it is for our environmental security. Every business that impacts the environment must accommodate the fact that the environment will have an important impact on its business.[18]

MNEs are regarded as decisive contributors to the developmental process. Management of their assets and the environmental impact of their processes and products is therefore of crucial importance for sustainable development.[19]

However, multinationals also have negative effects on a developing country's environment. For example, more than 50 percent of global greenhouse gas emissions are created by MNEs. The bulk of biotechnological research worldwide is financed by MNEs, and they are extensively involved in natural resource exploitation activities (e.g., oil drilling, mining, and forestry). In ASEAN (Association of Southeast Asian Nations), pollution levels are increasing dramatically. As a result the consequences of environmental degradation are mounting in the form of increased health costs, higher mortality rates, and loss of biodiversity.[20]

Events such as the horrendous chemical explosion at a Union Carbide chemical plant in Bhopal, India, and the exportation of hazardous and highly toxic waste to West African nations by several European corporations do little to change the perception of MNEs as bad actors on the environmental scene.

Japanese MNEs have gained much notoriety and negative publicity from their vigorous pursuit of tropical woods in Southeast Asia. Lacking abundant resources of its own, Japan is the world's largest importer of tropical timber, 92 percent of which comes from Malaysia.[21] This trading in forest products leads to massive deforestation and to a lack of true profits for the owners and/or concessionaires of the forest.

Forestry is a major industry in Southeast Asia and it represents far more than a simple source of income.

> Forestry is central to sustainable development because of the high numbers of people working in [this] area, the amounts of money generated, and the extensive, direct impacts that [it has] on renewable resources and the environment. . . . Especially in developing countries, the health of forestry and [its] resource base have a major impact on nutrition, energy supply, employment, population growth, and rural migration. . . . [There is] linkage to energy issues; forestry has energy needs, [while on the other hand] forest biomass is a vital domestic energy source in many developing countries.[22]

Forests are rapidly disappearing, covering only 30 percent of the earth's surface, less than half the area before settled agriculture began. Deforestation is accelerating between 17 million and 20 million hectares every year, 80 percent higher than a decade ago.[23] These forests are fast disappearing.

> Much of the serious deforestation in developing countries occurs as farmers abandon degraded, previously productive [agricultural] fields to clear new land. Cutting down trees, however, usually speeds the degradation process, since tropical forest soils are rarely suited to continuous cultivation and intensive grazing. Another important reason for deforestation has until recently been fast-growing cattle production. Since 1950, world meat production has tripled, . . . and in Latin America, 20 million hectares of tropical forest have been converted to pasture since 1970.[24]

What can be done to save the world's forests? Currently most forests are owned by national governments, but a large proportion of these are systematically logged (through either government enterprises or concessions). Quite often, due to inadequate government regulations and enforcement, forests are being torn down for farming or cattle grazing.

Reversing their previous actions, many MNEs are now investing their time and effort to improve the environment. MNEs typically allot 1 to 2 percent of sales revenues to environmental expenditures, and a substantial number contribute more than 25 percent of net income after taxes.[25] In addition, the potential of MNEs to solve environmental problems is extensive. MNEs "possess the technologies and research and development (R&D) capabilities that will likely provide the solutions to many environmental problems of today."[26] Following are some outstanding examples of corporate environmental integrity.

Ben and Jerry's Homemade Ice Cream Inc. of the United States has developed flavors that feature Brazil nuts, cashew nuts, and assai and cupuacu fruits indigenous to the Amazon forests, where they are harvested by indigenous people. An international cosmetics chain, The Body Shop, imports herbs for use in cosmetics. Both of these corporations have taken special care to ensure that local people benefit as much as possible from trade.[27]

The proliferation of environmental groups such the Rainforest Action Network, the Rainforest Alliance, Greenpeace, and JATAN (a Japanese rain forest group) is forcing MNEs to act more responsibly. In June 1992 government officials, politicians, environmentalists, business representatives, and researchers from all over the world gathered in Rio de Janeiro at UNCED. A major policy statement, Agenda 21, was issued, which recommended the following: (1) involvement of groups such as women, farmers or indigenous people in environmental solutions; (2) focusing on solutions to specific environmental problems, such as waste management, biotechnology, and management of toxic substances; (3) establishing criteria for which decisions should be made, who is to participate, and who is to pay.[28]

Although efforts to achieve environmental sustainability are increasing, as shown in Table 11.2, only 22 percent of MNEs are engaged in activities aimed at protecting the global commons, such as R&D programs for renewable energy, policies for protection of the rain forests, or programs for the protection of biodiversity.

Table 11.2
Corporate Policy Priorities: Corporate Activities on
Environment, Health and Safety, and Sustainable Development

Highest-Priority Activities	Percent of Respondents
Energy-related activities	
R&D for energy-efficient production	70.7
Policies for securing energy supplies	67.7
Policies for conserving nonrenewable resources	54.4
Energy conservation	54.0
Health and safety activities	
Worker health and safety	67.5
Accident prevention	60.3
Emergency preparedness	58.0
Hazard assessment procedures	56.9
Traditional environmental activities	
Water quality/pollution	48.1
Air quality/pollution	47.2
Noise pollution	41.1
Soil quality/pollution	31.2
Waste/disposal-related activities	
Recycling	84.5
Waste-handling procedure	56.3
Waste-disposal policies	51.6
Waste-reduction technologies	48.7

Lower-Priority Activities	Percent of Respondents
Genuine sustainable development activities	
Afforestation programs	40.4
R&D for greenhouse gas generation reduction	39.0
Renewable energy sources	22.0
Preservation of endangered species	15.8
Conservation of biodiversity	10.1
Policies for protection of wetlands/rainforests in LDCs	9.2

Source: Adapted from *Environmental Management in Transnational Corporations.* Report on the Benchmark Corporate Environmental Survey (New York: United Nations Publications, 1994): 29.

Because MNEs can make a positive contribution to sustainable development by maintaining economic growth while reducing environmental risk and resource exploitation, they are highly encouraged by UNCTC to follow the ten steps outlined below.

1. Create and publish a transnational, corporate, sustainable development policy statement (in all languages of affiliate enterprises) emphasizing sustainable growth, environmental protection, resource use, worker safety, and accident prevention.

2. Review procedures for strategic planning, resource acquisition, and operations for conformance to the sustainable development policy. Announce significant efforts to reduce natural resource consumption and waste generation.

3. Align corporate structure, lines of responsibility and internal reporting mechanisms to the sustainable development policy. Encourage overseas affiliates to modify procedures as needed to reflect ecological and social realities of their area.

4. Educate staff on effects of sustainable development and how they can utilize these criteria in their specific tasks. Reward employees who report environmental problems or who recommend environmentally sound innovations.

5. Prepare (and distribute to affiliates) sustainable development assessments of investment and operating decisions.

6. Perform an environmental audit of ongoing activities (especially in developing countries), and establish a scale to measure the comparative track records of affiliates.

7. Issue public reports on the most hazardous products, processes and emissions generated by the enterprise, and distribute information on the methods in place to reduce these hazards and plan for emergencies.

8. Institute research and development toward eliminating or reducing greenhouse gas generating products and processes, and make environmentally safer technologies available to affiliates without added internal charges.

9. Inform joint venture partners and subcontractors about the corporate sustainable development policy. Establish policies for severing relationships with associated firms that operate with disregard for these concerns.

10. Disseminate these criteria to other firms, and share the experiences with local governments, national authorities, and the United Nations.[29]

Thus, MNEs should make sufficient information public so that independent analyses can be performed on their products and processes. Furthermore,

> Since TNCs operate in many countries and jurisdictions, they should file disclosures of technical information with a central United Nations agency. The resulting database would enhance the ability of countries and communities to weigh the costs of proposed new energy development and industrial plants in economic and environmental terms. Such information could assist in the development of locally-based industries in poorer countries with otherwise limited technical resources. Generally speaking, a more informed debate about both environmental and economic issues would help increase the range of choices for development in an environmentally sound direction.[30]

SUMMARY

MNEs conduct and control productive activities in more than one country. They are considered important components of economic development because they introduce capital, technology, management know-how, and marketing to host countries. On the other hand, developing countries fear that MNEs can impose excessive environmental costs, as has happened with multinational firms in Southeast Asia that have contributed to massive deforestation.

Following the Earth Summit in Rio de Janeiro in 1992, many MNEs have attempted to introduce retroactive management policies of greening the investment environment in a number of developing countries. For example, a number of MNEs have been created through massive research and development programs that would provide solutions to existing environmental problems. Thus since MNEs could positively contribute to sustainable development by maintaining economic growth while reducing environmental risk, they are highly encouraged by the United Nations Center on Transnational Corporations (UNCTC).

REVIEW QUESTIONS

1. Compare and contrast MNEs and TNCs.
2. Discuss the reasons why MNEs are regarded as agents of development.
3. Discuss the negative impact of TNCs on the developing countries.
4. Discuss the strengths and weaknesses of the environmental management of TNCs.

CASE STUDY: TOYOTA

In Southeast Asia, Toyota Corporation maintains eight subsidiaries, including four automobile manufacturing companies, three automobile parts manufacturing companies, and a subsidiary that functions as a trading firm. In addition, Toyota possesses 400 dealerships in the ASEAN countries.[31]

At present the total automobile market for the entire ASEAN region is roughly 900,000 vehicles per annum.[32] In comparison with the 14 or 15 million vehicles manufactured in the United States and the 13 million vehicles manufactured in the European Union, the ASEAN market is rather small even though the market is growing.[33] Facing this circumstance, Toyota and ASEAN realized that without a strong domestic market there would be difficulties in competing internationally in the highly competitive automobile industry.[34]

In response to this problem, the ASEAN countries are striving to boost their automobile industry. As part of this effort, Toyota is promoting the division of labor and the integration of the parts manufacturing business. At present, the production of specific auto parts is delegated to the different ASEAN countries.[35] These parts are supplied to all the markets within the ASEAN region; some are also exported to Japan.[36] The demand in one country may not correspond with the volume of parts production. However, in this way full production that was not possible in one country is now financially attainable through these concerted efforts.[37] Also, this system steadily builds up the region's competitive power to export automobile parts to countries outside the system of ASEAN.[38]

In the future it will be very difficult to maintain the present high rate of economic growth in ASEAN through reliance on a strategy of low labor costs. Presently, wages are rising fast in these countries.[39] Manufacturing of products using high technology leading to high added value is key to maintaining competitiveness. Toyota believes that promoting the cooperative efforts of manufacturing operations is the proper way to contribute to local economies.[40]

Toyota strongly believes in contributing to local communities. For example, Toyota's development of environment-related human resources includes the creation of the International Center for Environment Technology Transfer, established at Yokkaichi City, Japan, in 1990.[41] Since Japanese technologies in the field of industrial pollution prevention are among the world's most advanced, its purpose would be to transfer these technologies to other countries.[42] As of the end of 1991, 350 Japanese engineers had already assisted in introducing pollution-preventing technologies in many countries.[43]

In 1992, following the Earth Summit in Rio de Janeiro, Toyota announced a research program to genetically engineer trees that will remove more of the carbon dioxide emissions from automobiles. Toyota hopes to plant these "super-trees" across the hills of Southeast Asia. In announcing this research program, Toyota has generated the image of an earth-friendly firm, in spite of the 5 million automobiles it produces annually. Toyota's environmental efforts illustrate not only the company's acceptance of their social obligations but also its conviction that people's demands for environmental integrity offer new business opportunities.[44]

Toyota is an example of an MNE that is committed to follow the path of social responsibility by transferring environmentally sophisticated technology to ASEAN. The company has recognized the imperative of including environmental considerations in their strategic decision making. Toyota's top management has realized how new industry opportunities will be driven by environmental change.

DISCUSSION QUESTIONS

1. What strategic reasons prompted Toyota to plant "super-trees" across the hills of Southeast Asia?
2. What are the strengths and weaknesses of the Toyota case?
3. What lessons can we learn from the Toyota case?

NOTES

This chapter was written with the assistance of Glomelyn E. Sosario, Amy Fisher, Yonny Savage, and Jerg Althaus, all of Dominican College, San Rafael, California.

1. United Nations Centre on Transnational Corporations, *Climate Change and Transnational Corporations* (New York: United Nations, 1992): 11, 26.

2. Theodore H. Moran, "Multinational corporations and the developing countries: An analytical overview," in Theodore H. Moran (ed.), *Multinational Corporations* (Lexington, Massachusetts: D. C. Heath and Company, 1985): 3.

3. See, for example, Jan S. Hogendorn, *Economic Development* (New York: HarperCollins, 1992): 176.

4. Moran, "Multinational corporations and the developing countries," 4.

5. Isaiah Frank, *Foreign Enterprise in Developing Countries* (Baltimore: John Hopkins University Press, 1980): 30–31.

6. World Bank, *World Development Report 1985* (Oxford: Oxford University Press): 127–28.

7. United Nations Centre on Transnational Corporations (now the Transnational Corporation and Management Division of the U.N. Department of Economic and Social Development), "Criteria for sustainable development management," *The CTC Reporter,* no. 30 (Autumn 1990): 1–3.

8. W. Dickerson Hogue, "The foreign investment decision making process," *Association for Education in International Business Proceedings* (December 29, 1967): 1–2.

9. See, for example, Asayehgn Desta, *International Political Risk Assessment for Foreign Direct Investment and International Lending* (Needham Heights, Massachusetts: Ginn Press, 1993): 41.

10. See, for example, Stephen H. Hymer, *The International Operations of National Firms: A Study of Direct Foreign Investment* (Cambridge, Massachusetts: MIT Press, 1976).

11. Neil Hood and Stephen Young, *The Economics of Multinational Enterprise* (London: Longman, 1979): 56.

12. Raymond Vernon, "International investment and international trade in the product cycle," *Quarterly Journal of Economics* 80 (May 1966).

13. For a thorough review of the literature, see John Dunning as quoted in Gerald M. Meier, *Leading Issues in Economic Development* (New York: Oxford University Press, 1995): 256.

14. Ibid.

15. Ibid.

16. Ibid.

17. Michael P. Todaro, *Economic Development,* 5th ed. (New York: Longman, 1994): 527.

18. "Interview with Maurice Strong, Secretary-General of UNCED," *Environmental Management in Transnational Corporations* (New York: United Nations Conference on Trade and Development, Programme on Transnational Corporations, 1993): 1.

19. Ibid.

20. Carter Brandon, "Reversing pollution trends in Asia," *Finance and Development* (June 1994): 21.

21. Stephan Schmidheiny, *Changing Course: A Global Business Perspective on Development and the Environment* (Cambridge, Massachusetts: MIT Press, 1992): 242.

22. Ibid., 135.

23. Ibid., 149.

24. Ibid.

25. "Interview with Maurice Strong, Secretary-General of UNCED."

26. Ibid., 3.

27. Ibid., 154.

28. Ibid., 6–7.

29. Adapted from United Nations Centre on Transnational Corporations, "Criteria for sustainable development management" (New York: United Nations, 1991).

30. United Nations Centre on Transnational Corporations, *Climate Change and Transnational Corporations,* 31.

31. Francois Gipouloux, *Regional Economic Strategies in East Asia* (Tokyo: Maison Franco-Japonaise, 1994): 212.

32. Ibid., 214.

33. Ibid., 215.

34. Ibid., 214.

35. Ibid.

36. Ibid.

37. Ibid.

38. Ibid.

39. Ibid., 215.

40. Ibid.

41. Ibid., 216.

42. Ibid.

43. Ibid.

44. Brandon, "Reversing pollution trends in Asia," 21.

Technology and the Environment

Some patterns of development are self-defeating in the long run in the sense that they would lead to an environmental collapse.

—Daniel Resendiz-Nunez[1]

For centuries, the development and diffusion of new technologies has been a major stimulus to economic growth and an important contributing factor in international economic and political integration. As early as the Neolithic revolution some 15,000 to 20,000 years ago, several human communities with marked increases in population experienced such rapid technological innovation that the social and political fabric of these human groups underwent a corresponding increase in complexity and economic prosperity.[2] Particularly, LDCs have shown an increasing preference "to adopt the proved Euro-American model of broad-spectrum industrialization as a panacea for expeditiously solving the problems that arise out of poverty, illiteracy, rapidly expanding populations with diminishing food resources, and the use of unprocessed, non-commercial energy for cooking."[3]

However, cases of environmental degradation in both developed and developing countries demonstrate that as technology improves there are concomitant environmental threats. Some forms of technological progress may be inherently incompatible with a healthy environment. New environmental policies may be needed to reduce the existing bias toward income-producing technology rather than environment-saving technology.

The purpose of this chapter is to map out the theoretical basis for the relationship between technology and economic growth. New technologies are examined that embody both the income-producing and environment-saving elements which are so fundamental to sustainable development. Finally, a case study involving Japan is used to show the association between technology and the environment.

THEORETICAL FRAMEWORK

As mentioned before, historically technology has been regarded as the bedrock of development and as an indispensable tool to effectively harness natural resources. Technology has permitted access to vast resources, substantially raising living standards in all societies capable of taking advantage of technological innovations. However, no matter how effectively resources have been utilized, technology has only partially solved humanity's development problems. Rampant deforestation and overintensive farming have been practiced for centuries with resultant environmental degradation, but in recent decades exponential increases in population and quantum leaps in industrialization have created a worldwide ecological crisis.[4]

Technology is multifaceted. It ranges from engineering specifications to human development and can result in unintended environmental effects. Generally, technology can be divided into four aspects:

1. *Engineering specifications,* such as master planning, product design, blue prints, documents, production and processing techniques
2. *Human capital and development* including training, demonstration, consulting, managerial and marketing skills, and quality circles
3. *Productivity* (high volume, cost-saving per capita product)[5]
4. *Unintended environmental effects*

Countries have several options in obtaining new technology. These alternatives are:

- The purchase of new equipment
- Direct foreign investment
- The purchase of technology licenses for domestic production of new products or the use of new processes
- The use of non-proprietary technology, including that obtained from purchasers of exports
- Acquisition of knowledge from returning nationals
- Domestic research and development and efforts in reverse engineering[6]

Early theorists in the field of economics were "technologically optimistic." They were mainly concerned about quantitative growth, and saw technology as the vehicle of development. Adam Smith, David Ricardo, Karl Marx, and Joseph Schumpeter, though far from united on the determinants of economic growth, all agreed that technological progress must be encouraged in order to speed up capital accumulation in an underdeveloped economy. Smith argued for setting the "productive powers of labor" in motion, creating a spiraling effect whereby development is the result. His argument is based on greater division of labor and specialization, leading to, among other things, the invention of better machines and equipment.[7] Thus Smith viewed technological innovation as cumulative, creating greater efficiency and generating capital, and thereby resulting in economic progress.

David Ricardo refined Smith's analysis by including land and capital with labor as the driving force of economic development. His analysis focuses primarily on agriculture as the most important sector of the economy. "Ricardo and even later classical writers, such as John Stuart Mill, do not appreciate fully the important role that technological progress can play in increasing productivity in agriculture, thereby lessening the difficulty of feeding a growing population."[8] However, Ricardo did reinforce Smith's argument for the importance of technological improvements in relation to land and capital, not just labor.

Marx and Schumpeter "accept a rapid stream of new techniques and resource opportunities as 'givens.'"[9] Both argued in favor of the appropriate environment for technological opportunities to contribute successfully to development. Marx viewed technological progress as too labor-saving for the capitalist system to handle successfully. According to Joseph Schumpeter, capitalism performs successfully under the stimulus of technological improvements, but its very success undermines the proper social environment for capitalistic progress.[10]

Until the 1950s development theorists focused on technological innovation as the main vehicle of economic development. It was argued that the diffusion of Western technology into agriculture was the primary means of industrialization in the Third World countries. These theories had little to say about the intricate role and impact of technology on the economy and about the economic and political conditions of technological change.[11]

It was not until the mid-1950s that development theorists began to broaden their assessments of technology to include the industrial sector. A transformation of comparable significance evolved with the emergence of science-intensive industries based on chemistry, modern physics, and especially mathematics.

Arthur Lewis's two-sector model of development focused on the structural transformation of a subsistence agricultural economy to a modern industrial, service economy. Lewis emphasized the importance of economic infrastructure in developing countries and stressed the need for hard and soft technologies such as transport networks, communication systems, and educational facilities as prerequisites for growth.

Harrod and Domar concurrently developed an empirical variant of Lewis's economic growth model. (Their theory was later modified, formulated, and extended by Fei and Ranis in the mid-1960s.) Both Harrod and Domar considered technological progress as an expansion of natural resources. They looked at the importance of economic investment in spurring growth. There are direct linkages between the savings that are for technological innovation and the increased savings resulting from population growth. Domar and Harrod argued that advanced technology could not be utilized by an economy in the preliminary stages of development; advancement to the takeoff stage of economic development precedes the effective use of new technologies.

In response to the assumptions of the Lewis and Harrod/Domar models, W. W. Rostow defined the stages of economic growth. Rostow argued that growth is not as simplistic as described in previous growth theories. First, conventional theory provided no mechanism for the systematic introduction of noneconomic factors into the analysis of economic growth; it is quite clear that economic growth—most notably in its early phases but in fact in all phases—could not be understood except in terms of the dynamics of whole societies. Linkages between science, invention, and the production process were not elaborated. Mainstream theory provided no credible explanation for the effect of trend periods (longer than conventional business cycles) on prices of basic commodities relative to manufactures. Finally, there was no credible linkage of conventional business cycles to the process of growth.[12]

According to Rostow, the transition from underdevelopment to development must proceed in a series of economic stages of growth. These are (1) the traditional society, (2) the preconditions for takeoff, (3) the takeoff, (4) the drive to maturity, and (5) the age of high mass-consumption.

The 1970s marked a turning point in economic growth theories. It became apparent that giant tractors and crops requiring expensive fertilizers were of little use in regions where intensive agriculture prevailed at a bare subsistence level. Hand tools, small motors, and other implements of intermediate technology were more useful and accepted in such an environment. The role and impact of technology inspired new insights.

Simon Kuznets defined a country's economic growth as "a long-term rise in capacity to supply increasingly diverse economic goods to its population; this growing capacity is based on advancing and the institutional and ideological adjustments that it demands."[13] Kuznets states that economic growth results not only from the accelerated quantity and quality of resources and improved technology, but also from a social, political, and ideological structural transformation.

Robert Solow's economic growth model was "a theoretical construct that focuses on the role of technological change in the economic growth process."[14] The Solow model states that "technological progressiveness" (new production techniques, processes, methods, and products) plays a necessary role in offsetting diminishing returns to capital as the capital stock increases.[15] Solow's theory is a preliminary attempt to address growing development concerns about the interplay between capital flows and technology.

The technological gap theory looks outward to the changes in the pattern of international trade over time. It is based on a dynamic sequence of technology and product innovation and diffusion from the domestic to the international marketplace. The theory argues that advanced countries with a high propensity to innovate offer sophisticated new products in world markets, initially unobtainable from other sources. Over time this technology is diffused and adopted by less technologically advanced countries, which themselves eventually produce and supply more technologically advanced products to the world market. The result is an increase in international trade for the duration of the lag time. This theory provides a sophisticated analysis of the role and impact of technology on the global balance of capital flows.

The period from the early 1970s through the 1980s also marked a preoccupation by development theorists with the symmetry between basic human needs and economic growth. The concept of "technology assessment" (anticipating the impact and effects of new technology on economic progress) became a topic of great interest.

Peter F. Drucker, on the other hand, argued against these assessments, explaining that it is a "delusion" to think that man can predict the impact of new technology on development: "What needs to be watched is 'young technology,' one that has already had a substantial impact, enough to be judged, to be measured, to be evaluated."[16] It is a managerial responsibility to monitor technological progress but not to forecast that which is unpredictable.

Ann Johnston and Albert Sasson argue for successful transfer of technology to any society deemed capable of generating major social and economic change. Their strategy requires a policy of technical education and research that is suited to the economic and social conditions of the country.[17]

Jean-Jacques Salomon and Andre Lebeau explain that while technological advances may speed the process of modernization (contributing substantially to improving technology and living standards) in isolated instances, they cannot induce the social transformation that is a prerequisite of development. Scientific research and technological innovation can be effective only where social structures, institutions, and habits have first eliminated the "blocking factors" that are characteristic of traditional societies.[18]

THE RELATIONSHIP BETWEEN TECHNOLOGY AND SUSTAINABLE DEVELOPMENT

In the past two decades, we have witnessed a wave of theories of sustainable development. These theories center on technology as a remedy for problems of economic development. A. L. Alm relates that concern for the environment, awakened in the early 1970s, occurred at a time when technology was viewed as a rapacious force out of control. Economic growth, as exemplified by such technological marvels as nuclear power, supersonic transport, and new chemical products, was often thought to be in opposition to a healthy environment. At the same time, technological growth with its accompanying high-wage jobs is often viewed as the very essence of economic development, which in turn can lead to a reduction of environmental threats. In other words, to prevent environmental damage resulting from technological progress, one needs more technological progress.[19] Intellectual polarization between two extremes, the technological optimists and the technological pessimists, was commonplace during the 1970s.

Proponents of technology feared that retreatist, antitechnology prophets of doom would exert undue influence leading to a collective suppression of technological innovations. Alternatively, technological pessimists believed that uncritical technological optimism could lead to neglect of worsening global environmental problems, overshooting limits to growth, and missing an invaluable opportunity to create a human-scale society in balance with nature. In pessimistic minds, the ultimate (negative) outcome is near.[20]

In defining environmentally advanced technology, R. L. Olson believes these six characteristics must be present.

1. Sustainability: the capacity to meet present and future needs without jeopardizing the environment
2. A safe and inexhaustible supply of energy from the sun or fusion
3. Highly efficient use of energy and other resources
4. Efficient recycling and use of byproducts
5. Use of artificial intelligence and smart materials
6. Complex, living machines that emulate nature itself and can self-repair or self-adapt to changing environmental conditions[21]

On the other hand, some sustainable development theorists argue that in the search for high-tech solutions, logical and inexpensive low-tech solutions are overlooked. To overcome this problem, representatives from more than eighty developed and developing countries met in Geneva in March 1994 and agreed to transform the Global Environment Facility (an experimental program) into a permanent financial mechanism that would provide grants and concessional funding to developing countries for programs aimed at protecting the global environment. The focus of the program includes coverage, decision making, and governance. Specifically, the Global Environment Facility was set up to assist developing countries in dealing with the following global environmental problems.

1. Global warming, particularly the effects on the world's climate of greenhouse gas emissions resulting from the use of fossil fuels and the destruction of carbon-absorbing forests
2. Pollution of international waters through, for example, oil spills and the accumulation of wastes in oceans and international river systems
3. Destruction of biological diversity through the degradation of natural habitat, and the "mining" of natural resources
4. Depletion of the stratospheric ozone layer from emissions of CFCs, halons, and other gases
5. Land degradation (primarily desertification and deforestation) will also be eligible insofar as it relates to one or more of the four main focal areas above.

Decision making would take place primarily on the basis of consensus, but when this is not possible, a vote may be taken to forestall an impasse. Differences between the UN system, based on one country/one vote, and the Bretton Woods approach, where voting rights reflect economic strength, were resolved with the introduction of a "double majority" system. This requires a 60 percent majority of all member countries as well as approval by donors representing at least 60 percent of contributions; in effect, this gives both developed and developing countries veto power.

Governance would be handled by a new arrangement of unique UN and Bretton Woods practices. A universal assembly would meet every three years to review the Global Environmental Facility's policies, and a designated thirty-two-member council would meet twice a year (sixteen members from developing economies, fourteen from developed economies, and two from economies in transition). A functionally independent secretariat would be administratively supported by the World Bank but would report directly to the Global Environment Facility's council.[22]

This program raises the question: What kind of assessment techniques need to be undertaken by developing countries if they desire to achieve sustainable development by acquiring environmentally sound technology?

According to the Organization for Economic Cooperation and Development guidelines, technological assessment processes could involve (1) a preparatory phase, (2) an assessment study, (3) mapping out of exogenous and international factors and constraints, (4) presentation of complete alternative options for actions, and (5) quality control of technology assessment studies and reaction of interested parties. Nonetheless, as stated by Gunter Krober, technology assessment in the field of engineering includes four phases that represent the successive assessment processes.

1. Defining and structuring the problem
2. Analyzing the consequences
3. Evaluating the consequences
4. Making a decision

Defining and structuring the problem involves (1) outlining the objectives (i.e., determining technological solutions for given social or economic problems, and weighing the objectives with regard to their respective advantages or disadvantages) of the assessment; and (2) finding out whether a problem-generated assessment is required (that is, assessing a given technological solution with regard to its consequences, and comparing it with other possible solutions). Of course, the definition of the problem must be reproducible and discussable, and must be reviewed by other subject specialists. The problem must be explicitly stated, and at least the consequences should be considered. As stated by Krober,

> It is also important during this phase to have a clear idea of the variables and constant characteristics of the process, as well as to know, for example, what information and data are needed, and how to get them. Furthermore, it is important to define: the economic, political, ecological or social context under consideration; the time horizon of the assessment; and the underlying criteria of the evaluation.[23]

Analyzing the consequences involves forecasting the changes in the economic, social, or ecological areas that will result from the given technology. "There are several quantitative or qualitative methods available for this task: trend extrapolations; expert hearings; brainstorming; risk analyses; cost-benefit analyses; morphological classifications; historical analogies; and others."[24]

Evaluating the consequences means describing expected future changes resulting from the introduction of a certain technology. "This evaluation presupposes a set of values that may have different weights for different social groups, individuals or institutions."[25]

Making a decision is to a large extent a political act. Nevertheless, it depends on which objectives, values, needs, and interests are accepted by (or prevailing in) the community. The Centre for Sustainable Technology Acquisition Systems recommends the following economic assessment module for the technological assessment techniques shown in Table 12.1:

Table 12.1
Technoeconomic Assessment Module

- Impact of technology (environment, safety, energy, cost-benefit)

- Identification of remedial technologies

- Economic features and effects of remedial technologies

- Availability of materials and inputs

- Operational and maintenance standards for the plant, as well as safety standards of plant and community

- Quality of management

- Assessment of training requirements of managerial, technical and scientific personnel

- Product quality and competitiveness in relation to optimally functioning similar industries

- Assessment of industrial environment within which the identified remedial technology would operate

- Regulatory and legislative framework

- Institutions affecting operational level of industry

- Basic industrial and financial structures

Source: Sonia P. Maltezou, "Constraints to clean technology transfer to developing countries," *Environmentally Sound Technology for Sustainable Development* (New York: United Nations, 1992): 174.

> First, identification of the effect of the technology on the environmental, safety, energy and profitability factors of an industry will be assessed. Furthermore, appropriate technology that will minimize negative effects and optimize efficiency of the technology will be identified. Following the preliminary identification of replacement or new technologies, there will be further assessment of their respective effects, and of the availability of materials or inputs.[26]

At the same time it is necessary to assess the safety standards of the plants and the community concerning the operation and maintenance, thus providing a further screening device for the potential optimal application of contemplated technology changes. To facilitate the introduction of such changes and undertake the required assessment evaluations, it is important to assess the quality of management and adopt an integrated quality approach. Furthermore, it is important to provide rigorous training of managerial, technical, and scientific personnel to deal effectively with technology improvements or changes.[27]

From the above analyses we may conclude that if developing countries want to satisfy the needs of the present generation without compromising the needs of future generations by using clean and appropriate technologies, they must first accumulate a pool of skilled human resources. These endogenous capabilities could be used for elaborating and evaluating the environmental soundness of transferred or newly developed technologies. In addition to skilled human resources, other factors essential for the transfer and application of clean and appropriate technologies to developing countries include appropriate information, the cost factor of clean technology, legislative and regulatory frameworks for promoting clean technologies, and infrastructures.[28]

SUMMARY

Historically, technology has been regarded as an indispensable tool to effectively harness natural resources. However, along with technological improvements come unintended environmental effects—as is clearly shown in case after case in both developed and developing countries.

To protect the global environment, representatives from more than eighty developed and developing countries met in Geneva in March 1994 and agreed to transform the Global Environment Facility and provide grants and concessional funds mainly to developing countries. Also, the Global Environment Facility was given a mandate to develop policy regarding climate change, destruction of bio-diversity, pollution of international waters, and ozone depletion.

REVIEW QUESTIONS

1. Define technology. Describe ways in which technology is transferred to a country or a firm.

2. What are the differences between income-producing and environment-saving technologies?

3. Why are early economists regarded as technology optimists? How do they differ from technology pessimists?

4. Discuss the advantages and disadvantages of the Global Environment Facility.

CASE STUDY:
TECHNOLOGY AND THE JAPANESE ENVIRONMENT

In the development of the Japanese economy, rice farming and other agricultural pursuits, fishing, and textile production preceded mining. But as industrialization proceeded coal, copper, lead (for bullets), zinc, gold, silver, sulfur (for gunpowder), and cadmium mining assumed great importance. Because of unfavorable trade treaties imposed on Japan from the 1850s and 1860s, Japan could scarcely afford to pay for the import of badly needed machinery, transportation equipment, steel, and other materials necessary to begin industrial development.

With the buildup of Japan's military and industrial strength, production of consumer goods stagnated and the cost of imports remained high. Intractable "old-line" merchants forced the government to intervene by bringing in machinery, technology, and instructors to set up model plants for production of paper, glass, cotton and wool textiles, soap, sugar, beer, and other commodities. It is said that "in the Meiji era before 1890 virtually all manufacturing of major foreign-style products in Japan was the result of government subsidy rather than private initiative."[29]

Of particular note was government subsidizing of silk production and manufacture intended for overseas markets. Silk production required power-driven foreign machinery, silk-reeling mills, and spinning and weaving facilities that soon dominated the world's production of raw silk. This financed the foundation of other light industries, especially cotton for yarn and fabric. Government policies favored development of a Western-style paper mill industry, a machine-making factory which led to steam engine production for seagoing vessels or factories, a machine-tool industry, a lightbulb industry, and a vertically integrated cotton industry that even underpriced Manchester, England—at the time the world's leading producer.[30]

The Japanese government perceived that the best way to industrialize was to give full support to those businessmen deemed most likely to succeed.[31] Thus, the government encouraged the formation of the zaibatsu system, which modernized business practices and sought new and innovative technology. In 1901 Japan's iron works installed their first modern blast furnaces, and the Japanese steel industry became a reality, furnishing an excellent foundation for basic industrial development. Korean and Manchurian holdings provided cheap cooking coal and iron ore and boosted trade and manufacturing. According to John G. Roberts' account:

> The annexation of new territories brought on a phenomenal boom in trade and manufacturing in Japan itself. Protective tariffs and increasing self-sufficiency in steel gave impetus to the shipbuilding, engineering, rolling stock, munitions, chemical, and machinery industries. Factories and railways were electrified, many city streets and homes were electrically illuminated, and thermal and hydroelectric power generation grew by leaps and bounds. The surge in trade with the mainland of Asia created strong demands for shipping, and the merchant marine grew rapidly. Japanese shipbuilding technology had progressed in step with the growth of the merchant marine, and by 1917 some sixty percent of the steam vessels in service were products of Japanese yards.[32]

While still lagging behind the West in technology for heavy industry and manufacture which required sophisticated techniques, the zaibatsu left the strategic industries of steel, naval shipbuilding, munitions, railway transportation, and communications in the hands of the government. However, the zaibatsu continued to acquire foreign processes, patents, and machinery essential for competitive production.

During World War I, Japan supplied Russia with the arms for attacking Germany. An "insatiable" demand for munitions, allowing the Mitsubishi and Kawasaki zaibatsus to lead the way in Japan's heavy industries, was coupled with huge shortages of civilian goods. Overseas markets that had been dominated by colonial powers fell into Japanese hands. Japan's merchant marine fleet, protected by the Navy, became indispensable to the Allies. By the end of the war, Japan's exports had tripled, the merchant marine fleet had doubled, Japan's income from sea transportation increased elevenfold, textile makers expanded, paper manufacturers became gigantic by international standards, and Japanese entrepreneurs were subsidized to enter new fields, especially heavy industry. Japan's chemical industry expanded into industrial chemicals, explosives, fertilizers, pharmaceuticals, and synthetic dye stuffs, which freed Japan's textile-dying industry from foreign dependence. Advances were made in Japan's artificial fertilizers industry. An automatic loom and a strong, economical thread allowed Japan's textile mills to become the world's most modern and efficient.[33] During the 1930s, the Japanese economy shifted to a war footing that further expanded Japanese industry.

Japanese industry suffered massive destruction toward the end of World War II. The American occupation forces dissolved the zaibatsu system but encouraged the reconstruction of the Japanese economic system for political and ideological reasons during the Korean War. Through hard work, protectionism, foreign technology, and reinvestment, the economy grew through light and then heavy industries into a modern industrial structure that includes much offshore manufacturing, with the greatest emphasis on cutting-edge technologies.

Early Japanese industrial development efforts also resulted in serious pollution problems, from the operations of copper mining, iron and copper ore smelting, and cement-processing and coal-burning industries. One famous incident occurred at the turn of the century when wastes from a copper mine poisoned the drinking water and cropland of several hundred farmers.[34]

During the 1960s and 1970s, air pollution was so bad that pictures of urban Japanese people with handkerchiefs over their faces were commonplace. Between 1960 and 1977 there was an elevenfold increase in automobiles in Japan, from 3 million to 33 million.[35] Toshio Hase points out that the air was so polluted that public health was endangered and that "virtually no natural vegetation [grew] in the major metropolitan areas of Tokyo and Osaka."[36] Between 1960 and 1970 agricultural land was lost at a rate of 0.55 percent annually. There had been mercury poisoning cases in Minamata and Niigata, severe air pollution problems in Yokkaichi, Kawasaki, Osaka, and Tokyo, cadmium pollution in Toyama, and noise pollution created by new airports and trunk roads. Douglas C. McGill attributes these outbreaks to "unchecked economic hypergrowth."[37]

According to McGill, in Tokyo during the 1960s some traffic officers used oxygen masks and children fainted in schoolyards. In 1970 strong antipollution laws were finally passed.

> [These laws] were effective in addressing the most severe cases of air and water pollution, but continued economic growth in Japan has overwhelmed many of those gains. The 1970 laws . . . sharply reduced the allowable limits for polluting emissions from individual automobiles.
>
> But the increase in the number of automobiles has pushed air pollution levels back to hazardous levels in the big cities. Nitrogen dioxide levels in many cities have increased above 1970 levels and, according to a recent

report from Japan's Environment Agency, have been linked to increasing rates of asthma in schoolchildren.[38]

By 1980 Tokyo Bay, Seto Inland Sea, and Ise Bay, all surrounded by large metropolitan areas and factories, suffered water quality destruction.[39] Hase describes the most well-known case of industrial pollution from Japan, the mercury poisoning at Minamata.

> The Chisso Corporation in Minamata, Kyushu, poisoned plankton and fish with mercury for more than 20 years. As a result of eating the fish, several thousand fishermen and their families suffered the agonies of mercury poisoning— aching limbs, partial paralysis, and partial blindness. This illness was also discovered in the Niigata Prefecture in Northern Japan, where the Showa Electric and Chemical Company also polluted the river with mercury-laden wastes; in this case, 50 people died and 669 were crippled, according to official estimates. But the number of injuries is probably far greater, as the government used a very narrow, rather too precise definition for the identification of Minamata disease.[40]

In Minamata Bay not only did the Chisso Company deny any wrongdoing, the mercury-laden Minamata Bay was never "cleared" of industrial waste, and the company continued its operations. It was also true that the workers were anxious to keep the plant open and were hostile to those who directly suffered and their supporters. Eventually, however, the company reached the brink of bankruptcy because of the claims for compensation.

McGill relates that Japan is under increasing attack for exporting polluting industries. "The trend began in the 1970s, when the combination of Japan's growing economy and strict new environmental laws led hundreds of manufacturers to look for lower rates and more lenient environmental laws in the developing countries of Asia. Since then, numerous Japanese export pollution cases have cropped up."[41]

When Japanese university students were asked to give examples of what they considered major environmental problems, two answers were "bad breath" and "old men on bicycles." These responses reflect the fact that the Japanese word for "pollution" is literally "public nuisance" and refers generally to a disruption of the smooth flow of civil life: traffic jams, drought, the loss of light or view by construction of a new building. It has little to do with nature in its wild state, which is not valued as such. McGill writes, "Most Japanese value nature the way Westerners admire a painting or sculpture — for the artful layering on of human workmanship and design. 'Wild' nature has no more value than a lump of clay before a sculptor shapes it."[42] He continues:

> Environmental problems have been discussed in terms of land rights, compensation claims, breaches of social contracts and reparations. Saving scenic beauty for human enjoyment, or protecting wilderness, or preserving the plants and animals indigenous to a region—the standard repertory of Western environmental goals—has, until recently, not been part of the discussion in Japan.[43]

Thus to expect the Japanese to take a real lead in saving the earth or to push the issue of biodiversity may be unrealistic at this time. The Japanese government has enacted some of the world's strictest antipollution laws and Japanese industries have adhered to them (at least in Japan, for the most part), but the value system to enthusiastically support these regulations is wanting.

Finally, McGill discusses how, at the Rio de Janeiro Earth Summit, Japan pledged $7.7 billion over a five-year period for a variety of environmental foreign aid programs and was thus cast in the role of being the champion of the "technofix" approach to environmental problems—"the idea that in better technology lies the salvation of the environment."[44] Japanese construction companies have begun researching a number of "global super projects" that reflect the technofix attitude.[45]

The Japanese case study demonstrates that the subject of the environment and technology will continue to be strongly debated because technology relates directly to the quality of life itself. Thus before new technology is developed or upgraded its environmental impact must be assessed carefully.

DISCUSSION QUESTIONS

1. Japan is showing a commitment to the "technofix" approach to environmental problems and is the only major industrial nation to have the means to finance its commitment. Should Japan be "subsidized" by the other industrialized nations to take the lead in developing the technologies that will overcome environmental problems? If there were to be a shared responsibility, should Japan still be given the leadership position when one considers its perceived environmental value system?

2. Because new technologies often pollute in new and more complex ways, toward what ends should technology be moving?

3. What are the strengths and weaknesses of the case study?

4. What lessons did you learn from this case study?

NOTES

This chapter was written with the assistance of Laura van Galen and Russell Scherf, both of Dominican College, San Rafael, California.

1. Daniel Resendiz-Nunez, "Sustainability and the nature of development," *Environmentally Sound Technology for Sustainable Development* (New York: United Nations, 1992): 13.

2. "Technology" entry in *The New Encyclopedia Britannica: Macropedia*, 15th ed., vol. 28 (Chicago: Encyclopedia Britannica, 1993): 442.

3. Rajendra Kumar, "Bridging the energy-environment chasm in developing countries: some technical options," *Environmentally Sound Technology for Sustainable Development* (New York: United Nations, 1992): 13.

4. Ibid.

5. See, for example, Asayehgn Desta, *International Political Risk Assessment for Foreign Direct Investment and International Lending* (Needham Heights, Massachusetts: Ginn Press, 1993).

6. Howard Pack, "Technology gaps between industrial and developing countries: Are there dividends for latecomers?" *World Bank Economic Review Supplement—1992,* 295–99.

7. Gerald M. Meier and Robert E. Baldwin, *Economic Development: Theory, History, Policy* (New York: John Wiley & Sons, Inc., 1962): 21.

8. Ibid., 25.

9. Ibid., 129.

10. Ibid.

11. Otto Hieronymi, "Reflections of technology, international order and economic growth," *Technology and International Relations* (1987): 74.

12. See, for example, W. W. Rostow, *Theorists of Economic Growth from David Hume to the Present* (New York: Oxford University Press, 1990): 429.

13. Simon Kuznets as quoted by Michael P. Todaro, *Economic Development in the Third World,* 4th ed. (New York: Longman, 1989): 121.

14. See, for example, Christopher Pass et al., *The HarperCollins Dictionary: Economics* (New York: HarperCollins, 1991): 487.

15. Ibid.

16. Peter F. Drucker, "New technology: predicting its impact," in Albert H. Teich (ed.), *Technology and Man's Future* (New York: St. Martin's Press, 1981): 255.

17. Ann Johnston and Albert Sasson, *New Technologies and Development* (Paris: UNESCO, 1986).

18. Jean-Jacques Salomon and Andre Lebeau, *Mirages of Development: Science and Technology for the Third Worlds* (Colorado: Lynne Rienner, 1993).

19. A. L. Alm, "Technology: Villain turned hero," *Environmental Science and Technology* 24(35) (1990).

20. See, for example, E. T. Smith, "Growth vs. environment," *Business Week* (May 11, 1992): 66–70.

21. R. L. Olson, "The greening of high tech," *The Futurist* (May 11, 1991): 28–34.

22. See, for example, Mohamed El-Ashry, "The new global environment facility," *Finance and Development* (June 1994): 48.

23. Gunter Krober, "Environmentally sound technology assessment in the context of sustainable development," *Environmentally Sound Technology for Sustainable Development* (New York: United Nations, 1992): 77.

24. Ibid.

25. Ibid.

26. Sonia P. Maltezou, "Constraints to clean technology transfer to developing countries," *Environmentally Sound Technology for Sustainable Development,* 170.

27. Ibid.

28. Ibid.

29. John G. Roberts, *Mitsui: Three Centuries of Japanese Business* (Tokyo: Weatherhill, 1989): 122.

30. Ibid., 124–26.

31. Ibid., 129–30.

32. Ibid., 170.

33. Ibid., 200–203.

34. Toshio Hase, "Japan's growing environmental movement," *Environment,* No. 23 (March 1981): 14–20.

35. Ibid., 15.

36. Ibid., 14.

37. Douglas C. McGill, "Sour technology's stain with technology," *The New York Times Magazine* (October 4, 1992): 33.

38. Ibid., 33.

39. Keikichi Kihara, "Japan's environmental policies: the last 10 years," *Japan Quarterly,* No. 28 (October 12, 1981): 502.

40. Hase, "Japan's growing environmental movement," 16.

41. McGill, "Sour technology's stain with technology," 33.

42. Ibid., 32.

43. Ibid., 33.

44. Ibid.

45. Ibid., 33.

International Trade and
the Environment

I t is generally assumed that international trade is vital to the economic development of a nation. According to the theory of comparative advantage, international trade remedies shortages of domestic commodities, instills new desires and tastes, and transfers technology, skills, and entrepreneurship. Trade can also induce innovation, increase productivity, expand foreign exchange, create capital accumulation, and accelerate the learning curve.[1] Moreover, with the globalization of market trends, it is assumed that trade policies can encompass environmental goals.

On the other hand, some economists argue that the gains from trade favor the advanced countries, and do not facilitate industrial development, resulting instead in income inequality in the LDCs.[2] Although a nation's trade structure (based on comparative advantage) can be assumed to be effective in a static sense, its dynamic effect is highly questionable. For example, the environmental effect of international trade on a country's growth pattern has become very debatable. Environmentalists claim that free trade leads to environmental problems.

> An example might be when industrial economies import products from tropical forests in quantities that encourage deforestation in the exporting country without building up other forms of capital. The importing country effectively imports sustainability, while the exporting country exports it. The import and export of sustainability are partly an issue of international inequality.[3]

The problem, therefore, is how the relationship between trade and the environment can be managed to create sustainable development.

This chapter introduces the most prominent theories of trade and development, followed by an outline of the linkages between trade and the environment. A case study looks at international trade patterns in China and their effect on that country's environment.

THEORETICAL FRAMEWORK

> The promotion of increased volumes of commodity exports has led to cases
> of unsustainable overuse of the natural resource base. While individual cases
> may not fit this generalization, it has been argued that such processes have
> been at work in ranching, fishing in both coastal and deep-sea waters,
> forestry, and the growing of some cash crops. Moreover, the prices of com-
> modity exports do not fully reflect the environmental costs to the resource
> base.[4]

In the following sections we will examine the classical and neoclassical theories
of trade, trade strategies of development (import substitution and export promotion), and some alternative strategies of trade for the developing countries.

Classical Trade Theory

Generally speaking, international trade theories have attempted to answer the
following questions.

- What constitutes the basis of trade—that is, why do nations export and import
  certain products and services?
- At what terms of trade (relative prices) are products and services exchanged
  in the world market?
- What are the gains from international trade in terms of production and consumption?[5]

In light of these questions, what are some of the international trade theories
that affect the developing countries?

Absolute Advantage Trade. Adam Smith, using the principle of absolute advantage in free trade theory (open markets, with many buyers and sellers and no
government intervention), proposed in his 1776 book *The Wealth of Nations*
that each nation benefits by specializing in the production of the good which it
can produce at the lowest cost while importing the goods it produces at a cost
higher than other nations. Stated differently, Smith argued that a nation could
use its excess resources to produce a surplus of goods for export. Trade could be
used to vent surplus capacity that otherwise could not be used at home. Smith
based his argument on the following assumptions.

> In a two-nation, two-product world, international trade and specialization
> will be beneficial when one nation has an absolute cost advantage (that is,
> uses less labor to produce a unit of output) in one good and the other nation
> has an absolute cost advantage in the other good. For the world to benefit
> from an international division of labor, each nation must have a good that
> it is absolutely more efficient in producing than its trading partner. A nation
> will import those goods in which it has an absolute cost disadvantage; it will
> export those goods in which it has an absolute cost advantage.[6]

Comparative Advantage Trade. According to Smith's absolute advantage theory,
each nation is required to be the lowest-cost producer in at least one product for

export. Unlike Smith, however, David Ricardo in his 1817 book *The Principles of Political Economy and Taxation* showed that a nation could have an absolute advantage in all products. According to Ricardo's argument:

> [E]ven if a nation has absolute cost disadvantage in the production of both goods, a basis for mutually beneficial trade may still exist. The less efficient nation should specialize in and export the good in which it is relatively less inefficient (where its absolute disadvantage is least). The more efficient nation should specialize in and export that good in which it is relatively more efficient (where its absolute advantage is greatest).[7]

To demonstrate comparative advantage trade theory, Ricardo (building on Adam Smith) posed the following model (based on a description by E. Wayne Nafziger).

- A world of two countries—for example, an LDC and a DC [developing country]
- Two commodities (e.g., textiles and steel)
- Productive resources (land, labor, and capital) that can only be combined in the same fixed proportion in both countries
- Full employment of productive resources
- Labor is the only factor of production and is homogeneous
- Given degrees of technical knowledge
- Given tastes
- Perfect competition in the two markets
- Free movement of labor and capital within the domestic market, but no movement between countries
- Equal export and import value for each country
- No transportation costs[8]

Ricardo's comparative advantage theory is essentially a classical trade theory. It has been modified in modern times to become the determinant of major patterns of trade. Comparative advantage trade theory asserts that a country can have a relative advantage over another if in producing a commodity it can do so at a relatively lower opportunity cost in terms of the forgone alternative commodities that could be produced.[9] It is further assumed that every trading country is able to enjoy a higher real income by specializing in production according to its comparative advantage and by trading even without any increase in resources or technological changes. Exports allow the country to "buy" imports on more favorable terms than if produced directly at home.

Ricardo's theory of comparative advantage provides a useful framework for analyzing international trade. It is rich in its implications about the gains from international trade for developing countries because it assumes that:

> (1) Any country can increase its income by trading, because the world market provides an opportunity to buy some goods at relative prices that are lower than those which would prevail at home in the absence of trade. (2) The

smaller the country, the greater this potential gain from trade, but all countries benefit to some extent. (3) A country will gain most by exporting commodities that it produces using its abundant factors of production most intensively, while importing those goods whose production would require relatively more of the scarcer factors of production.[10]

Some of the limitations of comparative advantage trade theory are:

- Increased mass production achieved through specialization is not necessarily beneficial, because it may leave untouched the realization of such critical goals of economic development as universal education, social equality, personal fulfillment, and national independence.
- Comparative advantage theory does not consider the environment.

According to the theory, LDCs may have a comparative advantage if they wish to exploit their few resources and sustain environmental damage (some two-thirds of the exports of renewable resources are sent to the industrial world).

Thus this theory needs to take into account the external effects and user costs of trading in natural resources. Among other things, the relationship between trade and sustainability depends on "(a) the balance between the trade and the resource endowments of the countries involved, (b) the extent to which revenues from exported resources are converted into other forms of capital, and (c) the extent to which the trade takes place at international prices that reflect the true social costs of resource depletion in the exporting country."[11]

Neoclassical Trade Theory

Comparative advantage trade theory based on labor productivity was further expanded in the 1920s to include factors such as labor and capital by neoclassical economists Eli Heckscher and Bertil Ohlin. This theory, known as the Heckscher-Ohlin or factor-endowment trade theory, was formulated to explain why different nations have comparative advantages in producing different goods. The factor-endowment trade theory states that comparative advantage can be explained exclusively by differences in supply conditions between countries. In particular, this theory highlights the role factor endowments (such as land, labor, capital) play as the principal supply factor underlying comparative advantage. Like all theories, the Heckscher-Ohlin theory relies on several simplifying assumptions.

- All nations have identical tastes and preferences (demand condition).
- They all use factor inputs that are of uniform quality.
- They all use the same technology.[12]

According to the factor-endowment trade theory, relative price levels differ among nations because (1) Countries have different relative endowments of factor inputs, and (2) different commodities require that the factor inputs be used with different intensities in their production. Given these situations,

[A] nation will export that commodity for which a large amount of relatively abundant (inexpensive) inputs are used. It will import that commodity in the production of which relatively scarce (expensive) inputs are used. That is why land-abundant nations (such as Canada and Australia) export land-intensive goods such as wheat and meat, while labor-abundant nations (such as South Korea and Hong Kong) export labor-intensive goods such as textiles and shoes.[13]

Based on factor-endowment theory we can try to explain the kinds of goods exported and imported by developing countries. LDCs have lower labor costs while developed nations have relatively cheap capital. This means that the LDCs should specialize in labor-intensive products, while developed countries should specialize in capital-intensive products. For example, Indonesia exports oil and natural resources while the United states exports capital-intensive products such as chemicals, computers, and aircraft. Though suggestive, the theory has limitations that

> fail to explain growth and structural change because [the theory] excludes growth in the stocks of productive factors, as well as improvements in the quality or productivity of those factors. The theory thus provides no mechanism to explain how economies evolve over time and change the composition of their outputs, their consumption, and their trade.[14]

Though factor-endowment trade theory encourages LDCs to concentrate on labor and land-intensive primary products for export, the theory seems to justify the exploitation of Third World people by claiming that it is natural for a country to maintain its comparative advantage based on low-skill labor. In fact, "[t]his free trade doctrine also served the political interests of colonial nations searching for raw materials to feed their industrial expansion and for market outlets for their manufactured goods."[15]

Moreover, the theory does not take into consideration the outcome of export enclaves (mainly mining and agricultural plantations) in the developing countries which were controlled by foreign or domestic interest groups who freely transferred their profits abroad. As Pari Kasliwal states, the export enclaves had very few economic linkages with the rest of the economy, and such production would not produce significant economic growth because it would induce minimal technological change. He provides as examples the copper industry of Chile or Zaire, both of which have "few externalities apart from generating useful foreign exchange," provide "little business to domestic suppliers," and serve few domestic customers.[16]

To summarize, classical and neoclassical economists saw no conflict between a country's conformity with its comparative advantage and the acceleration of its development. They believed that the differences in endowments of labor, capital, and natural resources among nations account for the pattern of international trade. However, it needs to be pointed out that because of the existence of similar tastes in the developed countries, about one-fourth of world trade is intraindustry trade, that is, the exchange of automobiles for automobiles or office machines for office machines.[17] A number of the LDCs did not gain new technology, and growth from trade was hardly realized. These nations faced the choice of shifting to a closed economy and developing self-sufficient systems or of remaining dependent on developed nations.

TRADE STRATEGIES FOR DEVELOPMENT

Before the 1950s conventional wisdom stated that the road to development could be traversed most rapidly by pursuing policies based on comparative advantage trade theory. Arguing from the interventionist (structuralist) view of development, Paul Prebisch, then-director general of the Economic Commission for Latin America, and Hans Singer, associated with the United Nations Department of Economic and Social Affairs, proposed that the prices for developing country exports were falling relative to the prices for LDC imports of manufactures from developed countries. Along these lines, a study by the World Bank from 1965 to 1988 indicates "[t]he barter terms of trade fell a significant 50 percent over the period, while the income terms of trade rose 50 percent until the late 1970s and fell 50 percent from then until 1988."[18]

To account for the terms of trade (the purchasing power of exports in terms of trade), the Prebisch-Singer hypothesis used the net barter terms of trade—the average price of a country's exports divided by the average price of its imports. However,

> [T]he net barter terms of trade tell us little about income or welfare, which ought to be the basis for judging changes in world trade conditions. A better measure of the income effect of price changes would be the **income terms of trade**, T_i, which measures the purchasing power of exports by comparing an index of export revenues to an index of import prices. This is equivalent to the net barter terms of trade multiplied by the volume of exports (Q_x), or $T_i = P_x Q_x / P_m$.[19]

The terms of trade in LDCs have declined; that is, exporting countries must export more just to maintain consistent levels of foreign exchange earnings. A number of developing countries have attempted to industrialize using a strategy which tries to balance import substitution (where domestically produced commodities substitute for "expensive" foreign imports) against export promotion (outward-looking methods).

Import Substitution

While countries may be classified as using either import substitution industrialization (ISI) or export promotion industrialization (EPI), many economies make use of a combination of policies at different times. Countries which choose export promotion strategies usually begin to trade by exporting primary products such as agricultural products and raw materials, and later develop the capability to export manufactured products. Primary products continue to make up 70 percent of the world's export earnings.[20] Primary product exports have grown more slowly than total world trade except for petroleum and a few minerals. Developing countries derive 40 percent of their export earnings from primary products (nonfood agriculture and raw materials). However, the drawbacks of this strategy from the demand side are:

- Income elasticities of demand for primary product and non-fuel commodities is low.
- Populations in developed countries are near replacement levels, so there will be little increased demand to drive growth.
- The development of synthetic substitutes for commodities is very high.

From the supply side, the structural rigidity of Third World rural production (limited resources, poor climate and soil, antiquated rural institutions, and backward social and economic structures) is unmanageable. Also, large corporate capital-intensive farms exist side by side with thousands of fragmented, low-productivity peasant holdings.[21]

As the world market for primary products declined, leading to a growing balance of payments deficit, a number of LDCs turned to import substitution industrialization techniques or inward-looking strategies to replace imported commodities (usually manufactured consumer goods) with domestic sources of production and supply.[22] In short, the inward-looking strategies focused on agricultural self-sufficiency and then turned to manufacturing to provide their own products as substitutes for imports. ISI was expected to provide capital accumulation and spur technological progress, based on learning by doing in the protected industries. Tariff barriers or quotas protect the infant industries, which are established with heavily borrowed funds, until they are able to compete in world markets. The protected industries are usually joint ventures with foreign investors. The goal is to reduce the balance of payments deficit and develop large scale industries capable of competing in world markets. In reality, the ISI strategy by itself has not proven to be very successful because of the following weaknesses.

- Prices were generally higher for the protected industries than those in world markets. For example, the prices of machinery and other intermediate imports needed for domestic industry were generally higher than the prices of exported products.
- The principal beneficiaries of import substitution have been foreign firms able to locate behind tariff walls and take advantage of liberal tax and investment incentives.
- Import substitution industries rarely become cost-efficient, and cannot compete in world markets.
- Overvalued home currencies make exports more expensive and imports cheaper in terms of local currencies.
- The ISI approach never considered environmental implications or consequences.

Export Promotion

The theoretical platform of EPI, as advocated by neoclassical counterrevolutionaries, involved purposeful government efforts to expand the volume of a country's exports through export incentives and other means to generate more foreign exchange and improve the current balance of payments. In addition, advocates cite the efficiency and growth benefits of free trade and competition, and the benefits of large world markets over limited domestic markets.[23]

In looking at the success or failure of developing countries over the past fifty years, one sees that neither export promotion or import substitution strategies have prevailed exclusively. Much depends on the overall world economy. During the period of world economic expansion from 1960 to 1973, the outward, open economies of the LDCs experienced more economic growth than the closed economies. However, during the slow growth period from 1973 to 1977, most closed economies did better, with the exception of the NICs of Asia (Hong Kong, Taiwan, South Korea, and Singapore), which practiced a combination of both strategies. From 1973 to 1983, changes in trade policy appear to have had little or no effect. Thus, it is possible to say that differences in trade policy alone do not account for higher levels of inequality in some countries than in others. Contrary to the position of the World Bank, an outward-oriented policy is not necessarily a valid policy for all LDCs. It is the power structure of a country that determines how economic gains are distributed within a society.[24]

As mentioned above, the sustained economic growth recorded over a prolonged period in the "East Asian economic miracle" countries (often referred to as the Four Tigers or Gang of Four) was due to export-promotion policies. It is worth pointing out that in the early stages of development, the NICs protected their economies with protectionist policies in order to allow them to gain strength before competing in world markets. The experience of the Asian NICs illustrates the need for cooperation between public and private sectors of the economy and for a balanced trade strategy.

Alternative Trade Strategies

Trade policy that combines both outward- and inward-looking aspects in the developing countries is either South-South trade or regional economic integration.

South-South Trade. Historically trade among the LDCs has been relatively meager (about 7 percent of total world trade). But by 1990 South-South trade represented almost 33 percent of all Third World exports, against 25 percent in 1965. Trade in manufactures has risen from only 5 percent in 1960 to almost 35 percent of all exports in the early 1990s.[25] If the present levels are maintained, they can help to compensate for weak demand and growing protectionism in the developed world. LDCs may find it much easier to grant trade preferences to other developing countries than to lower barriers to the developed countries. Many development economists argue that Third World countries should orient their trade more toward each other than to the developed countries because there are greater dynamic gains to be realized, export instability can be reduced, and "collective self-reliance" can be easily accomplished.[26]

Regional Economic Integration. A variant of South-South trade patterns is regional economic integration. "Economic integration occurs whenever a group of nations in the same region, ideally of relatively equal size and at equal stages of development, join together to form an **economic union** or **regional trading bloc** by raising a common tariff wall against the products of nonmember countries while freeing internal trade among members."[27]

This approach can take various forms such as free-trade areas (external tariffs against outside countries differ among member nations while internal trade is free), customs unions (free internal trade and common external tariffs), and common markets (free internal trade and common tariff against nonmembers plus the free movement of labor and capital among the member countries).

Economic integration can have both static and dynamic effects. The static effects include trade creation (shift from the consumption of higher-cost domestic products to lower-cost products of other member states), and trade diversion (shift from the consumption of lower-cost nonmember countries' products to higher-cost member countries' products). The dynamic effects of regional trade creation take place over the long run and include increased competitiveness, economies of scale, and industrial planning according to dynamic comparative advantages.

Such economic cooperation between countries of similar size and levels of development may benefit small, poor nations who cannot prosper in isolation or in the very unequal world economy. Third World countries at similar stages of industrial development, with similar market size, political orientation, and commitment and currency clearing mechanisms, can benefit most from economic integration, and their regional cooperation can act as a buffer to the overwhelming world market.[28]

THE EFFECTS OF TRADE ON THE ENVIRONMENT

As discussed above, trade has been a very efficient means of economic growth for some developing countries. On the other hand,

> [T]rade liberalization is likely to produce negative environmental externalities. . . . The negative association between freer trade and environmental degradation does not imply that freer trade should be halted. It does suggest that the most cost-effective policies should be adopted to optimize the externality. Restricting trade is unlikely to be the most efficient way of controlling the problem, especially if trade retaliation may occur. The losses can best be minimized by firm domestic environmental policy designed to uncouple the environmental effects from the economic activity. This firm environmental policy may itself have international trade effects.[29]

However, there are some aspects of economic growth that benefit the environment, as when poverty is reduced, per capita income increases, and some types of environmental pollution decrease. Increased per capita income is associated with decreased population growth leading to reduced pressure on the environment. In addition, increased income raises educational standards and increases demand for less pollution.[30]

But by and large, economic growth is generally accompanied by environmental damage. For instance, it is generally agreed that world trade frequently precipitates resource depletion in developing countries.[31] In industries such as cattle ranching, fishing, forestry, and farming, resources are usually compromised. In addition to resource loss, the developing countries usually do not receive adequate compensation in export prices to offset the environmental costs. Some products suffer less from permanent depletion (e.g., tea, coffee, cocoa, and citrus), but are more vulnerable to unstable prices; the terms of trade are usually not as beneficial to the exporting country.[32]

When income from resource rents is reinvested and contributes to capital accumulation in the exporting country, there is at least some movement toward sustainable development. Policies within the developing countries have the most significant influence on the amount of environmental damage caused by trade. Each of the following activities by the developing countries advances the possibility of achieving sustainable development.

- Reducing environmentally damaging subsidies
- Enforcing communal or private property rights
- Regulation of pollution
- Promotion of development and transfer of technologies
- Conservation of natural capital by encouraging sustained-yield resource development
- Ensuring that the gains from trade are funneled into measures promoting sustainable development[33]

A case in point is Southeast Asia, where the hardwood trade is almost completely unsustainable. Productive forests in 1985 amounted to 828 million hectares, with only one million hectares in a sustained-yield management plan. In the Philippines the forests are exhausted, despite efforts to ban logging. In 1983 the International Tropical Timber Organization was created to "encourage the development of national polices aimed at sustainable utilization and conservation of tropical forests and their genetic resources and at maintaining the ecological balance in the regions concerned."[34] It had set the year 2000 as the target date for reaching complete sustainability. Such goals always require many short-term sacrifices, and it remains to be seen if sustainability is possible any time soon.

It is unlikely that sustainable development will occur in the LDCs unless there is substantial funding from the developed countries for research and development of clean technologies (including solar and wind), biotechnology, reduced use of CFCs, family planning, debt relief in the form of debt-for-nature or debt-for-farmland swaps, rural development projects, and financial and technical assistance in environmental regulatory programs. In addition, sustainable development requires removal of trade barriers to the products of poor countries.

Although there is a lot of controversy about whether a given country has the right to dictate environmental policy to another country, there are global pollution problems, such as ozone depletion and global warming, that need international cooperation. A case in point is the Montreal Protocol, signed in 1987 by twenty-four countries to protect against atmospheric ozone reduction.[35]

The Montreal Protocol called for an international 50 percent reduction in CFC production over a period of ten years beginning with a baseline established in 1986. The Protocol gave concessions to poor countries locked into current levels of low consumption because these nations were not responsible for the global problem as it existed then. Developing countries were given a ten-year grace period to conform, and wealthier nations were urged to set up an assistance fund to ease transition. China and India did not originally sign on because of the benefits of cheap refrigeration from CFCs. However, a 1990 revision of the treaty was signed by ninety-three countries and required rich countries to establish a fund of $260 million to finance the adjustment to CFC replacements in poor countries, with $60 million from the United States, which is the primary CFC producer. This induced India and China to join.[36]

Although there are other CFC-producing countries who did not sign the Montreal Protocol, the agreement provides for trade sanctions against "free riders," those countries that benefit from the reduction of CFCs without having to change their own practices.[37]

Five factors that made the agreement possible were:

1. confirmation of the ozone hole over Antarctica
2. simplified monitoring of the phaseout, since only six major corporations are involved in CFC production
3. rapid development of clean non-CFC substitutes as the ban became imminent
4. creation of a compensation fund by the wealthy countries to assist the developing countries
5. trade sanctions in the case of noncompliance.[38]

The Rio Agreement on Biodiversity is another important symbolic step, although nonbinding. Rich countries again formally acknowledged the need for a transfer of resources to protect biodiversity.

INTERNATIONAL REGULATORY ORGANIZATIONS AND THE ENVIRONMENT

Since 1947, the General Agreement on Tariffs and Trade (GATT) has served as the primary framework for international trade and a forum for regulation and resolution of disputes. GATT regulates tariffs and other monetary barriers to free trade, and covers goods and raw materials, with a few major exceptions such as agricultural products. For example, if a country believed that one of its trading partners was violating a GATT regulation, it could ask the Geneva-based bureaucracy that administered the GATT to investigate. If GATT investigators found the complaints to be valid, member countries could request that the offending party country change its policies. As a result of the GATT, tariffs have been cut in industrial countries from an average of 40 percent in 1947 to 5 percent in 1990.[39] Another function of GATT is to furnish member nations a mechanism whereby disputes concerning trade policy can be settled. There are 117 current signatories, with another eight countries adhering to the agreement, without the formal status of "contracting parties." All of the world's major trading nations are members with the exception of China, Taiwan, and Russia (Taiwan and China have requested membership).

The World Trade Organization (WTO) was established in Geneva to replace the 47-year-old GATT. As a legal institution similar to the United Nations, it is charged with adjudicating disputes under the GATT and executing the rules in the Final Act Text. It is staffed by unelected trade officials with greatly expanded powers of enforcement. The new WTO is one of the most powerful and least accountable economic bodies in the world. Under the new rules there are four changes in dispute resolution: a party is guilty until proven innocent; participation in side agreements is mandated; there is a second layer of approval residing in a panel with the power to make rulings; and the GATT supersedes all national laws. Decision making under the GATT is by consensus; any nation can choose not to participate or abide by a particular provision. The new WTO operates according to a two-thirds vote, and all nations are forced to accept the decisions. The rule forces countries to accept trade in areas that might be undesirable or to forgo participation in the world trading system.[40] In short, from the perspective of Third World nations, the three major provisions of the new accord are as follows.

1. Developed countries will cut tariffs on manufactures by an average of 40% in five equal annual reductions. Tariffs will be eliminated in 10 major sectors (beer, construction equipment, distilled spirits, farm machinery, furniture, medical equipment, paper, pharmaceuticals, steel, and toys). Developing countries in turn agreed to not raise tariffs by "binding" in recent trade reforms.

2. Trade in agricultural products will come under the authority of the of the WTO and be progressively liberalized. Developed-country nontariff barriers are to be converted into tariffs and reduced to 36% of the 1986–1988 level by the year 2000. Agricultural subsidies will also be reduced.

3. For textiles and apparel, the Multi-Fiber Arrangement (MFA), which has long penalized exports of developing countries, will be phased out by 2005, with most of the reductions taking effect toward the end of the period.[41]

Certainly the adoption of the Uruguay Round of the GATT by the United States and Japan and the resulting creation of the WTO could be seen as a decisive victory for free traders. For example, proponents of free trade claim that free markets will create such a great expansion in the world economy that all people will ultimately benefit. Molly Ivans, political commentator for the *Texas Star,* commented that while the free traders' claim is true in the long run, "by then we'll all be dead."[42] Many who support free trade in general and the new WTO in particular have asked for better international environmental controls.

The imperatives of economic growth versus environmental protection are nowhere in such conflict as in Asia. The economic dynamism of the Asia Pacific nations has brought millions out of poverty, but the price is wanton environmental destruction. Such environmental losses are treated as the price of economic growth. However, it is now becoming clear that the resultant environmental degradation is costly as well as unhealthy and unaesthetic. World Bank studies show that 1 percent of Jakarta's annual GDP is spent on boiling the contaminated water supply, and in Bangkok some studies suggest that the average child loses four or more IQ points by the age of seven because of lead exposure, with enduring implications for adult productivity.[43]

Conflict over the importance of the environment pits North against South, developed nations against developing nations. The most outspoken proponents of development—Malaysia, China, and India—argue that alleviating poverty is the most important first step in solving environmental degradation. They insist that environmental concerns should not dampen economic growth in any way. They want technology transfers at affordable prices, new definitions of intellectual property rights, and large amounts of "green" aid to pay for environmental protection.[44] Free traders from the developed countries argue that if developing countries could export more textiles, their need to sell their timber would be less desperate and therefore less environmentally destructive.[45]

Many industries have acted responsibly when locating offshore production facilities in developing countries and have actually enforced higher standards than the host country requires. In India, following the Bhopal catastrophe, many chemical companies upgraded local standards to meet the more stringent standards practiced in the United States. However, not all corporations can be relied upon to act responsibly.

It is imperative that the WTO be brought in line with the goals of the June 1992 Rio de Janeiro Earth Summit. This can be accomplished by convening the newly established environmental committee of the WTO for the purpose of updating and clarifying environmental aspects of the free trade organization.[46]

SUMMARY

International trade theories are very vital to the economic development of a nation. For example, the classical, comparative, neoclassical and neoclassical counterrevolutionary theories argue that unrestricted free trade remedies can remove shortages of domestic commodities and transfer new technology and skills. Also, trade is expected to induce innovation, increase productivity, expand foreign exchange, and create capital accumulation.

Absolute advantage, comparative advantage, and factor endowment (Heckscher-Ohlin) trade theories hypothesized that the differences in endowments of labor, capital, and natural resources among nations account for patterns of international trade. On the other hand, the neoclassical counterrevolutionaries argued for purposeful government support to promote exports through subsidies and to limit imports through tariffs and quotas.

Although trade has been a very efficient means of economic growth for some developing countries, it can be argued that economic growth in the NICs has been mainly accompanied by resource depletion. Thus, if sustainable economic growth is expected to be accomplished in the developing countries, there should be substantial grants from the advanced countries for research and development of clean technologies. Particularly, the WTO needs to find a path to development that does not deplete the resources upon which the future economic well-being of the world depends.

REVIEW QUESTIONS

1. What is the difference between absolute advantage and comparative advantage?
2. Why do LDCs face declining terms of trade?
3. What is the difference between import substitution and export promotion? Which strategy should LDCs follow to expand trade?
4. What is the difference between South-South trade and Economic Integration for LDCs?
5. Discuss the linkage between trade and the environment.
6. How can the WTO facilitate sustainable development in the LDCs?

CASE STUDY: SUSTAINABLE DEVELOPMENT IN CHINA

For more than a decade, China's GDP grew at more than 9 percent per annum.[47] Similarly, between 1980 and 1992 its exports grew at 11.9 percent and its imports grew at 9.2 percent. China represents 20 percent of the world's population but subsists on just 7 percent of the world's arable land. This ratio indicates a challenging relationship between nature and human development. When China's economic growth is factored into this equation, sustainable development becomes an explosive question. As Xia Kumbao of China's National Environmental Protection Agency (NEPA) has pointed out, "The major source of environmental pollution is industrial growth."[48]

To best understand China's environmental policies, or lack thereof, it is necessary to examine the trade strategies practiced by China during the country's drive to economic growth.

Since China opened its doors to the world in 1979, it has maintained a "fundamental philosophy of import substitution."[49] That is, China continued to impose barriers to imports, despite its stated goal of reforming and liberalizing its trade regime. These barriers include not only high tariffs but also stringent import-licensing requirements, import quotas, restrictions and controls, and standards and certification requirements. By the mid-1990s, however, China made a number of unilateral reforms to improve its trade regime. It agreed to eliminate the use of import substitution policies and measures and "promised not to subject any imported products to such measures in the future, nor will it deny approval for imports because an equivalent product is produced in China."[50]

Though not overtly, China started promoting exports. It claimed to have abolished direct subsidies for exports on January 1, 1991. However, many of China's exports continued to receive indirect subsidies through guaranteed provision of energy, raw materials, labor supplies, and bank loans that have lengthy or preferential terms. Import/export companies also cross-subsidized unprofitable exports with earnings from more lucrative products. Tax rebates became available for exports, as well as duty exemptions on imported inputs intended for export production. In addition, China's swap markets allowed exporters to exchange their foreign currency holdings at a higher rate than the official one.[51]

In recent years China seems to have been leaning toward a policy of specialization once import restrictions are totally lifted. For example, China's export profile in 1993 consisted of textiles, garments, telecommunications, recording equipment, petroleum, and minerals, and totaled $99.5 billion. In 1993, China's imports totaled a nearly identical $99 billion, and included specialized industrial machinery, chemicals, steel, textile yarn, fertilizer, and natural resources such as coal, iron ore, crude oil, mercury, tin, tungsten, antimony, manganese, molybdenum, vanadium, magnetite, aluminum, lead, zinc, and uranium.[52]

China's Environment

Given the trade pattern described above, how has China managed the environment?

The costs of economic development are perhaps nowhere more visible than in China. Ecological nightmares, such as air pollution and water shortages, threaten to stunt industrial growth. Some of the serious environmental problems facing China today are outlined below.

Solid Waste. With industrial growth outstripping even its urban population increase, China churned out more than 587 million tons of industrial waste in 1992 alone. Residential and commercial garbage (municipal waste) reached 100 million tons in 1993. Alarmingly, only 3 percent of it is being recycled, as evidenced by overflowing trash heaps and urban landfill.[53] This solid waste leaks toxins into the ground water. Now the water in many rivers does not meet bathing standards, much less drinking standards.[54]

Wastewater. China's total wastewater reached 36.65 billion tons per year in 1992 (a 9 percent increase in a single year). This excludes wastewater from township and village industry enterprises. It was projected that this number would rise to more than 130 billion tons per year as a result of China's modernization drive. In 1990 thirteen of the fifteen major rivers flowing near Chinese cities were seriously polluted.

Energy and the Use of Coal. China's energy consumption ratio in the early 1990s was: coal, 76 percent; oil, 17 percent; natural gas, 2 percent; and hydropower, 5 percent. With coal as the main energy source (both in terms of consumption and production), a tremendous environmental toll is taken.[55] As noted by observers, the new coal mining operations in China do not appear to take into consideration environmental protection measures.[56]

Ozone-Destroying Chemicals. China's production of 25,000 tons of CFCs ranked ninth in the world in 1991, but the demand for CFCs or substitutes was expected to triple within a five-year period.[57]

Land. Erosion and silting affect 15 percent of China, while desertification is calculated to grow at a rate of 1560 square kilometers a year.[58] As Lester Ross summarizes, "For years, China's environmental authorities have been like a muzzled dog: plenty of bark but little bite."[59]

Between 1982 and 1993, at least thirteen major pieces of environmental legislation were passed in China, involving the protection of marine life, forests, fisheries, grasslands, mineral resources, wildlife, soil, and agriculture, as well as protections against air and water pollution.[60] However, the key question is whether the legislation will be effectively enforced.

During the eighth Five-Year Plan (1991–1995), environmental protection was planned at 0.85 percent of annual GDP. In 1991 only 0.7 percent was spent. NEPA officials have estimated 1.5 percent is needed to halt further degradation,[61] as comparable developing countries spend 1 to 2 percent on environmental protection.[62] Based on what is allocated, it can be said that China is not practicing sustainable development. Aside from lax environmental protection laws and a meager budget, China's environmental policy suffers from "weak, non-comprehensive regulations and standards and inadequate enforcement of regulations that do exist."[63] The following facts seem to back up that assessment.

- Some policies, specifically those conferring liability for the use of polluting technologies and disabling pollution controls, can be interpreted to apply only to government work units, not to non-state and private enterprises.[64]

- The environmental protection bureau cannot shut down offending operations without the approval of the local government, which is typically more concerned about economic development with its attendant government revenues than about environmental standards.[65] Some issues, most notably solid and hazardous waste management, are not even covered by specific legislation.[66]

China needs legal tools with real teeth in them to hold polluters fully accountable for their actions. In 1992 a local township pharmaceutical plant in Zhejiang province was fined only $740 for dumping chemical waste, yet in half a year the plant had inflicted losses worth $180,000 to local seafood breeders.[67]

Legislative changes are needed to strengthen a number of outdated regulations. For example, China relies heavily on pollution or effluent fees to discourage industrial pollution. However, the great disparity between the marginal amount of the fees and the marginal costs of implementing pollution control measures limits their effectiveness.[68]

Although Article 33 of China's 1989 Environmental Protection Law states that "the production, storage, transportation, sale and use of toxic chemicals and materials containing radioactive substances must comply with the relevant state provisions so as to prevent environmental pollution," NEPA officials acknowledge that few specific controls exist to administer toxic substance control.[69]

The conclusion reached from analyzing the link between trade and the environment in China is that trade is not the real culprit in environmental degradation. In fact, commodity trade can actually help improve the environment, especially when environmentally sensitive technologies are part of the process. However, environmental costs need to be properly priced and existing environmental laws need to be properly enforced.

DISCUSSION QUESTIONS

1. What is the link between comparative advantage theory and the environment in China?
2. What are the strengths and weaknesses of the Chinese case study?
3. What lessons can we learn from the Chinese case study?

NOTES

This chapter was prepared with the assistance of Christy Pichel, Fara O'Sullivan and Mary Irene Zemanek, all of Dominican College, San Rafael, California.

1. Gerald M. Meier, *Leading Issues in Economic Development* (New York: Oxford University Press, 1995): 460.

2. Ibid., 453.

3. David W. Pearce and Jeremy J. Warford, *World without End: Economics, Environment and Sustainable Development* (New York: Oxford University Press, 1993): 281.

4. World Commission on Environment and Development, *Our Common Future* (Oxford: Oxford University Press, 1987): 80–81.

5. Robert J. Carbaugh, *International Economics* (Cincinnati, Ohio: South-Western College Publishing, 1995): 17.

6. Ibid., 19.

7. Ibid., 19–20.

8. Adapted from E. Wayne Nafziger, *The Economics of Developing Countries* (Belmont, California: Wadsworth, 1984): 421–22.

9. Michael P. Todaro, *Economic Development,* 5th ed. (New York: Longman, 1994): 666.

10. Malcolm Gillis et al., *Economics of Development,* 2d ed. (New York: W. W. Norton, 1987): 408.

11. Pearce and Warford, *World without End,* 281.

12. Carbaugh, *International Economics,* 67–68.

13. Ibid., 68.

14. See, for example, Meier, *Leading Issues in Economic Development,* 455–56.

15. Todaro, *Economic Development,* 422.

16. Pari Kasliwal, *Development Economics* (Cincinnati, Ohio: South-Western College Publishing, 1995): 203.

17. Meier, *Leading Issues in Economic Development,* 455–56.

18. Pearce and Warford, *World without End,* 284.

19. Gillis et al., *Economics of Development,* 421.

20. Todaro, *Economic Development,* 487.

21. Ibid.

22. Ibid., 491–94.

23. Ibid., 485–89.

24. Ibid., 508.

25. Ibid., 509.

26. Ibid., 510.

27. Ibid.

28. Ibid., 512.

29. Pearce and Warford, *World without End,* 300.

30. Eban S. Goodstein, *Economics and the Environment* (Englewood Cliffs, New Jersey: Prentice-Hall, 1995): 419.

31. World Trade Commission on Environment and Development, *Our Common Future* (Oxford: Oxford University Press, 1987): 80–81.

32. Pearce and Warford, *World without End,* 282.

33. Goodstein, *Economics and the Environment,* 515.

34. Ibid., 293.

35. Ibid., 512.

36. Ibid., 513.

37. Marine Stetson, "Saving Nature's Sunscreen," *World Watch* (March–April 1992): 35.

38. Adapted from Goodstein, *Economics and the Environment,* 513.

39. Hilary French, "The GATT: Menace or ally?" *World Watch* (September–October 1993): 13.

40. Ralph Nader, "GATT threatens US environment," *Earth Island Journal* (Summer 1994): 30.

41. International Monetary Fund, *World Economic Outlook, May 1994* (Washington, D.C.: International Monetary Fund, 1994), annex 1, as quoted in Michael P. Todaro, *Economic Development,* 6th ed. (New York: Addison-Wesley, 1997): 488.

42. Molly Ivans in the *Texas Star,* as quoted in the *Santa Rosa Press Democrat* (December 3, 1994).

43. Adam Schwarz, "Looking back at Rio: Give us trade, not aid: environmental values vs. economic growth," *Far Eastern Economic Review* (October 28, 1993): 28.

44. Ibid., 52.

45. *The Economist* (January 26, 1991): 13.

46. French, "The GATT: Menace or ally?": 13.

47. The World Bank, *World Development Report 1994* (Oxford: Oxford University Press, 1994): 162–86.

48. Robert Nadelson, "The ruined Earth," *Far Eastern Economic Review* (September 19, 1991): 39.

49. U.S. Department of State, "Country reports on economic policy trade practices: People's Republic of China," *National Trade Data Bank* (July 25, 1994): 19940719.

50. Ibid.

51. Ibid.

52. Ibid.

53. International Trade Administration, "China—Solid Waste Management," *National Trade Data Bank* (July 25, 1994): 19940721.

54. International Trade Administration, "China—Coal Industry News," *National Trade Data Bank* (July 25, 1994): 19940317.

55. Ibid.

56. Ibid.

57. Sandy Hendry, "Policy reform when it suits," *Far Eastern Economic Review* (October 29, 1992): 42.

58. Nadelson, "The ruined Earth," 39.

59. Lester Ross, "The next wave of environmental legislation," *The China Business Review* 21(4) (1994): 30–33.

60. Ibid.

61. Hendry, "Policy reform when it suits."

62. Nadelson, "The ruined Earth."

63. Ross, "The next wave of environmental legislation."

64. Ibid.

65. Ibid.

66. Ibid.

67. Hendry, "Policy reform when it suits."

68. Ross, "The next wave of environmental legislation."

69. International Trade Administration, "China—Toxic Substance Regulations," *National Trade Data Bank* (July 25, 1994): 19940317.

External Debt and the Environment

I n the early part of the 1980s it became apparent that more than twenty-five developing country borrowers had experienced difficulty in repaying their international loans on time. For instance, in 1982 the Mexican government announced it would be unable to service its external debt. Following in the footsteps of Mexico, other heavily indebted and less developed countries announced that they could not pay their external debt service requirements. As discussed by Morris Miller,

> The immediate fear in 1982 was, of course, the devastating impact of such threatened defaults and moratoria on the financial viability of the world's major commercial banks, banks with Third World "accounts receivable" assets many times greater than their capital assets. This fear gave rise in turn to a reaction that brought on the very developments that were feared: lending by the commercial banks was abruptly cut back, creating a situation even more fragile and frightening. In the five years leading up to 1982, the flow of capital to the developing countries in the form of long-term lending from commercial banks, official lending, and concessional aid had amounted to $147 billion; from 1983 onward the flow was reversed.[1]

Some environmentalists assert that the international debt crisis has become the cause of environmental degradation in a number of developing countries. On the other hand, lending institutions argue that debt crisis and environmental crisis are both outcomes of the same cause, namely the drive for rapid growth by LDCs. For example, World Bank advisor John D. Shilling argues that "[i]n both instances, the culprit was the attempt to increase consumption above levels the economy and environment could sustain."[2]

This chapter treats the international debt crisis and environmental degradation. The first section focuses on the factors that precipitated the international debt crisis. The second section provides the linkage between debt crisis and the environment. Finally, the chapter examines a case study that deals with debt-for-nature swaps as a solution to alleviate both the debt and the environmental facets of the global crisis.

THE EXTERNAL DEBT CRISIS[3]

To put the debt crisis into perspective, we should briefly note the origin of the external debt problems of the LDCs. During the Great Depression of the 1930s, a large number of European and Latin American countries defaulted on their external debt obligations. Three decades after the international flow of capital almost came to a halt, private international intermediaries in the developed countries re-emerged as important sources of debt capital to the LDCs. Prior to the 1970s, however, Western commercial banks selectively channeled existing surpluses in the Eurodollar markets to those LDCs that passed credit-worthiness tests based on resource endowment or growth in the export of manufactured products. Since short-term maturity loans were used to finance long-term development projects, some LDCs were not able to service their external debts. In other words, some LDCs did not accumulate adequate foreign exchange reserves to enable them to retire their debt. Instead, the external debts were either rescheduled or restructured at higher interest and fee payments. Consequently, from 1955 to 1964, the external debts of LDCs grew from approximately $8 billion to $35 billion.[4]

Following the quadrupling of oil prices from 1972 to 1974, a significant change in the lending procedures of private international banks ensued. The surplus OPEC petro-dollars deposited in Western banks could not be absorbed locally because of economic recession in the industrialized countries. These funds were aggressively recycled, mostly to middle-income LDCs, which were then experiencing balance-of-payment problems due to past large price increases, inflation, bad harvests, and the deterioration of export earnings.[5]

For the first time, non-OPEC LDC governments used financial intermediaries for balance-of-payment financing on a large scale. The total disbursed loans from U.S. commercial banks to non-OPEC developing countries doubled from $23.8 billion at the end of 1974 to $47.7 billion at the end of 1977.[6] With the increase in the demand for loanable funds by LDCs, international earnings accounted for 95 percent of the increase in total earnings of thirteen U.S. banks between 1970 and 1975.[7]

Since 1974–1975, the medium- and long-term external financial needs of the LDCs have been fulfilled by commercial banks in the developed countries. By 1975 commercial banks had almost replaced multinational financial agencies and governments as the major lenders to LDCs because loans could be arranged quickly for large amounts. This avoided the political ties and the conditionalities attached to official credits, particularly those from the International Monetary Fund (IMF).[8] The IMF imposed austerity programs on the borrowing nations that included currency devaluation, monetary supply restrictions, reduction of government spending on social services, wage controls, increased taxes, and trade liberalization.

With an average increase of 20 percent per annum from 1971 to 1981, the total disbursed external term debt outstanding in about 150 developing countries was estimated to be $626 billion.[9] The dramatic increase in external debts also resulted in large debt service obligations. For instance, in 1982 annual interest payments accounted for 84 percent of official reserves compared with a 32 percent annual interest payment in 1972.[10] Interest rates soared because lending institutions preferred to make short-term loans and introduced several types of variable interest rates to counteract the cost of borrowing funds, thereby worsening the ability of the borrowing nations to service their debts according to the terms of the contracts. Economist Jeffrey Sachs estimates that in the years 1980 to 1983, while Latin America's debt servicing exceeded total exports, Asia's (with the exception of the Philippines) debt servicing fell below the level of exports. However, when current account deficits and capital flight are used as a measure of accumulated gross debt, the Latin American countries show a slightly greater proportion of debt to GDP than the Asian nations.[11]

As a result of the large flow of funds, the world debt crisis has become conspicuous and concerns have escalated. Recalling memories of the 1930s, many investors believed that "governments of developed and developing countries could not be relied on to give the highest priority to honoring their international obligations."[12] The possibility of domino-effect loan defaults, if one country after another should run into unsolvable debt servicing difficulties, is anticipated. As a result, a climate of uncertainty has arisen in the already volatile international financial markets. The poor-performing LDC loans have in fact caused the financial market to contract, and some investors have moved out of banks and have concentrated instead on buying blue chip stocks and government securities.

The magnitude of the international debt problem of the developing nations can be summarized as follows.[13] From 1978 to 1993, the external debt of non-oil-developing countries rose from $328 billion to $1,489 billion. As a percentage of the gross domestic product of developing nations, external debt rose from about 25 percent in the 1970s to as high as 34 percent in 1984 and 33 percent in 1989, then dropped to 27 percent in 1993. The debt service ratio (debt service/exports), which indicates the ratio of interest and payments of principal to export earnings, indicates that the ratio in developing countries decreased from 19 percent in 1984 to 14 percent in 1993. It is clear that the revenue earned from exports could not service the external debt. For example, in years sampled (1984, 1989, and 1993), the ratio of external debt to export of goods and services was well over 100 percent. Nonetheless, the net resource transfers "from the developing countries amounted in total to approximately $200 billion. . . . [I]n 1989 alone this outflow rose to its highest annual level, over $50 billion, an amount substantially greater than what they had received that year in official development aid (ODA)."[14]

THEORETICAL FRAMEWORK

> Who is to be held responsible for the debt crisis: commercial banks that behaved as imprudent lenders, or debtors from developing countries that misused the borrowed external funds?[15]

A review of the literature indicates that a combination of several trends and developments contributed to the debt crisis.

- Two oil price increases (1973–74 and 1979–80)

- Recycling of the petro-dollars to the countries with balance of payments deficits

- Misuse of the borrowed funds by many debtors to buttress consumption, delay adjustment, or invest in projects with low rates of return

- Deterioration in trade capabilities of borrowing countries throughout the 1980s

- Continued expansion of multinational enterprises, along with cross-border mergers and acquisitions and related borrowing needs

- The financial and economic policies of the industrial countries. In an effort to eradicate the severe inflationary tendencies they allowed to develop during the 1970s, these countries adopted measures that slowed their economic growth (thus reducing opportunities for debtor country exports) and sharply raised interest rates, further deteriorating the debtor nations' ability to service their debts.[16]

The factors contributing to the debt crisis of the developing countries can be examined using three approaches.[17] The first approach analyzes the LDC debt problem from the supply side and focuses on lending procedures of country risk assessment techniques used by international lenders. The imprudent lending policy argument is premised on two assumptions: (1) that either the ability and willingness of the borrowing countries to service their debt was not systematically assessed; or (2) that bankers, faced with fierce competition from rival banks, might have overextended themselves in setting the country ceilings to protect their market share.

The second perspective examines internal economic conditions, including the use and management of borrowed funds within sovereign borrowers during the loan period. The management of borrowed funds approach is based on the assumption that analysts might have systematically analyzed the economic and sociopolitical conditions of the borrowing countries, but inadequate internal economic policies and mismanagement of borrowed funds during the loan period exacerbated debt-servicing problems in the LDCs. The third perspective is based on the international interdependence concept and attempts to locate the LDC external debt within the international economic order. It assumes that the dramatic increase in the current account deficits of the LDCs, followed by the substantial increase in their overall indebtedness, is due to the persistent current account surpluses in certain developed and oil-exporting countries, as well as high interest rates and the concomitant economic slowdown within the developed countries. Table 14.1 indicates some of the variables that could be used to test the above perspectives.

PROPOSALS FOR DEBT REDUCTION

> There is an old saying, "it takes two to tango." In the run-up to the debt crisis, creditors and debtors acted as unwitting partners.[18]

Table 14.1
Variables That Could Be Used to Test the Debt Crisis Assumptions

Imprudent Lending Assumption

Annual gross domestic product (GDP) growth rate

Annual export growth rate

Annual import growth rate

Gross international reserves rate

Human development index (HDI)

Total long-term debt service/exports

Mismanagement of Borrowed Funds

Average domestic annual rate of inflation

Average money supply

Average annual growth rate as percentage of gross domestic investment

Government budget deficit as percentage of GDP

International Economic Interdependence

Average interest rate of borrowed funds

Terms of trade

Percentage of oil imports

Source: Modified from *International Political Risk Assessment for Foreign Direct Investment and International Lending Decisions* by Asayehgn Desta. © 1993 by Ginn Press. Published by Ginn Press, an imprint of Simon & Schuster Education Group. Used by permission.

A number of proposals were suggested to resolve the debt crisis of the 1980s. The first would modify the economic policies of the LDCs, enhancing their capacity to service debt. This would require macroeconomic adjustments to achieve higher productivity and growth through expanded levels of exports. In October 1985, U.S. Treasury Secretary James Baker proposed a plan that emphasized adjustment programs for growth which encouraged private and public lending. But this "takes time and can cause temporary hardships [lower consumption] . . . further, it may require going deeper into debt in order to finance the investments necessary for generating economic growth—a requirement that may be hard to meet since creditors are, in general, loath to lend more where existing loans are in difficulty."[19]

The second approach reduces the burden of debt servicing through rescheduling or refinancing or spreading debt obligations. The third approach involves some form of debt reduction, which might include a shrinking of the stock of debt, lowered interest payments, or a renegotiated settlement.[20]

Nonetheless, these approaches are not comprehensive and are not permanent solutions to LDCs indebtedness. In 1988 Japanese Finance Minister Kiichi Miyazawa suggested that creditor banks swap debt for guaranteed bonds. Specifically, he suggested:

> First, debtor countries would "securitize" part of their debt, with guarantees on the principal through liens on their exchange reserves and on the proceeds from the disposal of state-owned assets. Second, the remaining unsecuritized debt would be rescheduled with grace periods of up to five years, during which interest payments could be lowered, suspended or forgiven. Finally, multilateral and bilateral agencies would increase their lending to countries that had taken the first two steps.[21]

A second proposal was initiated by President François Mitterand of France. His plan included a new issue of Special Drawing Rights to back guarantees for new bonds issued by debtor countries. Specifically he proposed that

> a fund should be created in the IMF for the middle-income indebted countries. This fund would guarantee the payment of interest charged on certain commercial loans converted into bonds. The fund would help significantly lower the finance charges payable by debtor countries. In order to finance it, the developed countries would set aside their share of a new issue of Special Drawing Rights (SDRs) for use by the developing countries.[22]

In March 1989 U.S. Treasury Secretary Nicholas Brady suggested a debt service reduction plan to be supported by the IMF and the World Bank. His plan provided the following.

- Debtor countries maintain growth-oriented adjustment programs and take measures to encourage repatriation of flight capital.
- International financial institutions, such as the IMF and the World Bank, provide funding to countries for debt and debt-service reduction through:
  1. debt buybacks
  2. exchange of old debt at a discount for new collateralized (asset-secured) bonds
  3. exchange of old debt for new bonds at par value, with reduced interest rates

Twenty-five percent of normal fund- and bank-policy-based lending could be reallocated to help reduce the principal of outstanding debt, through debt buybacks and collateralized reductions of principal. In addition, special resources could be used to support interest payments on discounted and par value reduced-interest bonds traded for commercial bank debt. Over a three-year period, the IMF and World Bank would be expected to provide a maximum of $20 to $25 billion, divided roughly equally between special pools and reallocations. International financial institutions may lend to debtor countries for debt reduction operations before a financing package is complete but after these countries commit in principle to the agreement. This would facilitate new flows of commercial finance and related debt-reduction methods. Commercial banks would provide debt reduction and new money, and support the accelerated reduction of debt and debt service through a temporary and conditional relaxation of some conditions on current debt. Creditor governments would continue to reschedule or restructure their own loans through the Paris Club and maintain export credit cover for countries with sound reform programs. Tax, accounting, and regulatory impediments to debt reduction would be eliminated. Japan is envisaged as providing about $4.5 billion over the next several years as additional financing.[23]

It is very difficult to assess the various debt proposals as successes or failures, because "if the ability of the international financial system to withstand the debt crisis is the benchmark, the strategy can be regarded as successful. . . . [I]f, on the other hand, the test is the quick resolution of the debt crisis, with debtor countries returning to full debt servicing and regaining 'normal' access to capital markets, the debt strategy has not met its goal."[24]

Though the above suggestions are instructive and can result in temporary solutions, a long-lasting solution can occur in the indebted countries only if an open trading system is promoted for exports coming from the LDCs. A strong and sustained adjustment is also possible in the currently indebted countries if they can pursue adequate policy reforms and economic management. More importantly, the currently indebted countries need to have access to official development assistance to include technology, capital, and management know-how from MNEs, and foreign capital at reasonable rates from other multilateral organizations. But the indebted countries should be required to consider the environment as a partner in economic development.

ECOLOGICAL IMPLICATIONS OF THE DEBT CRISIS

> Without environmental policies, development will be undermined. Without development, environmental protection will fail.[25]

As mentioned above, there is consensus among environmentalists that the debt crisis has had a significant negative impact on the environment. Much LDC indebtedness was created by a desire to attain or match levels of prosperity in Western industrialized countries. To achieve Western industrial progress, the developing countries depended heavily on foreign capital. After the loans were assumed and the money was spent, there was strong international pressure for the LDCs to generate hard currency to meet crushing debt repayment schedules.[26]

Much of the pressure comes from the austerity programs of the IMF, which forced debtor countries to increase hard currency income. This often requires increasing exports of natural resources such as timber, oil, or agricultural products. At the same time that many LDCs tried to increase exports of commodities, prices dropped, which means that more had to be exported to increase revenues. The IMF also applies pressure to reduce government spending, which can result in further cuts in environmental programs already in place.[27] These practices of the LDCs were not sustainable environmentally or economically. But what are the causes of environmental degradation in the LDCs? As discussed by John D. Shilling,

According to many commentators, a significant share of the blame should be placed squarely on the debt crisis and related adjustment programs. Some even assert that debt alleviation, per se, will help solve environmental problems. This argument holds a bare grain of truth, so it is very appealing, particularly in the developing world. But it is potentially dangerous, because it confuses the cause and the cure; if acted upon, might lead to inequitable solutions, validate inappropriate behavior, create moral hazards.[28]

The widely accepted view is that debt repayment is but one of many economic and political factors which are behind unchecked environmental degradation. Inflation, population pressures, low or negative rates of economic growth, and continuous encroachment on undeveloped land are all factors in the lack of environmental protection. While environmentalists may disagree on the mix of factors that have resulted in the environmental and debt crises, they do agree on two points. First, much of the hard currency for debt repayment is generated by exploiting resources such as minerals, cattle, and timber products. Second, much of the debt is used to fund projects that directly or indirectly create environmental problems.[29]

On the other hand, some bankers argue that, while debt is not a cause of environmental degradation, the debt crisis and environmental crisis are outcomes of the same cause, namely the drive for rapid growth by LDCs. For example, debt crisis results

from the drive for rapid growth, which, given external circumstances and the accepted development models, led to levels of foreign borrowing that could not be sustained, particularly when the borrowed resources were not invested productively. Similarly, environmental degradation resulted from the drive for rapid growth, which given social structures and technologies, led to consumption of environmental resources beyond sustainable levels. In both instances the culprit was the attempt to increase consumption above levels the economy and environment could sustain.[30]

Thus it is argued that further development must occur if the environment is to be sustainable. As suggested by Thomas E. Lovejoy, an innovative program to help alleviate both the debt crisis and environmental degradation is debt-for-nature swaps. As suggested by the U.S. World Wildlife Federation in 1984, "debt-for-nature" involves a swap in which an NGO purchases from a bank a portion of an LDC's debt. The NGO then forgives the debt, or donates it to the country's central bank, in exchange for actions which will benefit that country environmentally. The first debt-for-nature swaps were instituted by Bolivia, Ecuador, and Costa Rica in 1987. Now many other countries are considering or have developed debt-for-nature swaps, including the Dominican Republic, Jamaica, the Philippines, Zambia, and Madagascar.[31]

Debt-for-nature swaps provide a popular, workable means for alleviating some of the debt burden while achieving modest environmental gains. Debt-for-nature swaps have captured the imaginations of many people worldwide, and in most cases provide positive press for all parties involved. Jan S. Hogendorn argues, "The concept of reducing debt while doing battle with pollution might be just the catalyst that could mobilize political support in both the developed countries and LDCs, convincing rich-country taxpayers and donors that their sacrifice is worthwhile, while persuading LDCs that environmental protection really pays."[32]

Though debt-for-nature swaps can be viewed as stepping stones to substantive progress in alleviating two of the world's most tenacious problems, there are limitations to them. The amount of debt retired has been very small relative to the overall external debt of the participating countries, and the amount of benefit to the environment has been minor relative to the investment needed for substantial gains. Countries also become very reliant on NGOs and therefore may not develop their own environmental agencies. Finally, the swaps have little impact on the continuing exploitation of the environment by private concerns in the short or medium run.[33]

There are other alternatives to debt-for-nature swaps. Conventional private sector debt swaps can include environmental criteria. In these situations, private parties purchase debt and either exchange it with the government for something of economic value or establish bonds with the central bank of the country used to fund development projects. There could be sustainability criteria or other environmental protection criteria attached to these commercial debt swaps.[34]

Two other alternatives to debt-for-nature swaps are promoted by the international environmental community. One alternative involves engaging in bilateral or multilateral negotiations for debt reduction. Ideas being discussed are (1) the repayment of some debt in national currency to be placed in an environmental fund, and (2) the forgiveness of debt based on environmental "good works" by developing countries. The other alternative is the inclusion of environmental criteria in Brady Plan debt renegotiations, which have become mired in controversy in many countries. While the stagnation of these talks provides an opportunity to increase the role of the environment in negotiations, no progress can be made unless negotiations are concluded.[35]

Although debt-for-nature swaps and similar strategies can bring about temporary relief to the indebtedness of LDCs—in other words, they may reduce the debt—they can have little lasting effect on the environment. Dynamic sustainable development in the indebted countries can be realized only if solutions lie in applying policies that are based on better development paradigms, not in loan cancellations.

> A key step in developing countries is to undertake national environmental assessments. . . . [I]ndeed, that is the best way to be sure to properly identify the critical environmental issues and determine priorities for subsequent action plans . . . [which] need to be closely integrated with the economic adjustment programs underway in most developing countries.[36]

SUMMARY

In the early part of the 1980s it became apparent that more than twenty-five developing country borrowers had experienced difficulty in repaying their international loans on time. The factors that contributed to the debt crisis of the developing countries at that time can be looked at using three approaches. The first approach focuses on the supply side, that is, on the lending procedures used by international lenders. The second perspective examines internal economic conditions and management of the borrowers. The third approach is based on the international economic conditions, such as high interest rates, economic slowdowns in advanced countries, terms of trade, and the high price of imported oil.

Three major proposals were suggested to resolve the debt crises. The first would modify the economic policies of the LDCs, enhancing their capacity to service debt. This would require macroeconomic adjustments to achieve higher productivity and growth. The second proposal suggests reducing the burden of debt servicing through rescheduling or spreading debt obligations. The third approach involves some form of debt reduction through lowered interest payments. Though the three methods of reducing international debt crisis are instructive, there is consensus among environmentalists that the debt crisis has to be seen in terms of environmental depletion. That is, much of the indebtedness of LCDs was originally created by the desire to attain or match levels of prosperity in the industrialized countries and now requires the developing countries to increase their exports of natural resources in order to pay their loans. Thus dynamic sustainable development in the indebted countries can be realized only if solutions lie in applying policies that are based on better development paradigms rather than the cancellations of existing loans.

REVIEW QUESTIONS

1. Describe the debt crisis and define the causes.
2. Critically review the proposals to alleviate the Third World debt crisis.
3. There is disagreement about the role external debt has played in the environmental deterioration of LDCs. What is your opinion?
4. It can be argued that LDCs must exploit natural resources in order to maintain good credit and relations with the IMF, commercial and noncommercial lending institutions and other international business and government concerns. At the same time they are criticized by the international environmental community for damaging the environment. How can indebted LDCs responsibly manage both their natural resources and their debt?

CASE STUDY: DEBT-FOR-NATURE SWAPS

Latin America's debt crisis has been the major cause of the destruction of its tropical rain forests and the rapid depletion of its other natural resources. In servicing their external debts, Latin American countries were compelled to reach into their green reserves and harvest their tropical forests.

Under a variety of cooperative arrangements, usually with conservation groups as mediators between debt-holding institutions and governments in both North and Latin America, there were many renegotiated agreements during 1986 and 1987 where a great amount of rain forest was saved and many of the indebted countries were able to reduce their debts. These debt-for-nature swaps seem not only to be effective and efficient on a short term basis, but they also have positive long term effects. Debt-for-nature swaps seem to suggest that, in the future, debt reduction strategies may shift focus from micro effects to overall resource policies.

As a result of investor or lender hesitation to extend credit to Latin American countries, a secondary market has come into existence where high-risk debts are sold at a discount. Banks desiring to hedge their risk and still have an investment foothold in Latin America are the major traders in these discounted debts which they can later exchange for equity or investment privileges in the debtor nations.

One of the founders of debt-for-exchange programs was Thomas Lovejoy, vice president for science at the World Wildlife Fund, based in the United States of America. In 1984 he suggested that "Third World debt might be turned into some sort of support for conservation."[37] He wrote in the *New York Times* that "under the best circumstances debtor nations find it hard to address critical conservation problems because of stimulation conservation while ameliorating debt would encourage progress on both fronts."[38]

In 1986 Barbara Bramble, director of the international division of the National Wildlife Federation, and Alan Weeden of the Frank Weeden Foundation, were responsible for designing one of the first debt-for-exchange programs when they learned about the existence of the secondary market for loans. They realized that, for pennies on the dollar, they could eliminate large amounts of debt for relatively small investments (usually available to conservation groups, charitable foundations, and commercial lenders). The second step was to have conservation organizations and debtor governments strike bargains where the newly purchased debts could be forgiven in exchange for commitments of equivalent sums in local currency to a conservation fund. Stated differently, debt-for-nature swaps work along the following lines: (1) The bank holding a country's debt sells it at a deep discount to conservationists and writes off the face value as a taxable deduction; (2) the country's central bank redeems the debt and issues local currency bonds equivalent to the total debt; and (3) debtor nation conservation organizations use bond interest to finance local environmental protection projects.[39]

Following the above steps, the first debt-for-nature swap was announced in July 1987. The two types of swaps are bond-based programs and government policy programs. In a government policy program, the national government directly commits to initiating a series of new environmental policies and programs. In a bond-based program, debt is retired in exchange for bonds issued by the central bank to the assigned NGOs. The interest paid on the bonds finances environmental projects and initiatives.

The Weeden Foundation provided Conservation International with $100 million, which was enough to purchase $650,000 worth of Bolivia's foreign debt, then sell it at about $0.15 on the dollar from a Swiss Bank. Citicorp Investment Bank acted as Conservation International's agent in the secondary market. In exchange, the Bolivian government agreed to provide the maximum protection for the Beni Biosphere Reserve, which is home to thirteen of Bolivia's endangered species, and to add 3.7 million acres to the adjacent protected areas. Furthermore, the government committed $250,000 in local currency to manage the Beni Reserve and its expanded buffer zones on a sustainable basis with special attention to retaining the traditional people of the Beni Reserve, the nomadic Chimane people. A Bolivian national commission included biologists, environmentalists, and local officials to monitor the new conservation programs, and U.S.-based Conservation International agreed to set up a local institution as its representative in Bolivia.

As described by Alan Patterson, the agreement was concluded with all parties satisfied with the terms. The problems were in the implementation, which was slow and difficult.[40] Implementation did not begin for two years. Most difficulties were the result of miscommunication by diplomats and misrepresentation by the foreign press, which led Bolivians to believe they were losing national sovereignty over large tracts of land as well as losing economic rights. Confrontations developed between opponents and supporters of the swap. Government matching funds were delayed because of Bolivia's economic problems. The Bolivian government lost the first year's interest due to these factors. Also, while the difficulties in implementation did not derail the process, Bolivian NGOs involved in the swap have not actively supported new deals.

Following the Bolivian swap was an Ecuadorian swap three months later. There were some significant differences and improvements in this second swap. Fundacion Natura, Ecuador's leading conservation organization, secured an agreement with Ecuador's government and its monetary board to offer up to $10 million in external debt in exchange for interest-bearing bonds issued in local currency.[41] The president of Fundacion Natura, Rogue Sevilla, pointed out that there were some favorable differences between the Ecuadorian and Bolivian Plans. With the Bolivian arrangement the founders and engineers of the swap were Americans, which resulted in some negative press in the Latin American national papers, whereas the Ecuadorian swap was designed solely by local and nongovernmental organizations. Ecuador also issued monetary stabilization bonds that would grow over nine years with market-based interest on the principal available for project funding.

Costa Rica is a country that has been able to implement effective programs for protecting its natural areas, but has little capital or cash to support it. Therefore, the country designed a swap in 1987 to suit their specific needs. Costa Rica's Central Bank, along with Costa Rica's minister of Natural Resources, Energy and Minerals approved a full scale debt program in which Costa Rica's National Parks Foundation would trade up to $5.4 million in external debt for local currency bonds, redeemable at 75 percent of the face value. These bonds would grow over a five-year period and bear 25 percent interest per year, providing financing for conservation projects.

These debt-swap programs seem to be effective in solving foreign debt pressures and deforestation, which are two interrelated problems in the Latin American countries. The debt-for-nature swaps are a means toward progress in conservation, education, health, and sustainable development. From these results we can see that they have some long-term positive effects.

As a result of these successes, other groups began to jump on the bandwagon. For example, in 1988 a financial group from Providence, Rhode Island, called the Fleet Norstar, donated $254,000 of Costa Rican debt for Nature Conservancy International, which could convert the donation to Costa Rican bonds valued at $190,000. Both principal and interest will fund land acquisition and land management programs for the 25,000 acres called La Selva, a protected zone in Costa Rica. Other donors followed, pledging more than $5.34 million, surpassing the ceiling that was previously set when the program was initially set up. The Costa Rican government then went on to set up a new program setting a new $50 million ceiling.

The World Wildlife Fund of the United States purchased $41 million in Ecuadorian external private debt at $0.35 on the dollar. Then the funds were converted into local currency bonds at full face value of the debt note and turned over to Fundacion Natura, which will use the principal of the matured bonds as an endowment, while the interest, which is 31 percent in the first year, is allocated to a variety of ongoing conservation programs.

Thus the bond-based program in Costa Rica was implemented smoothly and quickly. There were no political opponents. Interest payments went directly to a single NGO, which administered programs or distributed funds to other NGOs. Funds have largely been used by Fundacion Neotropico/Pargues Nacionales to purchase and operate parklands.

While swaps are regarded as inflationary, this drawback can be avoided by turning the donations into interest-bearing bonds. Also, as pointed out earlier, debt-for-nature swaps are not the ultimate solution to the dual problem of debt and resource degradation. For example, some feel that this program only puts a Band Aid on the situation and that no real action takes place.[42] However, the positive experiences in Costa Rica and Ecuador have led to further interest in debt-for-nature swaps in other countries. Thus, there are hopes that larger swaps can be implemented with substantial reductions in LDC debt and significant protection for the environment, and that other forms of debt renegotiation can include environmental criteria.

DISCUSSION QUESTIONS

1. What are the strengths and weaknesses of the above case study?

2. Although the total external debt of LDCs is more than $1 trillion, the amount that has been exchanged in debt-for-nature swaps worldwide is in the tens of millions of dollars. Is there any hope that debt-for-nature swaps can have any real impact on the crushing burden of foreign debt?

3. What lessons can be learned from the above case study?

NOTES

This chapter was written with the assistance of John Stayton, Farimah Banimahd, and Juliet Meehan, all of Dominican College, San Rafael, California.

1. Morris Miller, *Debt and the Environment* (New York: United Nations Publications, 1991): 13–14.

2. John D. Shilling, "Reflections on *Debt and the Environment*," *Finance and Development* (June 1992): 28.

3. This section of the chapter was adapted from Asayehgn Desta, *International Political Risk Assessment for Foreign Direct Investment and International Lending Decisions* (Needham Heights, Massachusetts: Ginn Press, 1993): 77–89.

4. Helen Hughes, "Debt and development: The role of foreign capital in economic growth," *World Development* 7(2) (1979): 107.

5. Miguel S. Wionczek, "The LDC external debt and the Euromarkets: the impression record and the uncertain future," *World Development* 7(2) (1979): 183.

6. Laurie S. Goodman, "Bank lending to non-OPEC LDCs: Are risks diversifiable?" *Federal Reserve Bank of New York: Quarterly Review* 6(2) (1981): 10.

7. Chandra S. Hardy, "Commercial bank lending to developing countries: Supply constraints," *World Development* 7(2) (1979): 190.

8. See, for example, Irving S. Friedman, *The World Debts Dilemma: Managing Country Risk* (Washington, D.C.: Council for International Banking Studies, 1983).

9. Ibid.

10. William C. Freund, "What's behind the debts of developing countries?" *Journal of Accounting, Auditing and Finance* (Fall 1983): 94.

11. Jeffrey D. Sachs, "External debt and macroeconomic performance in Latin America and Asia," *Brookings Paper on Economic Activity* 2 (Washington, D.C.: 1985): 523–53.

12. Morgan Guarantee Trust Company, "Debt Service in 1983," as quoted in Christopher A. Kojm (ed.), *The Problems of International Debt* (New York: Wilson Company, 1984): 10.

13. Most of the data in this paragraph are derived from International Monetary Fund, *World Economic Outlook* (October 1992): 157–64.

14. Miller, *Debt and the Environment*, 14.

15. Mario Henrique Simonen, former Brazilian Minister of Finance, as quoted in Miller, *Debt and the Environment*, 82.

16. Bahram Nowzad, "Lessons of the debt decade," *Finance and Development* (March 1990): 9–10.

17. See, for example, Desta, *International Political Risk Assessment for Foreign Direct Investment and International Lending Decisions*, 81.

18. Nowzad, "Lessons of the debt decade," 10.

19. Ibid.

20. Ibid.

21. Ibid.

22. Ibid.

23. Cited by Ishart Husain in "Recent experience with the debt strategy," *Finance and Development* (September 1989): 16.

24. Nowzad, "Lessons of the debt decade," 11.

25. Andrew Steer, "The Environment for development," *Finance and Development* (June 1992): 18.

26. Alan Patterson, "Debt for nature swaps and the need for alternatives," *Environment* 32(10) (1990): 6.

27. Walter Corson, *Citizen's Guide to Sustainable Development* (Washington, D.C.: Global Tomorrow Coalition, 1990): 46.

28. Shilling, "Reflections on *Debt and the Environment*," 28.

29. Patterson, "Debt for nature swaps and the need for alternatives."

30. Shilling, "Reflections on *Debt and the Environment*," 28.

31. Patterson, "Debt for nature swaps and the need for alternatives," 6.

32. Jan S. Hogendorn, *Economic Development* (New York: HarperCollins, 1992): 615.

33. Patterson, "Debt for nature swaps and the need for alternatives," 6.

34. Ibid., 12–13.

35. Ibid., 31.

36. Shilling, "Reflections on *Debt and the Environment*," 29–30.

37. Andrew N. Hultkrans, "Greenbacks for greenery," *Sierra* (November–December 1988): 44.

38. Ibid.

39. C. P. Work and G. Smith, "Using red ink to keep tropical forests green," *U.S. News and World Report* (March 6, 1989): 48.

40. Patterson, "Debt for nature swaps and the need for alternatives."

41. Hultkrans, "Greenbacks for greenery."

42. F. Bequette, "Who benefits from debt-for-nature exchange?" *UNESCO Courier* (September 1992): 27.

Selected Bibliography

Afsar, Haleh (ed.). *Women, Development, and Survival in the Third World.* New York: Longman, 1991.

Chenery, Hollis, and T. N. Srivinasan (eds.). *Handbook of Development Economics,* vol. 1. Amsterdam: North Holland, 1988.

Desta, Asayehgn. *International Political Risk Assessment for Foreign Direct Investment and International Lending Decisions.* Needham Heights, Massachusetts: Ginn Press, 1993.

Environmentally Sound Technology for Sustainable Development, ATAS Bulletin No. 7. New York: United Nations Publications, 1992.

Environmental Management in Transnational Corporations: Report on the Benchmark Corporate Environmental Survey. New York: United Nations Publications, 1994.

Gillis, Malcolm, Dwight H. Perkins, Michael Roemer, and Donald R. Snodgrass. *Economics of Development,* 2d ed. New York/London: W. W. Norton, 1987.

Goodstein, Eban S. *Economics and the Environment.* Englewood Cliffs, New Jersey: Prentice Hall, 1995.

Haddad, Wadi D., Martin Carnoy, Rosemary Rinaldi, and Omporn Regel. *Education and Development: Evidence for New Priorities.* World Bank Discussion Paper No. 95. Washington, D.C.: The World Bank, 1990.

Hogendorn, Jan S. *Economic Development,* 2d ed. New York: HarperCollins, 1992.

Kasliwal, Pari. *Development Economics.* Cincinnati, Ohio: South-Western College Publishing, 1995.

Kim, Iipoyong J. (ed.). *Development and Cultural Changes: Cross-Cultural Perspectives.* New York: Paragon House, 1986.

Lutz, Ernest (ed.). *Toward Improved Accounting for the Environment: An UNSTAT-World Bank Symposium.* Washington, D.C.: The World Bank, 1993.

Mazur, Laurie Ann (ed.). *Beyond the Numbers.* Washington, D.C.: Island Press, 1994.

Mclellan, David. *Karl Marx: Selected Writings.* New York: Oxford University Press, 1990.

Meier, Gerald M. *Leading Issues in Economic Development.* New York: Oxford University Press, 1989.

Miller, Morris. *Debt and the Environment.* New York: United Nations Publications, 1991.

Nafziger, E. Wayne. *Economics of Developing Countries,* 2d ed. Paramus, New Jersey: Prentice-Hall, 1990.

Pass, Christopher, et al. *The HarperCollins Dictionary: Economics.* New York: Harper-Collins, 1991.

Pearce, David W., and Jeremy J. Warford. *World without End: Economics, Environment, and Sustainable Development.* New York: Oxford University Press, 1993.

Qureshi, Zia, et al. *Indonesia: Sustaining Development.* A World Bank Country Study. Washington, D.C.: The World Bank, 1994.

Repetto, Robert, and William B. Magrath. *Wasting Assets: Natural Resources in the National Income Accounts.* New York: World Resources Institute, 1989.

Rostow, W. W. *Theories of Economic Growth from David Hume to the Present.* New York: Oxford University Press, 1990.

Schmidheiny, Stephan. *Changing Course: A Global Business Perspective on Development and the Environment.* Cambridge, Massachusetts: MIT Press, 1992.

Thirlwall, A. P. *Growth and Development.* Boulder, Colorado: Lynne Rienner, 1994.

Todaro, Michael P. *Economic Development,* 6th ed. New York: Addison-Wesley, 1997.

———. *Economic Development,* 5th ed. New York: Longman, 1994.

United Nations, Department for Economic and Social Information and Policy Analysis, Statistical Division. *Integrated Environmental and Economic Accounting.* New York: United Nations, 1993.

United Nations Development Programme (UNDP). *Human Development Report 1990.* New York: Oxford University Press, 1990.

———. *Human Development Report 1993.* New York: Oxford University Press, 1993.

———. *Human Development Report 1996.* New York: Oxford University Press, 1996.

United Nations Environmental Programme (UNEP). *Poverty and the Environment.* Nairobi, Kenya: UNEP, 1995.

Vickers, Jeanne. *Women and the World Economic Crisis.* London: Zed Books Ltd., 1991.

Welsh, Brian W. W., and Pavel Butorin (eds.). *Dictionary of Development: Third World Economy, Environment, Society.* New York: Garland Publishing, 1990.

The World Bank. *World Development Report, 1990: Poverty.* New York: Oxford University Press, 1990.

———. *World Development Report, 1992: Development and the Environment.* New York: Oxford University Press, 1992.

———. *World Development Report, 1993: Investing in Health.* New York: Oxford University Press, 1993.

The World's Women, 1995: Trends and Statistics. New York: United Nations Publications, 1995.

Additional References Listed in Tables

Abramovitz, Moses. "Resources and output trends in the United States since 1870." *American Economic Review* 44 (1956): 5–23.

Aukrust, O., and J. Bjerke. "Real capital and economic growth in Norway, 1900–56." International Association for Research in Income and Wealth, *The Measurement of National Wealth,* Income and Wealth, Series VIII. London: Bowes & Bowes, 1959.

Bruno, M. *Interdependence, Resource Use and Structural Change in Israel.* Jerusalem: Bank of Israel Research Department, 1962.

Bruton, Henry J. "Productivity growth in Latin America." *American Economic Review* 57 (1967): 1099–1116.

Fuller, W. "Education, training and worker productivity: Study of skilled workers in two firms in South India." Ph.D. Thesis: Stanford University, 1970.

Gaathon, A. L. *Capital Stock, Employment and Output in Israel, 1950–59.* Jerusalem: Bank of Israel Research Department, 1961.

Hogan, Warren T. "Technical progress and prodction functions." *Review of Economics and Statistics* 40 (1958): 407–11.

Jamison, D., and L. Lau. *Farmer Education and Farm Efficiency.* Baltimore, Maryland: Johns Hopkins University Press, 1982.

Jamison, D., and P. Moock. "Farmer education and farm efficiency in Nepal: The role of schooling, extension services and cognitive skills." *World Development* 12(1): 1984.

Levine, Herbert S. "A small problem in the analysis of growth." *Review of Economics and Statistics* 42 (1960): 225–28.

Lockheed, M., D. Jamison, and L. Lau. "Farmer education and farmer efficiency: A survey." *Economic Development and Cultural Change* 29(1): 1980.

Maddison, Angus. *Economic Progress and Policy in Developing Countries.* London: Allen and Unwin, 1970.

Massell, Benton F. "Another small problem in the analysis of growth." *Review of Economics and Statistics* 44 (1962): 330–35.

Massell, Benton F. "Capital formation and technological change in United States manufacturing." *Review of Economics and Statistics* 42 (1960): 182–88.

Min, W. "The impact of vocational education on productivity in the specific institutional context of China: A case study." Ph.D. Thesis: Stanford University, 1987.

Niitamo, Olavi. "The development of productivity in Finnish industry, 1925–52." *Productivity Measurement Review* 33 (1958): 30–41.

Patrick, G., and E. Kehrberg. "Costs and returns of education in five agricultural areas of eastern Brazil." *American Journal of Agricultural Economics* 55(2): 1973.

Reddaway, W. B., and A. D. Smith. "Progress in British manufacturing industries in the period 1948–54." *Economic Journal* 70 (1960): 6–37.

Robinson, Sherman. "Sources of growth in less developed countries: A cross section study." *Quarterly Journal of Economics* 85 (1971): 391–408.

Solow, Robert. "Technological change and the aggregate production function." *Review of Economics and Statistics* 39 (1957): 312–20.

Index

About the Author

ASAYEHGN DESTA is Professor of Business Economics at Dominican College of San Rafael, California. He also serves on the faculty of San Francisco State University. He is the author of several articles and the book *International Political Risk Assessment for Foreign Direct Investment and International Lending Decisions* (1993).